Food Systems Governance

Sustainability and food production represent a major challenge to society, with both consumption and supply sides posing practical and ethical dilemmas. This book shows that food governance issues can occur in many ways and at many points along the food chain. The risks and impacts, particularly with the increasing globalization of food systems, are often distributed in unequal ways.

It is the role of law to form the pivot around which these issues are addressed in society in the form of food governance mechanisms. The chapters in this book address a range of issues in food governance revolving around questions of justice, fairness, equality and human rights. They identify different issues regarding inequality in access and control over food governance. Some address generic governance and institutional issues across a range of international contexts, while others present case studies, including from Argentina, China, India, Indonesia, Thailand, the UK and West Africa. The book offers directions for reform of the law and legal institutions to mitigate the dangers of inequality and promote greater fairness in food governance.

Amanda Kennedy is an associate professor and the Deputy Director of the Australian Centre for Agriculture and Law, University of New England, Australia.

Jonathan Liljeblad is a lecturer at the University of New England Law School, Australia. He was a Fulbright Scholar, Myanmar (2014–15).

Routledge Studies in Food, Society and the Environment

Street Food
Culture, economy, health and governance
Edited by Ryzia De Cássia Vieira Cardoso, Michèle Companion and Stefano Roberto Marras

Savoring Alternative Food
School gardens, healthy eating and visceral difference
Jessica Hayes-Conroy

Human Rights and the Food Sovereignty Movement
Reclaiming control
Priscilla Claeys

Food Utopias
Reimagining Citizenship, ethics and community
Edited by Paul Stock, Michael Carolan and Christopher Rosin

Food Sovereignty in International Context
Discourse, politics and practice of place
Edited by Amy Trauger

Global Food Security Governance
Civil society engagement in the reformed Committee on World Food Security
Jessica Duncan

Civic Engagement in Food System Governance
A comparative perspective of American and British local food movements
Alan R. Hunt

Biological Economies
Experimentation and the politics of agri-food frontiers
Edited by Richard Le Heron, Hugh Campbell, Nick Lewis and Michael Carolan

Food Systems Governance
Challenges for justice, equality and human rights
Edited by Amanda Kennedy and Jonathan Liljeblad

Food Literacy
Edited by Helen Vidgen

For further details please visit the series page on the Routledge website: http://www.routledge.com/books/series/RSFSE/

Food Systems Governance

Challenges for justice, equality and human rights

Edited by Amanda Kennedy and Jonathan Liljeblad

Routledge
Taylor & Francis Group
LONDON AND NEW YORK

earthscan
from Routledge

First published 2016
by Routledge
2 Park Square, Milton Park, Abingdon, Oxon OX14 4RN

and by Routledge
711 Third Avenue, New York, NY 10017

First issued in paperback 2018

Routledge is an imprint of the Taylor & Francis Group, an informa business

British Library Cataloguing-in-Publication Data
A catalogue record for this book is available from the British Library

Library of Congress Cataloging in Publication Data
Names: Kennedy, Amanda (Law teacher), editor. | Liljeblad, Jonathan, editor.
Title: Food systems governance : challenges for justice, equality and human rights / edited by Amanda L. Kennedy and Jonathan Liljeblad.Description: London ; New York : Routledge, 2016. | Series: Routledge studies in food, society and environment | Includes bibliographical references and index.
Identifiers: LCCN 2015042337| ISBN 9781138939431 (hbk) | ISBN 9781315674957 (ebk)Subjects: LCSH: Right to food. | Agricultural laws and legislation.Classification: LCC K3260 .F665 2016 | DDC 363.8--dc23LC record available at http://lccn.loc.gov/2015042337

ISBN 13: 978-1-138-61829-9 (pbk)
ISBN 13: 978-1-138-93943-1 (hbk)

Typeset in Bembo
by Saxon Graphics Ltd, Derby

Contents

Notes on contributors

Anke Brons is a studying for a master's in international development studies at Wageningen University, the Netherlands. Her fields of expertise are food governance and sustainability. She holds a BA (*summa cum laude*) in liberal arts and sciences from Utrecht University.

John T. Eshleman is a Ph.D. candidate in rural sociology and the human dimensions of natural resources and environment at the Pennsylvania State University, USA, and is currently a research associate at North Carolina State University. His work focuses on the sociology of agriculture, social movements theory, and community food security.

Irene I. Hadiprayitno is a political scientist and human rights scholar with special interests in socio-economic equality, social movement and governance as well as legal and political changes in Indonesia and South-East Asia. She works as a lecturer in International Studies, Faculty of Humanities, Leiden University, the Netherlands.

Otto Hospes is an associate professor at the Public Administration and Policy Group of Wageningen University, the Netherlands. His fields of expertise include food governance, sustainability governance and human rights. He holds a Ph.D. degree in agricultural and environmental sciences from Wageningen University.

Kristal Jones is a research scientist at the National Socio-Environmental Synthesis Center at the University of Maryland, USA. She received her Ph.D. in rural sociology and international agriculture and development. Her work focuses on the social dimensions of agricultural production and natural resource management.

Amanda Kennedy is an associate professor and the Deputy Director of the Australian Centre for Agriculture and Law, University of New England, Australia.

Jonathan Liljeblad is a lecturer at the University of New England Law School, Australia. He was a Fulbright Scholar, Myanmar (2014–15). He holds a Ph.D. and a JD from the University of Southern California. His research interests are in human rights and environmental issues.

Chidi Oguamanam is a Full Professor in the Faculty of Law (Common Law Section) of the University of Ottawa, Canada. He teaches contract law, intellectual property and human rights, agricultural knowledge systems, biodiversity, and food security. His research interests include intellectual property and technology law with an emphasis on biodiversity, biotechnology, and knowledge systems. He is a member of the Nigerian Bar Association and the Nova Scotia Barristers' Society.

Mark Perry is Professor of Law at the University of New England, Australia. His research interests are in intellectual property.

Qin Tianbao is Professor of Environmental Law and International Law, and Assistant Dean for International Affiliations for both the School of Law and the Research Institute of Environmental Law at Wuhan University, China.

Elise Wach is a research and learning adviser at the Institute of Development Studies, a Ph.D. researcher at the Coventry University Centre for Agroecology, Water and Resilience and a part-time food grower, based in the UK. She engages in action research to understand the pathways for transitioning to food systems with better social, economic, nutritional and ecological outcomes.

Wei Lele is a Ph.D. candidate at the Research Institute of Environmental Law, Wuhan University, China.

Xiaobo Zhao holds a Ph.D., and is a lecturer at the School of Law and Justice, Toowoomba Campus, University of Southern Queensland (USQ), Australia. His research interests includes comparative environmental law and Chinese environmental law.

Acknowledgements

The idea to produce this volume arose from fruitful presentations and discussions at the Food Systems Governance conference held in Beijing in May 2014, hosted jointly by the Beijing Foreign Studies University and the University of New England (Australia). We owe much to our colleagues from Beijing Foreign Studies University for co-hosting this event, in particular Dean Meng Wan and Julie Wan. From the University of New England, the support of Professor Michael Stuckey, Jackie Su and Trudy Page is also gratefully acknowledged.

Following the conference, the dedicated staff at Routledge have played a central role in bringing this volume to life. We would like to acknowledge in particular Tim Hardwick (Senior Commissioning Editor) and Ashley Wright (Senior Editorial Assistant). Martin Barr and Amy Cosby provided invaluable editorial assistance to bring this work to press, for which we are also truly grateful. We also thank the authors and various reviewers for producing the chapters included in this volume.

Amanda Kennedy and Jonathan Liljeblad
January 2016
University of New England, Armidale, Australia

1 Introduction

Amanda Kennedy and Jonathan Liljeblad

Introduction

Food is essential for life, yet for many, access to adequate food is denied. While the past 50 years have witnessed growth in food production, sustained population growth will continue to increase the global demand for food. Indeed, the Food and Agriculture Organization (FAO) found that 805 million people suffered from chronic hunger from 2012 to 2014,[1] raising concerns about the capacity to feed a projected world population of 9 billion[2] by 2050. When coupled with growing competition for the land and water needed to produce such food, as well as environmental issues and the overarching threat of climate change, the pressing challenge of feeding 9 billion people becomes quite complex.[3]

Arguably, this conundrum is one of the most difficult social and environmental issues facing society at present, with the demand and supply of food raising critical ethical and practical questions. This multifaceted problem poses enormous challenges for the governance of food systems, demanding innovative approaches to ensure fair access to adequate, safe food. In this sense, governance refers to the resolution of trade-offs, through the interactions between the laws, institutions, policies and other social norms that frame and influence decision-making.

As several scholars have noted, food systems governance is in a state of 'crisis'.[4] Innovation has been scant, regulatory arrangements are 'fragmented and complex', and now intersect with a multitude of private standards and corporate initiatives across both national and global scales.[5] Scholars have increasingly called for greater attention to the architecture of food systems governance to ensure a sustainable and safe global food supply into the future.

This volume aims to bring focus to this issue by examining the changing regulatory and institutional landscape, and proposing new directions for food systems governance. The chapters in this volume are largely based upon presentations made at the 'Food Systems Governance' conference held in Beijing in May 2014 hosted jointly by the Beijing Foreign Studies University and the University of New England (Australia). The papers presented at this forum covered a broad range of issues in food governance linked to overarching questions of justice and fairness. Specifically, the papers identified different issues regarding inequality in access and control over food governance, and sought to offer directions for reform of the law and legal institutions to mitigate the dangers of inequality and promote greater fairness in food governance.

The present volume opens with a systematic literature review of food systems governance from Otto Hospes and Anke Brons. For readers new to the subject of food systems *governance*, Hospes and Brons carefully detail the development of the literature on this subject, assessing how food systems governance has been addressed in academic publications, and identifying the weaknesses as well as desired options for change. They begin by exploring the concept of food systems more generally, finding that there has been little effort to articulate a comprehensive definition of 'food systems'. The authors find that while there has been some recent developments in defining food systems – including the use of broader systems-based conceptions to understand the complex dynamics of food systems – the available literature has paid limited attention to the interaction of 'politics, polity and policies', failing to fully appreciate governance issues.

Nonetheless, food systems governance is emerging as a conceptual field. Hospes and Brons focus on the growing literature, and organise the body of research into four key framings of governance – food policy, food regimes and private governance, urban governance, and multilevel governance. Each of these framings concentrate on different aspects of governance; for example, the literature on food policy distinguishes the actors who influence food decisions, and the drivers that influence policy change, whereas research around food regimes and private governance focuses upon WTO-led initiatives and the role of the private sector in particular. The literature on urban governance specifies more of the citizen and community-led collaborative attempts to govern food systems (such as local food policy councils); while the research on multilevel governance examines vertical linkages between levels of government to manage food systems. Each of these fields of research into food systems governance identifies weaknesses in approaches. Within food policy, approaches are fragmented, dominated by economic and agricultural interests, and offer limited opportunities for public participation. Likewise, the literature on urban governance points to the lack of public participation and local control, as well as highlighting the tension between urban and rural perspectives on food system governance. The literature on food regimes and private governance point more to the power of corporate entities, and their ability to set the agenda of food systems (including food safety), given the relative lack of government coordination and regulatory oversight. The research on multilevel governance, which overlaps with some of the other areas of research, notes the many challenges of allocating decision-making power across different levels of government and across borders.

Following their survey of the literature, Hospes and Brons lay out an agenda for research on food systems governance, noting pathways researchers should pursue to tackle the challenges identified and produce desired food system outcomes. To develop the research field of food systems governance, they identify the need to look to the broader concept of adaptive governance as a framework for scholarship. Drawing insights from a range of disciplines is necessary to deal with the complexities arising from socio-ecological food systems, and increasing the resilience of these systems to respond to pressure. Within this general framework, Hospes and Brons then propose specific governance strategies which warrant further investigation to mitigate inequality in food systems; namely, policy integration, resistant governance and reflexive governance. Policy integration across a broad spectrum – including environmental and health issues – can realise a more 'coherent and sustainable' food policy; resistant governance which seeks to vest power in the hands of consumers can work to minimise corporate domination of food systems; and reflexive governance – which goes beyond recognising the complexity of food systems, and seeks to identify non-dominant narratives in these debates – can open up more comprehensive policy spaces to respond to the uncertainties posed by food systems.

Hospes and Brons thus establish a framework within which the remaining chapters of this volume proceed. The other contributors to this text go on to examine specific aspects of the emerging scholarship of food systems governance – such as the use of resistant governance to overcome practices of exclusion, and the development of new, pluralist policy spaces which incorporate a rich notion of deliberation – identifying challenges and opportunities relevant to the governance of food. The remaining chapters in this volume are briefly explored below.

Resistant governance and reflexive governance

The propensity for the risks and impacts of food systems to be distributed in unequal ways, especially in light of globalisation, has stimulated a dialogue around rights-based approaches to food systems governance. The concept of 'food justice', which seeks to 'establish healthy food as a fundamental right and to eliminate barriers to its access', has begun to receive attention in legal scholarship;[6] similarly, as Hospes and Brons note, the notion of food sovereignty has also been used to 'resist agro-industrial capitalist powers and neo-liberal thinking on food and agriculture', proposing a counter-frame to corporate dominance. Alternative food movements have emerged, initially as 'disparate localized reactions to the disembedding and disenfranchising effects of neo-liberal economic and trade policies', and more recently embodying a broader social movement which employs a common language of resistance and 'self-determination' (Jones and Eshleman, Chapter 2). The contributions from Kristal Jones and John T. Eshleman, Elise Wach, Irene I. Hadiprayitno, and Jonathan Liljeblad each highlight the complexities that arise in cases that reflect aspirations of resistant governance and reflexive governance.

However, while the rhetoric of food sovereignty positions it as a resistant force against neo-liberalism and the commodification of food, the practical reality of alternative food movements and the lived experience of farmers suggest that a radical framing of interests might serve to exclude certain perspectives, and inadvertently generate new inequalities when decisions are made as to whose goals and values are prioritised. Seeds, and the notion of 'seed sovereignty', have become a particular focus of food governance debates. In Chapter 3, 'Food Sovereignty: governance and exclusion in an alternative social movement', Kristal Jones and John T. Eshleman present a case study of contemporary seed system development in West Africa to illustrate this phenomenon. As they note, while certain organisations have adopted the language and framing of global food sovereignty movements – seeking to resist the exclusionary impact of market institutions, and genetically modified crops, for example – this has not necessary reflected the lived experience and desires of individual farmers. Consequently, 'food sovereignty' becomes a 'homogeneous alternative frame', which may serve to exclude individuals and organisations who nonetheless seek to challenge the dominant frame.

In the case discussed by Jones and Eshleman, an influx of donor money, alongside the introduction of genetically modified crops, saw the seed system in West Africa move towards formality in the interests of achieving 'food security'. 'Food sovereignty' (in the sense of local knowledge and control) has since been mobilised as an organising frame by various farmer groups to resist the food security 'frame' posed, characterising attempts to formalise the seed system as constraining of community seed saving and exchange practices common in the region. But the reflections of individual farmers indicate a more nuanced reality, and demonstrate a desire to minimise the exclusionary effects of singular systems. Farmers have begun to engage in adaptive governance mechanisms, such as non-monetary seed exchanges and information sharing, which has the potential to bring about more integrated, rather than singular, methods of governance. Overall, their example provides some pertinent lessons for food systems governance, emphasising the potential for alternative frames to become homogeneous and possibly exclusionary of those who seek to broaden opportunities beyond dominant perspectives.

In Chapter 4, 'Seed sovereignty and inequality: an analysis of seed systems and their impacts on small-scale farmers', Elise Wach also uses seeds as a lens to explore the potential of resistant governance and reflexive governance. Like Jones and Eshleman, she notes the development and dominance of formal seed systems over informal seed systems. She finds that the promotion of formally bred seeds and the development of formal seed systems generally have resulted in 'path dependent lock in situations' for small-scale farmers, creating risks to seed variety diversity, as well as diminishing farmer knowledge of seed saving and storage. Overall, this has reduced small-scale farmer resilience to broader threats, such as climate change, which has in turn resulted in negative impacts upon farmer livelihoods.

Wach argues that while the seed sovereignty movement has the potential to challenge the dominance of formal seed systems, it has been 'typically misused or misinterpreted' to advocate for a romanticised, decentralised and farmer-led approach in opposition to formalised seed systems. Such approaches have tended to recognise farmers as having a uniform perspective, including resistance to genetic modification and intellectual property rights systems, and have failed to recognise how such an approach might have an impact on the rights and livelihoods of small-scale farmers (including improvements to their farming operations). Wach notes that small-scale farmers are the most affected by decisions regarding seed systems, yet have little opportunity to define these systems; indeed, seeds have an impact not only on the nutrition of these farmers, but also their livelihoods, and in some cases, their cultural well-being. She provides a detailed analysis of both formal and informal seed systems, and the opportunities for small-scale farmers participate in them. She finds that formal seed systems seem to create greater inequity for small-scale farmers, inhibiting farmer agency and access to information.

In order to overcome the inequities of formal seed systems and to increase the agency of small-scale farmers, Wach suggests that farmers must be given the opportunity to define their own seed systems. Furthermore, these informal seed systems must be given support from formal systems, rather than being undermined by the structures imposed. The author points specifically to the importance of robust and meaningful deliberative processes for farmers to actively participate in seed system governance. As with Jones and Eshleman's contribution, this chapter notes the potential of resistant governance, but is cautionary with respect to its limitations. Reflexive governance approaches seem to offer greater potential to cultivate rich deliberation, incorporating the many actors within food systems (including farmers, consumers, corporations and the government), and their broad and nuanced perspectives.

Moving away from seed systems to focus on food policy more generally, in Chapter 5, 'Transnational legal processes of the right to food: lessons learned from Papua, Indonesia', Irene Hadiprayitno explores the invocation of the 'right' to food as a transnational legal process to address injustices arising from agricultural modernisation currently underway in Merauke in Papua, Indonesia. While ostensibly agricultural modernisation programmes offer benefits in terms of development opportunities in poorer countries, land grabs can also result in a loss of access and control over the land for local people. Hadiprayitno defines transnational legal processes as those which see the interaction of a range of stakeholders across state borders to interpret and enforce international laws, which ultimately may have a normative impact within a nation state if international laws are internalised.

In this chapter, Hadiprayitno examines the Merauke Integrated Food and Energy Estate agricultural modernisation project which aimed to increase food production and safeguard its availability. There has been much resistance to the project, with indigenous peoples and other groups relying upon human rights discourse to articulate the injustices experienced. Economic and political marginalisation is feared, along with other sociocultural vulnerabilities. Those opposed to the project evoked the vernacular of the human right to food to argue for land rights. Many civil society groups have led advocacy and training workshops, which have become a central component of the knowledge transfer aspect of the transnational legal process. Several reports and requests for assistance have been made to the international community regarding indigenous and human rights violations associated with the project.

Hadiprayitno evaluates the effectiveness of the 'right to food' transnational legal process within the Merauke case. Overall, she finds that the complex interaction between the extant Indonesian human rights legal framework, the regulations governing the agricultural modernisation project and customary laws have challenged the internalisation of norms from international laws. While transnational legal processes such as human rights based concepts serve as a source of inspiration for local actors, they may offer a false sense of comfort where the domestic political climate enables corporations to adapt and adopt human rights norms themselves.

In contrast to Hadiprayitno, Jonathan Liljeblad questions the value of the international human right system itself. In Chapter 6, 'Foucault's evaluation of the UN call for human rights in global food governance', he finds that aside from questions of norm internalisation there is another question of whether the structure of the international human rights is suitable for resolving the inequalities in food systems. Responding to a call from the United Nations High Commissioner for Human Rights (UNHCHR) to integrate human rights into food governance, Liljeblad begins by presenting a basis for the UNHCHR's position. Liljeblad observes that the trends in global food governance have historically followed three paradigms: approaches that focus on state-centric international institutions, privatised free-market approaches, and public–private 'stakeholder' arrangements. These paradigms involve a panoply of actors consisting of states, international institutions, non-governmental organisations (NGOs), or corporations. Missing from such a slate are individuals and groups. Liljeblad notes that human rights ostensibly apply to individuals and groups, and so has the potential to aid actors who have historically been excluded from food governance.

Liljeblad then turns to critique the UNHCHR's position. He argues that the international human rights system is not sufficient to empower individuals and groups against the full slate of actors in global food governance. Applying the theories of Michel Foucault, Liljeblad finds that the international human rights system is focused on protecting individuals from the actions of states, and so offers little against the actions of international institutions, NGOs or corporations. Liljeblad goes on to find that even against states, the instruments comprising the international human rights system exercise individual complaint mechanisms that are anaemic in force, limited in access or restricted in application. As a result, the potential for human rights to aid subordinate voices in global food governance is throttled by weaknesses within the existing international human rights system.

In order to realise the UNHCHR's goal, Liljeblad argues that as much as there needs to be changes in food governance there also needs to be changes within the United Nations system of human rights. Unfortunately, he sees the likelihood of such changes as dubious, since the United Nations comprises states unlikely to concede their powers or status. Instead, Liljeblad suggests that a better strategy for subordinate voices may be to avoid legal approaches like human rights and instead mobilise to pursue political approaches that 'democratise' governance by decentralising decision-making and making it more inclusive towards a broader array of actors – including individuals and groups marginalised in a global food system dominated by states, international institutions, NGOs, and corporations.

Integrated food policy

Another of Hospes and Brons's recommendations for future research in the food systems space is to examine how food policy might integrate a range of policy domains, and move beyond productionist approaches to embrace ecological, health and other concerns. The contributions from Mark Perry, Chidi Oguamanam, Xiaobo Zhao, and Qin Tianbao and Wei Lele present a range of perspectives indicative of the idea of integrated food policy. Each one, in making their respective arguments, advances Hospes and Brons's position for more policy integration in multiple areas of food governance.

Chapter 7, by Mark Perry, 'Sustaining food production in the Anthropocene: influences by regulation of crop biotechnology' demonstrates how the potential for genetically modified crops has been undermined by fragmented and productionist-oriented regulatory approaches. As Perry notes, there are many conflicts surrounding the need for and the risks associated with using biotechnology to improve (and potentially increase) food supply. However, he argues that current challenges facing the global food supply require consideration of methods that will increase food crop productivity, but there is a need to do so in a manner which adequately contemplates the risks and benefits offered by new technologies. He reviews the promise of various biotechnologies – from improved breeding, to gene and trait mapping, and recombinant DNA techniques – noting that while a great deal of controversy surrounds these technologies, they offer significant potential.

Perry then focuses on current regulatory approaches to these technologies, and surveys approaches across a number of jurisdictions. A vast difference in methods is noted, with some countries focused on the method of crop creation and production as the basis for regulation (e.g. the European Union, Japan and Australia); while others focus more on the novelty of the plant product regardless of the methods used to create it (e.g. Canada). Many developing countries simply lack regulatory systems to deal with agricultural biotechnology – which, as noted in some of the earlier chapters, raises issues around seed access for small-scale and subsistence farmers. Overall, Perry argues that the approach to regulating agricultural biotechnology at the international level has been reactive, fragmented and based largely around the notion of production, which has stimulated much objection. Given that world trade now deals in crops as another commodity, and the nature of crop trading, the international community needs to come together to address the issues surrounding the application of new technologies to crops in a fashion that provides greater consensus, and recognition of a broader range of policy perspectives.

Chidi Oguamanam, in Chapter 8, 'Plant genetic resources interdependence: reintegrating farmers into the global food system', continues the exploration of plant biotechnology as an area where a plural food policy space might be nurtured. He argues that food security involves increasingly diverse issues beyond supply, including social and ecological concerns: 'food, culture and identity' intersect – especially within indigenous and local communities – and local knowledge is of significant worth. Yet, as Oguamanam details in his chapter, regulatory approaches to plant genetic resources fail to recognise these values. Intellectual property regulations are limited in their scope and application, generally aimed at formal scientific crop improvement techniques. Moreover, equitable application of the principles of common heritage and free and unrestricted access to plant genetic resources has been slow to garner support.

Oguamanam asserts that the concept of food security has largely been focused upon increased production through agricultural technology, which has witnessed a decline in agro-biodiversity and the depletion of natural resources within indigenous and local communities. Moreover, the move to more formal food systems has effectively marginalised many informal and non-industrial actors (as Jones, Eshleman and Wach observe in their earlier chapters). This has relocated power and influence away from the land, and from traditional small-scale agriculturalists to a more complex network of actors. The industrialisation of agriculture not only diminishes agro-biodiversity and agro-ecological sustainability, but can also result in the 'de-ruralisation' of societies, displacing populations and having an impact on local culture and agricultural identity. With 80 per cent of the world's hungry dependent upon small-scale agriculture for their food, there is a need within the regulatory space to address the other impacts of agro-biotechnology beyond production.

Overall, Oguamanam argues for the need to curb the trend towards plant monoculture across all communities, and suggests that the achievement of agro-biodiversity can be better obtained through practices which reinvigorate farmer-centred agricultural practices, particularly within indigenous and local communities. He notes that a holistic approach to food sovereignty has the potential to realise a reflexive governance model that is capable of beyond singular policy dialogues. Keeping in mind the concerns raised in earlier chapters from Jones, Eshleman and Wach, Oguamanam also cautions that a food sovereignty approach should not be used to deny plant genetic resources independence. It should, however, as a matter of principle reject the strategic exclusion of small-scale farmers as stakeholders in agricultural systems, and seek to implement more reflexive methods of governance which integrate farmers as key stakeholders. Oguamanam concludes by arguing that improved participation has the potential to shift the policy discourse beyond production to take into account social and cultural considerations, health and nutrition, as well as environmental sustainability.

The final two chapters, both concerning food safety in China, also illustrate the potential for better policy integration which moves beyond singular aspects – such as food production – to incorporate diverse perspectives to bring about more effective governance of food systems. Xiaobo Zhao, in Chapter 9, 'Contaminated land law of China: a possible way to achieve food safety?', notes that food safety has become a significant concern in China, particularly around issues of soil contamination. Land contamination from both industrial and agricultural activities has increased dramatically in recent years. While there are no specific regulatory instruments that deal with land contamination, several existing laws and policies – including the Constitution, and recently revised environmental protection laws – can be applied to problems of soil pollution and land contamination. However, this is a fragmented approach to what Zhao describes as an 'emerging crisis', which is exacerbated by a lack of administrative experience in the area of land contamination, and an absence of appropriate conflict resolution approaches and mechanisms for public participation.

Zhao argues that because land contamination is inextricably linked to food safety, there is a compelling case to consider these issues together within an integrated policy framework. Rather than relying solely upon environmental protection legislation to regulate contaminating activities, he recommends a comprehensive framework which incorporates a systematic land remediation mechanism, liability and financial assistance schemes to improve food safety outcomes.

In Chapter 10, 'Life-cycle regulation of food safety in China: a legal perspective', Qin Tianbao and Wei Lele examine similar issues, and propose the concept of 'life-cycle regulation' to deal with food safety concerns. In their chapter, the authors note that while there are laws relating to particular aspects of food production, these are fragmented and do not span the entire life cycle of food – from the initial growth and production of raw materials through to distribution and eventual consumption and disposal. For example, Qin and Wei point to the existing food safety regulatory framework. While there are several comprehensive instruments, food safety issues still persist (with soil contamination, as discussed by Zhao, a significant concern). Food production, storage and transportation are also regulated; yet food safety concerns have continued, largely as a result of limited supervision and enforcement of penalties against violations. On the other hand, regulation of other aspects of food production, particularly the disposal of waste foodstuffs, has not been adequately regulated. Overall, Qin and Wei find that the present food safety governance framework in China is deficient: regulations are fragmented, and do not coordinate well with other relevant laws (e.g. environmental law); and food safety standards are inconsistent, and their enforcement is lacklustre. Assessing approaches from other jurisdictions, Qin and Wei conclude that a life-cycle approach to food safety regulation, which covers all stages of food production, would be a more comprehensive approach.

Conclusion

A unifying element among the various contributions to this volume is a shared undercurrent of tension between structure and agency. A theme tied to social science literature, structure and agency centre on the nature of human behaviour, with structure being the forces that set or constrain choices and agency being the efforts by individuals to make choices independent of structure.[7] Each of the contributions to this volume can be framed as a commentary regarding structure and agency in that they involve subjects wherein the rise of transnational and national governance mechanisms has operated to marginalise local concerns by reducing the ability of individuals and groups within communities to exercise agency. Each of the chapters point out the dysfunction that can result, and asserts that such dysfunction aggregates to a scale that endangers the food governance structure itself. In response, the authors suggest lessons that share a common implication of a need to enable greater agency via means that are more inclusive and empowering of subordinate voices.

Hospes and Brons, in asserting an agenda of policy integration, resistant governance and reflexive governance follow this theme, in that they seek to promote agency that mitigates the existing inequalities of food systems structures. Hospes and Brons's proposal for policy integration directed at a 'coherent and sustainable' food policy seeks to expand the arena of issues, and hence the voices tied to those issues, involved in food policy. Their call for resistant governance looks to reduce corporate dominance to enable consumer power over food systems. Their directive for reflexive governance goes further to seek and include marginalised voices within food debates. All of these elements operate to encourage changes that aspire to address the inequalities in food systems by endowing subordinate voices greater agency over decisions in food policy.

Jones and Eshlemann caution that such efforts are at risk of generating new inequalities that perpetuate marginalisation and exclusion. But here too they reflect a desire to reduce inequalities within food systems structures and reveal a concern for the expression of subordinate voices in response to such inequalities. This latter sentiment is echoed by Wach, who argues for opportunities that allow small-scale farmers to have greater ability to define seed systems. This is the essence of agency, in that Wach sees a need for small-scale farmers to have greater power to articulate and pursue their own seed systems. Wach, however, goes further to issue her own caution that for these efforts to constitute substantive participation in governance they must be supported by existing food systems via inclusive deliberative processes.

To a degree, the agency of subordinate voices can be promoted through the international human rights system, which ostensibly endeavours to defend marginalised perspectives through a body of rights promoting human dignity. Hadiprayitno and Liljeblad both temper the potential role of human rights within food systems. Hadiprayitno shows that the international human rights system is a structure that can be manipulated by dominant powers to impose or maintain inequalities. Liljeblad observes that even in the absence of manipulation by the powerful, the international system of human rights itself limits individual claims and so proscribes the extent to which individuals can use human rights as a means of agency against dominant interests. For both Hadiprayitno and Liljeblad, the concern regards agency, with both seeing a disjuncture between the purpose of human rights to protect disempowered voices and the consequences of power relations tied to human rights that marginalise voices. Hadiprayitno and Liljeblad observe that the association of human rights with food systems does not eliminate, and indeed serves to emphasise, a need to focus on the issue of agency by subordinate perspectives as the requisite means of addressing the structural inequalities in food systems.

These cautionary sentiments extend to hopes for a technological fix to food systems. Perry and Oguamanam note that the promise of technology is a function of those who control it, and hence that technology is subject to persistent issues of access and exclusion that drive inequalities. Perry sees such inequalities as directing technologies regarding food productivity, Oguamanam sees them as influencing technologies regarding crop diversity. Both, however, share a common argument that extends to food policy in general: a need for a broader discussion regarding the presence of technology in food systems via an expansion in the number and diversity of perspectives involved in food policy. This essentially represents a call for agency by marginalised voices, since it asserts a need for inclusionary processes that promote participation by all interests associated with food governance.

The contributions from Zhao, and Qin and Wei follow these themes, with the two chapters both critical of state-centric policy approaches as suffering from fragmentary actions that fail to fully address the complexities of food systems. For Zhao, and Qin and Wei, expectations that power inequalities can be benign as a result of competent and comprehensive control by dominant actors are misguided. Their chapters show that the nature of food systems issues are on a scale of complexity that overwhelms the capacities of any governing authority, and that a more promising solution is to match the complexity of food systems with a corresponding expansion in public participation that encompasses a greater range of resources and perspectives. In arguing for such expanded inclusion, Zhao, and Qin and Wei effectively look to empower a broader array of voices in food systems.

Conceptualisation in terms of structure and agency is useful not only in recognising the common undercurrent running throughout the chapters in this book, but also in terms of looking for ways to move forward past the issues highlighted by the contributors. In particular, the structure–agency debates pose the possibility of structuration in the sense that as much as power structures may determine the choices and forces directing the behaviour of actors, those actors can also behave in ways that influence the composition and outcomes arising from power structures.[8] This is, in essence, what the chapters imply, with their prescriptions for greater inclusion of diverse perspectives working on a belief that participation within food systems governance will allow marginal voices to influence the policies towards food systems. The implied admonition for other aspects of food governance is to develop such connections between decision-making structures and participatory agency, such that food systems work towards the lessons given by the contributors in this volume: engagement of marginal voices that increases the diversity in perspectives involved in food policy.

Notes

1 FAO, IFAD and WFP (2014), 'The state of food insecurity in the world 2014', FAO.
2 United Nations Department of Economic and Social Affairs (2009), 'World population prospects: The 2008 revision', UN Doc. ESA/P/WP.210.
3 Godfray, H., Charles J., Beddington, J.R., Crute, I.R., Haddad, L., Lawrence, D., Muir, J.F., Pretty, J., Robinson, S., Thomas, S.M. and Toulmin, C., 'Food security: the challenge of feeding 9 billion people', *Science*, 327 (5967) (2010): 812–18.
4 Isshii-Eiteman, in Clapp, J. and Cohen, M. J. (eds), *The Global Food Crisis: Governance Challenges and Opportunities* (Wilfrid Laurier University Press, 2009), p. 217.
5 Havinga, T., van Waarden, F. and Casey, D., *Changing Regulatory Arrangements in Food Governance* (Edward Elgar, 2015).
6 Purifoy, D. M., 'Food policy councils: integrating food justice and environmental justice', *Duke Envtl. L. & Pol'y F.*, 24 (2104), 375–99, 380; see also Rebecca L. Goldberg, 'No such thing as a free lunch: paternalism, poverty, and food justice', *Stan. L. & Pol'y Rev.*, 24 (35) (2013): 48–9.
7 See for example: Bourdieu, P., *Distinction* (Routledge, 1984); Talcott Parsons, *The Structure of Social Action* (vols 1–2) (Free Press, 1967); Simmel, G., *The Metropolis and Mental Life: The Sociology of Georg Simmel* (Free Press, 1976).
8 See for example: Archer, M., *Realist Social Theory: The Morphogenetic Approach* (Cambridge University Press, 1995) and *Structure, Agency and the Internal Conversation* (Cambridge University Press, 2003); Berger, P.L. and Luckmann, T., *The Social Construction of Reality: A Treatise in the Sociology of Knowledge* (Anchor Books, 1966); Giddens, A., *New Rules of Sociological Method* (2nd edn) (Stanford University Press, 1993) and *The Constitution of Society* (Polity Press, 1984); Mouzelis, N., *Sociological Theory: What Went Wrong?* (Routledge, 1995).

2 Food system governance

A systematic literature review

Otto Hospes and Anke Brons

Introduction

Over the past decade, both scientists and policymakers have called for the development of new governance for food systems to address global challenges in the field of food security, environmental change and poverty reduction. One of the major triggers for this call was the world food price crises of 2007/2008 and 2010 that prompted scholars and policymakers to reflect on the deeper, more structural causes of the crisis. Isshii-Eiteman concludes that, 'We have not so much a food crisis today as a food system crisis' (in Clapp and Cohen, 2009, p. 217). Gustafson and Markie call for a stronger global architecture for food and agriculture because, 'it has become apparent that the international governance framework for food and agriculture has failed to provide a sustainable food supply that is accessible to all' (in Clapp and Cohen, 2009, p. 179). Similarly, Von Braun and Islam (2008) of the International Food Policy Research Institute (IFPRI) observe that, 'the current world food and agricultural policy system is in disarray'. Their list of symptoms shows that this system has not been able to adequately respond to a wide range of problems in the field of food, agriculture and nutrition:

> Incoherent or inadequate responses to exploding food prices; the slowdown in agricultural productivity growth; looming water problems; a disorderly response to higher energy prices; rapid concentration in multinational agribusiness corporations without the necessary institutional innovation to guide them; lack of progress in addressing scarcity; adverse impacts of climate change on agriculture; widespread nutrition problems, including hunger, obesity, and chronic diseases; and agriculture-related health risks, such as avian influenza.
>
> (Von Braun and Islam, 2008)

To stimulate a dialogue on what the future global institutional architecture and governance of agriculture, food and nutrition might look like and how it might be achieved, Von Braun and Islam (2008) present three options for change. The first option is to maintain the current global organizations and make marginal improvements. Strengthening the UN and CGIAR system for agriculture, food and nutrition in terms of their governance and resources is one way in which to do this. The second option is to form an innovative government network that will strengthen government-to-government systems for decision-making. The third option is to expand the current system to engage the new players in the global food system: the private sector and civil society. Von Braun and Islam (2008) add that the three options are listed in order from 'quite realistic to rather utopian'.

Scholars that have explored the interactions between global environmental change and food security have called for more attention to be paid to the governance of food systems (Ingram, 2011a; Ingram et al., 2010; Ericksen, 2008). In her comprehensive conceptualization of food systems, Ericksen (2008) lists 'the nature of institutional processes and food system governance' as one of the priorities for future research.

The aim of this chapter is twofold: first, to assess how food system governance has been addressed in academic publications since the world food price crisis of 2007 and the call for more research into food system governance to better understand interactions between global environmental change and food security was made; second, to generate an agenda for conceptual and empirical research on food system governance on the basis of this assessment. For this purpose, we conduct a two-step systematic literature review. The first step is focused on food systems and the second step on the governance of food systems. The reason for this is that we assume that the way in which food systems are described and assessed matters for or affects the governance of food systems. In both parts, we use two kinds of questions to review the literature: the first is ontological, exploring how the nature of food systems or governance is understood, framed and conceptualized; the second is judgemental, presenting what researchers consider the major weaknesses and desired properties of food systems and the governance of food systems.

For reviewing how the nature of food systems is understood, we use some generic properties of a system: components, boundary, scale and interconnectedness between different components and systems. To identify how food systems are scientifically framed or conceptualized, we search for definitions and key analytical notions. For reviewing the nature of governance of food systems, we focus on actors and authorities; laws and policies; coordination mechanisms; and scalar dimensions.

Our two main questions are: how has food system governance been conceptualized and diagnosed in academic literature? What proposals can be distinguished to change and strengthen food system governance? Our specific questions are:

1 How have food systems been conceptualized in the literature in terms of components, scales and interconnectedness?
2 What are considered the main weaknesses of the food system(s)?
3 What are seen as desired outcomes and properties of food systems?

4 How has governance of food systems been conceptualized in terms of actors, power, policies and institutional mechanisms?
5 What are considered the main weaknesses in the governance of the food system(s)?
6 What are seen as desired properties and required changes to food system governance?

Methodology

To source scientific publications, Scopus and then Google Scholar were used. Additional publications were identified for review through backward and forward reference checking.

Scopus

The search engine Scopus was used to identify relevant journal articles. The selection was conducted with a specific set of search terms (Box 2.1). For alternative terms of 'governance', the list of synonyms as used by Candel (2014) in his systematic literature review on food security governance was used. The search terms had to appear in the title (TITLE), abstract (ABS) or key words (KEY), with (synonyms of) 'governance' occurring within a distance of five words (W/5) from 'food system'.

Box 2.1 Search terms

'food system'	'governance'; 'government'; 'administration' 'handling'; 'management'; 'stewardship'; 'superintendence'; 'policy-making'; 'policy formation'; 'regime'; 'guidance'

The exact query was: 'food*system*' W/5 *governance* OR government* OR administration* OR handling OR *management* OR stewardship OR policy-making OR 'policy formation' OR superintendence* OR regime OR guidance) in TITLE-ABS-KEY. This query resulted in 131 publications that were then downloaded into Endnote.

All abstracts were read and then accepted or declined by using inclusion and exclusion criteria. The inclusion criteria are:

1 Language: in English and Dutch.
2 Research methods: empirical and theoretical; qualitative and quantitative.
3 Time-frame: unlimited.
4 Focus: papers that reflect on and provide insights into food system governance.

The exclusion criteria are:

1 Language: other languages than English or Dutch
2 Focus: paper is not about food systems, or no part of the paper is about food systems.
3 Focus: paper does not reflect on food governance arrangements or on food system governance.

As a result, the selection was downsized to 87 potentially relevant sources. Consequently, a further selection was made on the basis of reading the full text of the articles. This reduced our selection to 55 publications.

Google Scholar

To identify scholarly work that has not been published in refereed journals, the search engine Google Scholar was used. For sourcing and selection, we used the term 'food system governance'. This led to a total of 121 hits. We scanned the titles and, if relevant, read the abstracts, using the exclusion and inclusion criteria. This resulted into 16 additional publications to be systematically reviewed. Finally, another 17 articles were included through backward and forward referencing. Appendix 2.1 provides a list of these articles and how they have been traced. Altogether, our search queries led to a final total of 88 publications to be systematically reviewed.

The systematic literature review

This section of the chapter consists of two main parts. The first part presents some general characteristics of the selected literature in terms of years of publication, disciplines of the journals, country focus and methodologies used. The second part reviews the selected literature in greater depth by answering the six specific questions.

General characteristics

A great majority (n=79) of the selected literature has been published after 2006, with a steady increase in the number of publications observed over the 2007–2014 period (see Figure 2.1). First of all, this shows that the subject of food system governance is a fairly recent topic of academic research and debate. Second, this suggests that the calls – after the outbreak of the global food price crisis of 2007/2008 – to reflect on new architecture and governance of agriculture, food and nutrition have not gone unnoticed, and have prompted academic research and debate (Gustafson and Markie in Clapp and Cohen, 2009; Von Braun and Islam, 2008).

The selected literature includes 66 journal articles. Only three journals published more than three selected articles: *Agriculture and Human Values* (n=7),

Environmental Science and Policy (n=4); and *Global Environmental Change* (n=4). The other 22 selected sources consist of books, PhD theses, policy briefs and online research papers.

The articles have been published in 41 journals. Some 30 of these journals have a natural science profile, considering their subject categories: 'environmental sciences' (14 journals), 'agriculture' (13 journals) and 'health and nutrition (6 journals).[1] A modest number of journals have 'social sciences' (6 journals) or 'policy science' (3 journals) as a subject category (see Figure 2.2).

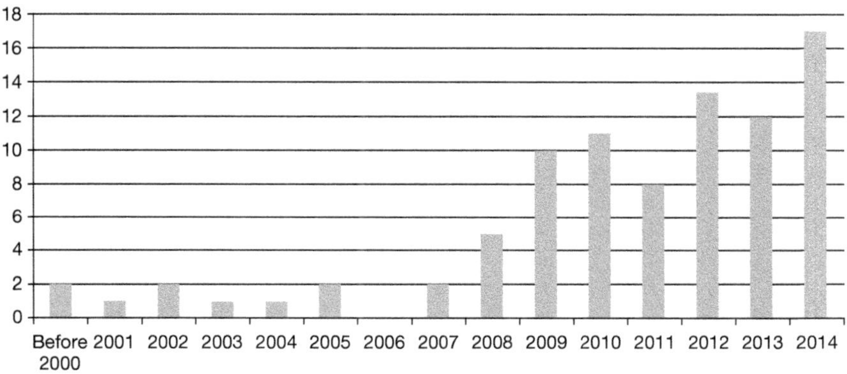

Figure 2.1 Publications per year

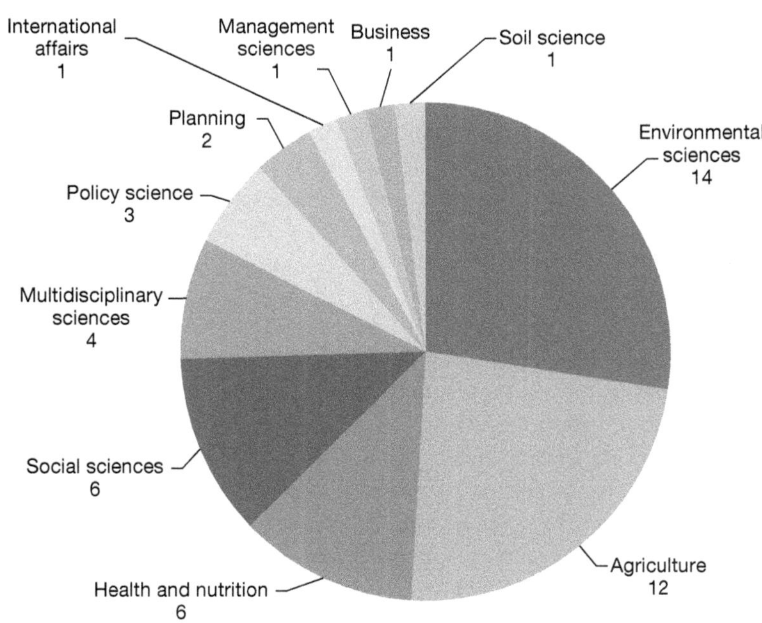

Figure 2.2 Journal subject categories

A total of 39 of all selected publications have a specific-country focus. Some 29 of these are focused on Canada (n=8), USA (n=7), UK (n=5), South Africa (n=5) or Brazil (n=4).

Some 24 publications are based on qualitative data collection through interviews and/or observations. In many of these and other selected texts, (further) empirical research into food systems and their governance is considered needed, timely or relevant.

Specific characteristics

Understanding and framing of food systems

In this section we review how food systems have been understood in terms of components, scale and interconnectedness. For this purpose we present definitions of food systems and review full texts on these dimensions. Based on these definitions, reviews and on the identification of key concepts, we distinguish two scientific frames of food systems.

Components

Definitions of food systems are relatively scant. We found 11 definitions in our selected literature (see Box 2.2). At least four different components of food systems can be distinguished in these definitions: the first component is activities, ranging from production to consumption. This component is explicitly mentioned in all definitions, except in the one of Hipel et al. (2010).

The other components are less commonly referred to, mentioned only in two or three definitions. The second component is outcomes of activities, not only in terms of food security but also environmental security and social welfare (see Box 2.2: definitions of Haysom, 2014; Pereira, 2014; Ericksen, 2008). The third and physical component is natural resources, environmental systems or bio-geophysical environments (see Box 2.2: Herforth et al., 2014; Hipel et al., 2010; Ericksen, 2008). The fourth and non-material component is institutions related to food, or governance of food chain activities (see Box 2.2: Olson et al., 2014; Vermeulen et al., 2012b).

Though activities presuppose actors, only one definition explicitly mentions them (see Box 2.2). Pereira (2014, p. 4) distinguishes three components of food systems, including specific actors: (1) value chain inputs, mechanisms and structures for food production (land, water, crops, marine stocks), processing, distribution, access, preparation, consumption, metabolism and waste; (2) participants in the food system, including producers, fishers, industries, labour, governments, purchasers (retailers and buyers, brands, manufacturers, traders), communities and consumers; (3) social issues inherent in food equity, food justice, and food sovereignty and political and spatial considerations on local, regional, national and global levels.

Box 2.2 Definitions of food systems in chronological order

1 The whole food production sector in the economy (including farms, processing and marketing for foodstuff), as well as the consumption of food (Sundkvist et al., 2005, p. 118).
2 Food systems include: (a) the interactions between and within bio-geophysical and human environments, which determine a set of activities; (b) the activities themselves (from production through to consumption); (c) outcomes of the activities (contributions to food security, environmental security and social welfare); and (d) other determinants of food security (stemming in part from the interactions in (a) (Ericksen, 2008, pp. 234–235).
3 The global food system is a system of systems and consists of a food supply chain and environmental, industrial and trade systems, which are themselves individual systems that are autonomous, heterogeneous and complex (Hipel et al., 2010, p. 13).
4 A series of interrelated processes, including production of raw food materials through farming and raising of livestock, processing and packaging for consumption, distribution and utilization by consumers (Hammond and Dubé, 2012, p. 12356).
5 The full spectrum of food issues including food production, food processing, food distribution, food access and food waste management (Mansfield and Mendes, 2012, p. 38).
6 Food chain activities (manufacturing and distribution of inputs, agricultural production, primary and secondary processing, packaging, storage, transport and distribution, marketing and retail, catering, domestic food management and waste disposal) and their outcomes and their governance (Vermeulen et al., 2012b, p. 197).
7 The food system combines food chains, food cycles, food webs, and foodsheds – and covers multiple stages: production, processing, distribution, acquisition, preparation, consumption and waste (Brinkley, 2013, p. 243).
8 Activities of commercial and non-commercial actors who grow, process, distribute, acquire and dispose of food, with activities (from production through to consumption) and outcomes (contributions to food security, environmental security, and social welfare) (Haysom, 2014, p. 6).
9 Process that turns natural and human-made resources and inputs into food (Herforth et al., 2014, p. 9).
10 Relations and processes that go beyond growing and harvesting to include other components such as research, transportation and consumption, as well as institutions related to food, such as markets and communities (Olson et al., 2014, p. 105).
11 Food systems comprise a complex set of interlinked activities and outcomes of the commodity chain of production through to consumption (Pereira, 2014, p. 4).

Scale

Limiting ourselves to spatial scale, about half of the selected publications (n=44) conceptualize food systems as multi-scale or multilevel (like Hammond and Haysom, 2014, Dubé, 2012, Thompson and Scoones, 2009, Ericksen, 2008). The next level of publications describe and analyse nationally scaled food systems (n=16) or locally scaled food systems (n=15), with the latter including seven publications on urban food systems (like Forster and Esceduro, 2014; Haysom, 2014; Sonnino, 2013; Mansfield and Mendes, 2012; FAO, 2011; Rocha and Lessa, 2009; Schneider et al., 2007). Smaller numbers of publications refer to international and regional food systems (n=6), or the global food system (n=6).[2] An interesting example of the latter is the study of Hipel et al. (2010) who define the global food system as a system of systems, consisting of a food supply chain but also environmental, industrial and trade systems (see Box 2.2).

Whereas many publications lack a clear definition of a food system, some speak of 'the food system', whereas others refer to a plurality of food systems. Authors who use the singular version often refer to a nationally or globally scaled food system. Yet, they do emphasize its complexity or interconnectedness with other systems (like Hipel et al., 2010) or refer to local resistance to the global food system (Hendrickson and Heffernan, 2002). Authors, who speak of systems, describe the coexistence of food systems at different levels, for instance, one at the global level, another at the national or local level. For instance, Blanc and Kledal (2012) analyse different kinds of food systems in Brazil that affect the organic sector: alternative, commercial and government-led food systems. Similarly, Friedmann (1995, p. 56) distinguishes regional, national and global institutional influences on local food systems, stating that '[t]o act locally entails acting at all levels'. Miller et al. (2013) identify a multiplicity of food system levels and emphasize that both local adaptations at farm level and food system planning at an international level are necessary to address climate challenges.

Interconnectedness

A total of 16 out of the 88 publications explicitly refer to and discuss interconnectedness as a dimension of a food system. They do so, however, in different ways.

Some authors point at interconnectedness *across scales*, for instance, when speaking of 'global interconnectedness' (Challies et al., 2014; Kirwan and Maye, 2013; Duit et al., 2010; Lang et al., 2001). As Kirwan and Maye (2013, p. 97) put it, 'it is problematic to define local and global in simple binary terms; neither the local nor … individual communities are isolated from wider processes, but are in fact highly interdependent across a range of scales'. Hendrickson and Heffernan (2002) place particular emphasis on the interconnectedness *between actors*, discussing interdependencies between producers and consumers within the food system, and arguing for a new kind of localized food community that recognizes this interconnectedness. Hipel et al. (2010) approach the concept from another angle and underline the interconnectedness *between systems*, including food, environmental, industrial and trade systems. Finally, researchers on the relationships between global environmental change and food security point at interactions *between and within biophysical and human environments* (Ingram, 2011a; Ingram et al., 2010; Ericksen, 2008).

Some scholars emphasize the need to incorporate different kinds of interconnectedness in the conceptualization of 'food systems thinking', or food systems for global environmental change. For instance, Haysom (2014, p. 2) quotes MacRae and Donahue (2013), who state that: '[f]ood system thinking reflects an awareness of how actions by one group in the system affect other groups, as well as influencing the environment, the economy, society, and the health of the population and ultimately consumers'. According to Ingram et al. (2010), the notion of interconnectedness is central to systems thinking. Such thinking is to acknowledge that various processes and components within food systems are highly interconnected, with dynamics, interactions and feedbacks occurring at multiple scales and levels (Thompson and Scoones, 2009). Ericksen (2008) distinguishes three kinds of interconnectedness in her conceptualization of food systems for global environmental change research. The first kind has been her topic of study: the interconnectedness between food provision and climate change. The second type of interconnectedness relates to interactions between and within biophysical and human environments. The third consists of interconnectedness across scales between biophysical and human processes.

To understand the dynamics and changes of the food system, Ericksen (2008) distinguishes basic constituents of the food system (activities and outcomes) and the drivers of socio-economic features and global environmental change. These drivers affect and are being affected by food system activities and outcomes (see Figure 2.3). Therefore, Ericksen points at different and complex interconnections, including not only interlinked activities, but also interactions between activities, outcomes, environmental change and socio-economic change.

The conceptualization of food systems by Ericksen (2008) is one of, if not the most comprehensive. However, after her publication, less comprehensive definitions have occurred focusing on activities and food chains, her conceptualization has been influential and been used by other authors (like Yu et al., 2012; Ingram, 2011a; Ingram et al., 2010; White et al., 2010). Ericksen's definition of food systems to include both activities and outcomes has been adopted by Haysom (2014), Pereira (2014) and Vermeulen et al. (2012b) (see Box 2.2).

Despite its comprehensiveness, Ericksen's conceptualization of the food system does not explicitly pay attention to actors and governance as both part and drivers of the food system. A critique by Haysom (2014) is that Ericksen does not consider how the food system shapes and is being shaped by policies. We could add that the conceptualization of Ericksen does not address polity and politics as two other dimensions of governance, next to policies (Treib et al., 2007). As shown in Box 2.2, only one author has explicitly mentioned

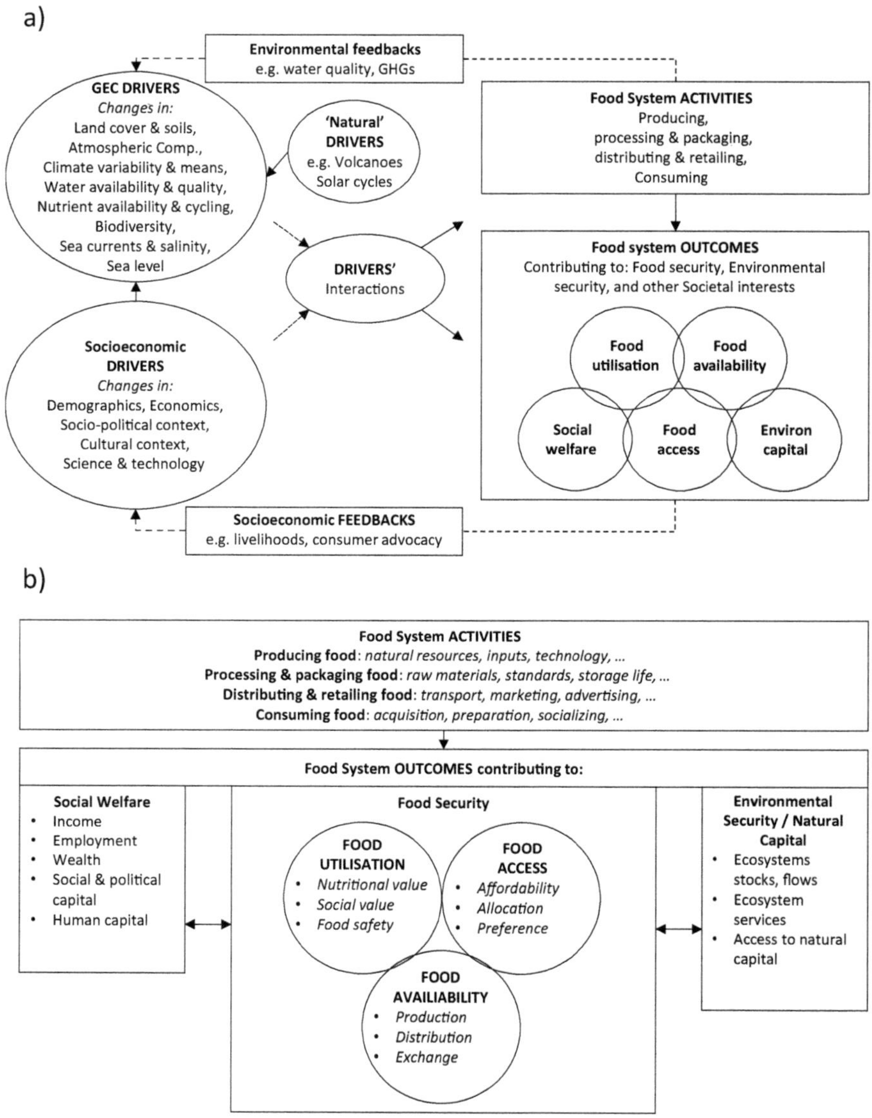

Figure 2.3 (a) Food systems and their drivers, (b) Components of food systems
Source: Ericksen (2008: 239).

governance as a component of the food system (Vermeulen et al., 2012b). Olson et al. (2014) refer to a polity as a dimension of governance, that is: 'institutions related to food' (see Box 2.2).

Scientific frames

Based on our review of key definitions and conceptualizations of a food system, different scientific frames of the nature of a food system can be distinguished. The first one is based on the notion that a food system is a series of interlinked activities, from production to consumption. We would like to coin this as the 'food chain' frame of food systems. This term is not new. There is a huge body of literature on global value chains and its governance (with seminal works of Gereffi et al., 2005; Humphrey and Schmitz, 2000). The central question in this literature is about the use and distribution of power in value chains. In our selection of literature on food system governance, the broader question of unequal power relations of the global agri-food system is dealt with in studies on global food regimes and private governance (see e.g. Pol, 2014; Sommerville et al., 2014; Challies, 2012; Henson, 2011; Konefal et al., 2005; Friedmann, 1995).

The second frame considers ecological processes and socio-economic change as interlinked drivers and outcomes of a food system. The scientific frame for this interconnectedness could be termed the 'social–ecological system' (SES), which is how Ericksen (2008) perceives a food system. An SES has been defined as: 'a coherent system of biophysical and social factors that regularly interact in a resilient, sustained manner' and 'a system that is defined at several spatial, temporal, and organisational scales, which may be hierarchically linked' (Redman et al., 2004, p.163). To further emphasize its dynamics, Pereira (2013) and Pereira and Ruysenaar (2012: 4) consider a food system as a complex adaptive system (CAS): a 'process-dependent, organic system with feedbacks among multiple scales and levels within it, and its emergent properties include having interactive and dynamic components that self-organize' (see also Folke, 2006; and Ison et al., 1997). According to Pereira et al. (2013) interconnectedness of a food system is best explained with the concept of 'emergence', which refers to 'the arising of novel and coherent structures, patterns and properties during the process of self-organization in complex systems' (Goldstein, 1999, p. 49).

By conceptualizing a food system as an SES or CAS, the complex, interactive and dynamic nature of a food system is emphasized. These understandings of a food system have major implications for conceptualizing and strengthening the governance of food systems. In the sections below we will review the different ways in which the governance of food systems has been conceptualized in the selected literature. Considering the conceptualization of a food system by Ericksen (2008) as a prime example of the use of an SES thinking, at this point we could say that the SES frame lacks an orientation and understanding of how politics, polity and policies – as three modes or dimensions of governance (Treib et al., 2007) – interact with and are part of food systems.

Main weaknesses of food systems

The inability to provide food security is considered the main weakness of the (current) food system(s) in nearly all selected publications. Nearly all authors refer to the definition of food security that was presented at the World Food Summit of 1996: food security exists 'when all people, at all times, have physical and economic access to sufficient, safe and nutritious food to meet their dietary needs and food preferences for an active and healthy life' (FAO, 1996).

While this definition of food security is commonly used, authors focus on a range of different issues when considering the current food systems. For instance, some scholars highlight health and nutrition risks (Clark, 2010; Story et al., 2009; Wahlqvist and Lee, 2007). Alternatively, Wegener et al. (2012) focus on lack of access to food. Again, other authors consider insufficient food production as a major problem (Johns et al., 2013; Miller et al., 2013).

The problems highlighted are not just limited to food insecurity but also address processes or drivers that may explain food insecurity. Global environmental change is considered a major threat to food security in many of our selected texts (see e.g. WRR, 2014; Vermeulen et al., 2012a; Vermeulen et al., 2012b; Hammond and Dubé, 2012; Vervoort et al., 2012; Thornton et al., 2011; White et al., 2010; European Science Foundation, 2009; Ericksen, 2008). At the same time, these scholars consider food systems as potentially undermining environmental security and social welfare. Some authors in particular express their concern in terms of threats to biodiversity (Johns et al., 2013; Lang et al., 2001). This has led to new problem statements and questions, like: how can food systems cope with global environmental change and at the same time provide food security, environmental security and social welfare? Other authors (Pereira, 2014; FAO, 2011) consider the processes of urbanization that has increased significantly over the past decades as the main threat of food security in the future.

Finally, several publications formulate the major problem of food systems in terms of lack of power of consumers and small food producers (Blanc and Kledal, 2012; Dubuisson-Quellier and Lamine, 2008; Hendrickson and Heffernan, 2002). In terms of principles and values to organize food systems, several authors consider the lack of a human rights-based approach to challenge neo-liberal thinking and organization of food and agriculture as the major problem of food systems (McMichael, 2011; Eakin in Ingram et al., 2010; Clapp and Cohen, 2009; Anderson, 2008).

These different problem statements suggest that a key challenge of food systems is to define and agree on what is the issue. Given the complexity of the issues of food systems and the lack of consensus of scholars on what is the cause, we can conclude that the problem of food systems is a wicked one (Rittel, 1973). A wicked problem is a problem that is hard to localize, is ill-defined, has many different layers and cannot be definitively solved. In several of our selected publications the problem of food insecurity and food systems has indeed been framed as a wicked problem (Brinkley, 2013; Pereira and Ruysenaar, 2012; Vervoort et al., 2012; Story et al., 2009).

Desired outcomes and properties of food systems

The perceptions of authors of desired outcomes of food systems reflect their problem statements of food systems. In nearly all the literature, food security is considered as the main aim and desired outcome of food systems. In the subset of literature on interactions between global environmental change and food security, two other major food system outcomes or functions are distinguished: social welfare and environmental security. Herforth et al. (2014) mention that the purpose of food systems is not only to generate nutritional quality but also economic viability and environmental sustainability (Miller et al., 2013; McMichael, 2011; Sundkvist et al., 2005). As regards the desired properties of food systems, four different proposals can be extracted from the selected literature. These proposals reflect the problem statements of authors regarding food systems but also their analytical views on the ontological nature of food systems.

The first proposal is that the adaptive capacity and resilience of food systems should be strengthened. This property is characteristic for those who conceive food systems as an SES or CAS. Gallopín (2006, p. 300) distinguishes two components of adaptive capacity of an SES: '(1) the capacity of the SES to cope with environmental contingencies … and (2) the capacity to improve its condition in relation to its environment(s) … or to extend the range of environments to which it is adapted'. Authors that have explored the adaptive capacity of food systems include Ericksen (2008), Fridman and Lenters (2013), Ingram et al. (2010), Pereira (2013), Thornton et al. (2014), Vermeulen et al. (2012a) and White et al. (2010). Pereira (2013) considers adaptive capacity as a vital asset of a well-functioning food system.

Publications on the resilience of food systems include among others WHO (2014); Johns et al. (2013); Miller et al. (2013); Pimbert (2012); Vermeulen et al. (2012b); White et al. (2010); International Human Dimensions Programme (2009); Story et al. (2009); Thompson and Scoones (2009). Carpenter et al. (2014) define resilience as:

> The amount of disturbance a system can absorb and still remain within the same state or domain of attraction, (2) the degree to which the system is capable of self-organization (versus lack of organization, or organization forced by external factors); and (3) the degree to which the system can build and increase the capacity for learning and adaptation.
>
> (p. 767)

Ingram (2011a) and Pereira (2013) warn that the resilience of food systems is threatened by differently scaled processes, including climate change, economic globalization, market policies and change in land rights.

Leach et al. (2010) pose critical questions about the concept of resilience itself and the social–political contexts in which it has been framed. They question the resilience of what, and for whom? In their view, the political nature of the concept of resilience has been ignored in scientific and policy debate. Duit et al. (2010) agree with this critical note and the need to recognize resilience as an inherently normative concept.

The second proposal is that food systems should be local or localized (see among others Forster and Esceduro, 2014; Sonnino, 2013; Mount, 2012; McMichael, 2011; Clark, 2010; Gillespie, 2010; Anderson, 2008; Dubuisson-Quellier and Lamine, 2008; Ganry et al., 2011; Schneider et al., 2007; Hendrickson and Heffernan, 2002). In their view, local food systems provide the best opportunities for a food system to be ecologically sustainable and socially just. Another major advantage of localized food systems is the proximity of food producers and consumers of food, which reduces 'food miles'. Localized food systems are also expected to provide social justice in the sense of advancing food democracy, giving communities and their small-scale farmers more control over the food they produce (Pimbert, 2012). Challies et al. (2014) provide another argument in favour of more localized food systems. Taking an SES perspective on food systems, their argument is that feedback loops function better in localized food systems, characterized by close ties between producers and consumers.

At the same time, however, a critical voice against the idealization of localizing food systems can be heard from within the literature. This voice warns against the so-called 'local trap', which is the idea that local systems are inherently good, for instance, in terms of provision of environmental or food security (Born and Purcell, 2006). Leach et al. (2010) warn against the depoliticization of the debate on scale and call for recognition of the interconnectedness of differently scaled systems. Based on the notion of interconnectedness across scales, Kirwan and Maye (2013) call for further research to address the question of how local food systems can be coordinated with (inter)national food systems, instead of imagining these systems as opposing and mutually exclusive. In a similar vein, several authors have emphasized the need for national support of local food systems in terms of building capacity, which could, for instance, be realized through technical assistance provided by ministries (Sonnino, 2013; Clark, 2010; Clapp and Cohen, 2009). Thornton et al. (2011) and Vermeulen et al. (2012a) point at the need of appropriate social, institutional and political support to strengthen the adaptive capacity of community food systems.

The third proposal is that food systems should be alternative or leave room for alternative food activities (Nigh and González Cabañas, 2014; Pol, 2014; Sommerville et al., 2014; Blanc and Kledal, 2012; Clark, 2010; Rocha and Lessa, 2009; Dubuisson-Quellier and Lamine, 2008; Hendrickson and Heffernan, 2002). The concept of 'alternative' is used in different ways: to refer to a food system that coexists with commercial food systems (Blanc and Kledal, 2012); to argue in favour of a local food system that challenges the dictate of the global food system (Hendrickson and Heffernan, 2002); to refer to new governance arrangements, or a combination. A key publication in this regard is Rocha and Lessa (2009), who studied the alternative food system (AFS) introduced by government agencies in Belo Horizonte, Brazil. It is a non-market-based system that is governed at the urban level through collaboration between the government, private sector and civil society. Clark (2010) reports a similar case in Venezuela, in which the government played a key role in organizing an alternative food system.

The fourth proposal is that food systems should be human rights-proof and reflect that access to food is a human right (Eakin in Ingram et al., 2010; Clapp and Cohen, 2009; Anderson, 2008). An example is the introduction by Anderson (2008) of rights-based food systems. Criteria of such systems are: democratic participation in food system choices affecting more than one sector; fair and transparent access by producers to all necessary resources for food production and marketing; multiple independent buyers; absence of human exploitation; and no impingement on the ability of people in other locales to meet this set of criteria.

Understanding and framing of food system governance

Those few authors that have conceptualized food systems for global environmental change research have not specifically addressed governance issues (Ingram, 2011a; Ingram et al., 2010; Ericksen, 2008). In various other fields of research on food systems, governance issues have been empirically studied in different ways and using distinctive key analytical concepts. We distinguish four groups of publications that each refer to a different understanding and framing of governance of food systems: (a) food policy; (b) food regimes and private governance; (c) urban governance; and (d) multilevel governance. Admittedly, some publications fit into more than one category.

Food policy

The first group of publications relates to food policy (i.e. Hospes, 2014; Pereira, 2014; WRR, 2014; Seed et al., 2013; Mansfield and Mendes, 2012; MacRae, 2011; Ingram et al., 2010; Maxwell and Slater, 2003; Barling et al., 2002; Lang et al., 2001; Friedmann, 1995). Food policy is the set of 'decisions that impact the ways that people produce, obtain, consume and dispose of their food' (Mansfield and Mendes, 2012, p. 38). Decisions that may impact food activities can be situated in various policy domains, like health, environment, agriculture, and economics. Lang (2005a; 2005b) distinguishes several key drivers of food policy, including health concerns, rising poverty and climate change.

Typically, in food policy studies different types of actors are distinguished, including government agencies, civil society organizations and food supply actors. The concept of the 'food policy triangle' (Seed et al., 2013) supposes that interactions between exactly three types of actors shape food policy. About half of the publications on food policy focus on national policies, whereas the other half addresses multiple levels of food policy (including the global level, e.g. WTO trade policy). As an exception, Mansfield and Mendes (2012) study food policy at a city level.

Food regimes and private governance

The second group of publications on governance of food systems relate to *food regimes and private governance* (Haysom, 2014; Hospes, 2014; Pol, 2014; Sommerville et al., 2014; McMichael, 2011; Ingram et al., 2010; Friedmann, 1995). Friedmann (1995, p. 30) defined a food regime as 'the rule-governed structure of production and consumption of food on a world scale'. Food regime traditionally takes an historical approach to identify underlying causes of current food crises, transformations and transitions, and to characterize different trends and periods. In her 1995 article, Friedmann signalled the rise of private global regulation and gradual transition towards more democratic public regulation. McMichael (2011) and many others would later qualify the rise of private global regulation as the emergence of the corporate food regime, that is based on neo-liberal thinking on food and agriculture, and assigns a key role to the WTO-led trade liberalization and the private sector in governing the global food system.

The focus on WTO regulation and the rise of governance arrangements in which non-state actors act as regulatory powers of the global food system, is particularly noted and discussed in studies on the 'agri- or agro-food system' (Olson et al., 2014; Sommerville et al., 2014; Challies, 2012; Henson, 2011; Hall, 2010; Konefal et al., 2005; Barling et al., 2002). These authors primarily conceive food system governance in terms of regulation, food standards, certification or labelling.

As a point of critique and signalling a new trend, Challies (2012) argues that it is difficult to clearly distinguish between public and private governance. Bavorová et al. (2014) use the term 'co-regulation' to describe the mix of public and private actors and regulations at different levels, which governs the agri-food system. Hall (2010), who studied the Japanese agri-food system and its governance, concludes that the government has actively supported private governance of the food system, leading to sounder monitoring of the quality and safety of food.

Urban governance

The third group of publications relate to urban governance (Clancy, 2014; Forster and Esceduro, 2014; Haysom, 2014; Blay-Palmer et al., 2013; Fridman and Lenters, 2013; Sonnino, 2013; Mansfield and Mendes, 2012; FAO, 2011; Clark, 2010; MacRae, 2011;, Rocha and Lessa, 2009; Schiff, 2008). These publications describe the collaborative efforts of citizens, civil society organizations and municipality governments in governing local food systems.

Case studies highlight alternative food systems and food policy councils. An example of the former is the city food system of Belo Horizonte in Brazil that is orchestrated by the Secretariat of the Municipality for Food Policy and Supply. Reportedly, this food system has successfully increased access to healthy food in the city by promoting urban agriculture through participatory community involvement and the use of agro-ecologically sustainable methods (Clapp and Cohen, 2009; Rocha and Lessa, 2009). Another example of urban governance that is considered a success story is the Toronto Food Policy Council (Forster and Esceduro, 2014; Haysom, 2014; Fridman and Lenters, 2013; Mansfield and Mendes, 2012; MacRae, 2011). This council developed the Toronto Food Strategy, which works towards a healthy and sustainable food system for the city. Its members include regional farmers, retailers, elected officials, community organizers, researchers and policymakers from different policy domains (Forster and Esceduro, 2014).

Multilevel governance

The fourth group of publications relate to multilevel governance (Forster and Esceduro, 2014; Sonnino et al., 2014; Miller et al., 2013; Pereira and Ruysenaar, 2012; FAO, 2011; Leach et al., 2010; International Human Dimensions Programme, 2009; Barling et al., 2002; Lang et al., 2001). For some authors multilevel governance basically refers to vertical linkages between different levels of government. For instance, the FAO (2011, p. 31) defines multilevel governance as 'governance continuum across levels of government'. Increasingly, broader definitions have been created, like the one of Termeer et al. (2010, p. 33) that is referred to by Pereira and Ruysenaar (2012) and Miller et al. (2013). Multilevel governance is

> the displacement of state power and control in three directions, that is: 1) upwards to international actors and organisations; 2) downwards to regions, cities and communities; and 3) outwards to civil society and non-state actors.

An example of multilevel governance is the nationwide food programme of Brazil called 'Zero Hunger' (Sonnino et al., 2014; Rocha and Lessa, 2009). This comprehensive programme has been designed along three main principles: a multilevel and multi-scale approach; a participatory attitude; and partnership of the government with both civil society and the private sector (Sonnino et al., 2014). A key strategy of the Zero Hunger programme has been decentralization, with devolution of powers from the federal to the state and municipality level, involving government officials, citizens and civil society organizations at all levels.

Main weaknesses of food system governance

In this section we present the main weaknesses of food system governance for each of the group of publications or fields of research as distinguished in the former section.

Food policy

In the literature on food policy, three main weaknesses of food system governance can be distinguished. First, food policy is fragmented. Food issues are dispersed over different policy domains (such as agriculture, health and society). Second, many food policies are dominated by the 'productionist' paradigm, tailoring food policy in terms of agricultural production and primarily considering trade and economic interests. Such policies ignore environmental, social and public health considerations (Maxwell and Slater, 2003; Barling et al., 2002; Lang et al., 2001). Food policies fail to 'reflect the essential reality of our biological and social dependence on food and the resources needed to produce it sustainably (MacRae, 2011, p. 424–425). Third, food policy studies report on the limited involvement of civil society in developing food policy (Seed et al., 2013). In the specific case of national councils for food security, there is a danger of 'eliticization of participation' (Sonnino et al., 2014), meaning that majority of members are relatively highly educated and wealthy.

Food regime and private governance

Three main weaknesses of current food system governance can be distinguished in the literature on food regimes and private governance. First, power imbalances in favour of corporate entities, or the lack of participation for the majority of the world's population in the governance of their own food (Pol, 2014; Sommerville et al., 2014; Challies, 2012; Henson, 2011; Konefal et al., 2005; Friedmann, 1995). Second, reluctance of transnational corporations in the prevailing corporatist food regime to address worsening global social and ecological crises in agriculture and food (Sommerville et al., 2014; Challies, 2012). Various authors are critical of private standards on food safety, quality and the environment and their role in preventing or reverting such crises (Challies, 2012; Konefal et al., 2005). These standards may, in fact, serve to 'reproduce and possibly deepen social and ecological inequalities' (Konefal et al., 2005, p. 299). The third weakness is the lack of coordination and regulation of large corporations by governments (Pereira, 2014; Challies, 2012; Pereira, 2013). Clapp and Fuchs (2009, p. 6) state that corporate actors 'are increasingly playing a role in setting the very rules that govern their activities'.

Urban governance

Two main weaknesses of urban governance can be distinguished in the selected literature. First, promises of increased participation and local control are not always met (Barungi, 2013; Thompson and Scoones, 2009). Second, urban food system governance is not always able to reconcile perspectives and priorities of the urban population with those of the surrounding rural population, upon which the former group is often dependent for its food production (Forster and Esceduro, 2014; FAO, 2011).

Multilevel governance

In the literature on multi-governance, the allocation of decision-making power across levels and across borders is generally considered the key issue (Clancy, 2014). At least five risks are related to this issue. First, there is the risk that choices may be politically influenced and result in, for instance, premature decentralization (FAO, 2011). Second, the authority of the state may become too dispersed, fragmented or even hollowed out (Pereira and Ruysenaar, 2012; Termeer et al., 2010). Third, voices at the local level may not reach decision-making process at the global level. Fourth, the weakness of one level of governance may negatively affect other levels. In Venezuela, for instance, opportunities for food system governance at a local level were not optimal because of an unstable and corrupt government (Clark, 2010). Fifth, due to these interdependencies between different levels of government, questions of accountability and legitimacy may easily occur (Biermann, 2009; International Human Dimensions Programme, 2009).

The complexity of the food system and risks of multilevel governance have prompted several authors to characterize food system governance as a wicked problem (Pereira, 2014; Brinkley, 2013; Miller et al., 2013; Pereira and Ruysenaar, 2012; Vervoort et al., 2012;, Story et al., 2009). For instance, Story et al. (2009) state that the governance of the US food system is a wicked problem due to its size and complexity.

Desired properties and changes in food system governance

Based on our literature review, in this section we present four main proposals from (groups of) scholars on what properties or changes of food system governance contribute to desired food system outcomes. The first proposal is to establish food policies that integrate different policy domains and are driven by ecological, health and food security concerns. The second is to establish food sovereignty to replace the global corporatist food regime. We refer to this as 'resistant governance'. The third is to organize reflexive governance and to create inclusive policy spaces. The fourth is to strengthen adaptive governance.

Policy integration

In the literature on food policy, several authors call for a 'new food policy' that goes beyond food production and includes, or is even primarily based on, environmental and health concerns (Gerlach and Loring, 2013; MacRae, 2011; Maxwell and Slater, 2003; Barling et al., 2002; Lang et al., 2001). For instance, Barling et al. (2002) propose that UK food policy draws on a new ecological public health model approach to replace the dominant productionist approach. To create a coherent and sustainable food policy, 'joined-up food policy' is proposed, that is, policy integration across discrete sectors (Barling et al., 2002, p. 558). The national nutrition councils of Norway and Finland are seen as institutional examples of joined-up food policy (Barling et al., 2002). Overall, food policy councils at both the national and local levels are seen as important institutional models for developing sustainable food systems (Forster and Esceduro, 2014; Brinkley, 2013; Gillespie, 2010; Rocha and Lessa, 2009; Clapp and Cohen, 2009; Schiff, 2008; Clancy, 2004).

Resistant governance

A main proposal in the literature on food regimes and private governance is not to adapt corporate food regimes and powers, but to move towards a totally different regime, with rights and powers vested in the hands of small food producers and consumers. To get away from an industrial capitalist agri-food system towards a more just and sustainable agri-food system (Challies, 2012; Konefal et al., 2005), scholars call for 'alter-geopolitics of food security and governance' (Sommerville et al., 2014) and the introduction of 'food sovereignty' (Hospes, 2014; Nigh and González Cabañas, 2014; Pereira, 2014; Pol, 2014; Sommerville et al., 2014; Pimbert, 2012; McMichael, 2011; Clark, 2010; Ingram et al., 2010; Clapp and Cohen, 2009; International Human Dimensions Programme, 2009; Thompson and Scoones, 2009; Anderson, 2008). Key roles for challenging corporate food regimes and establishing alternatives are assigned to farmer and social movements. As their resistance is critical, we coin their ideas on new food regimes as resistant governance.

The concept of food sovereignty was termed by the international peasant movement La Vía Campesina, as a response and counter-frame to neo-liberal policies and institutions marginalizing the voices and interests of small food producers all over the world. This movement defined food sovereignty as 'the right of each nation to maintain and develop their own capacity to produce foods that are crucial to national and community food security, respecting cultural diversity and diversity of production methods' (La Vía Campesina, 1996). Challenging the idea of food as a global commodity, farmer and social movements emphasize the notion of access to food as a human right.

Reflexive governance

In many scholarly publications, the call for democratization of food system governance can be heard (Sonnino et al., 2014; Kirwan and Maye, 2013; Pimbert, 2012; FAO, 2011; Clapp and Cohen, 2009; Dubuisson-Quellier and Lamine, 2008). For instance, Eakin in Ingram et al. (2010) propose

> a democratic forum in which alternative perspectives on food and its value to society have equal footing, and rules and norms are established to compensate for the differential power and political interests associated with different perspectives on food values.
>
> (p. 263)

Likewise, several authors call for new policy spaces or 'spaces of deliberation' that can help to articulate, reflect on and reconcile different views and values on food (Hospes, 2014; Sonnino et al., 2014; Eakin in Ingram et al., 2010; Leach et al., 2010). Leach et al. (2010) particularly emphasize the

> fundamental need to open up; to reveal and give voice to marginalized narratives and so enable pathways which do address poorer people's goals and take greater account of multiple dimensions of incomplete knowledge and of sustainability
>
> (p. 96)

Several authors have coined the governing of new policy spaces, deliberation and reflexivity as reflexive governance (Sonnino et al., 2014; WRR, 2014; Mount, 2012; Leach et al., 2010). Reflexive governance 'facilitates learning, adaptation and collaboration between stakeholders at different scales and stages of the food system' (Sonnino et al., 2014, p. 2). A few scholars have systematically used the concept of reflexive governance to analyse specific cases and forms of governance (Sonnino et al., 2014; Mount, 2012). Vervoort et al. (2012) have used the concept of reflexive governance to develop a 'reflexive interventionist multi-actor' scenario for food system governance, which is particularly meant to address the wicked problems of food systems.

Adaptive governance

The fourth main proposal on changing and strengthening food system governance relates to adaptive governance (Clancy, 2014; Fridman and Lenters, 2013; Pereira, 2013; Pereira et al., 2013; Pereira and Ruysenaar, 2012; Ingram, 2011b; Duit et al., 2010; Leach et al., 2010; International Human Dimensions Programme, 2009). The need for adaptive governance is particularly emphasized in those publications that conceptualize the food system as an SES. Adaptive governance is seen as a response to dynamics and uncertainties of the food system. According to Folke (2006), adaptive governance consists of four essential parts:

> (1) understanding ecosystem dynamics; (2) developing management practices that combines different ecological knowledge system to interpret and respond to ecosystem feedback and continuously learn; (3) building adaptive capacity to deal with uncertainty and surprise including external drivers; and (4) supporting flexible institutions and social networks in multi-level governance systems
>
> (p. 262)

Several authors emphasize that cross-scale and cross-level interaction in and beyond food systems require adaptive governance (Pereira, 2013; Pereira et al., 2013; Pereira and Ruysenaar, 2012; Ingram, 2011b). Quoting Lebel et al.

(2006), Ingram et al. (2010, p. 129) state that 'adaptive governance requires participation, polycentric institutions to manage across scales and levels, and strong accountability of authorities'.

In the literature on governance of food systems, the concept of adaptive governance is still a rather theoretical concept that has hardly been used and tested in empirical research. There is a lack of empirically grounded examples of adaptive governance. One of the few studies that uses adaptive governance as an analytical concept to describe a food policy or institution is the study of Fridman and Lenters (2013). This study highlights the flexible, governing role of the Toronto Food Policy Council that orchestrated community food initiatives, such as community kitchens, to contribute to food security. The small-scale character of these initiatives, well embedded in larger governance structures, suggests that any global or national project needs to foster local initiatives. The critical comment of Challies et al. (2014, p. 39) on grand projects has to be taken seriously: 'while governance of specific social–ecological subsystems seems plausible, grand projects of "earth system governance" or management of global systems, seem improbable'.

Conclusion

Food system governance is an emerging field of study. The key academic booster for this field has been the predominantly natural-science community that has studied interactions between global environmental change and food security. Ericksen (2008) was the first to conceptualize the nature and dynamics of food systems for global environmental change research in a comprehensive way. She conceived food systems as an SES. From this perspective, the interconnectedness between human and biophysical environments is seen as a complex driver of food activities and their outcomes. Governance was not part of Ericksen's (2008) definition and framework for analysing the complexity and change of food systems framework but tabled as a research priority.

Though declared a research priority by Ericksen (2008), we have found little conceptual work on food systems from an SES perspective that has integrated and elaborated on governance in definitions and frameworks to analyse the complexity and dynamics of food systems. Also, there is lack of empirical studies of the alternative ways in which differently scaled governance arrangements interact with biophysical environments and food activities to shape food outcomes.

Yet, the thinking on food system governance has certainly not stood still since the conceptually pioneering work of Ericksen (2008). In the literature on food systems as an SES, the concept of adaptive governance has emerged. This concept echoes the idea that food systems should be resilient and have adaptive capacity to cope with threats as a result of global environmental change and at the same time contribute to food security, environmental security and social welfare. Adaptive governance is considered critical for strengthening the adaptive capacity of food systems and designing governance arrangements across scales for different food activities and outcomes. As such, adaptive governance is not so much a descriptive–analytical, but a normative–directive concept. Also, the concept of adaptive governance has hardly been used and tested in empirical research.

To further develop food system governance as a research field, we first suggest prioritizing efforts to include governance in analytical frameworks on the complexity and dynamics of food systems as socio–ecological systems. Second, we recommend the use and testing of the concept of adaptive governance in empirical, multilevel, multi-actor and multi-site research of food systems. Third, we suggest learning and benefiting from three alternative proposals for food system governance that we have identified on the basis of our review. Every proposal has been developed in scientific research and scholarly debate, in which governance issues rather than food systems have formed the problem statement or primary object of study.

The first proposal is to seek policy integration across different sectors or domains (agriculture, health, environment, etc.). Scholars on food policy have developed this proposal. Their problem statement is that institutional fragmentation and one-dimensional, productionist approaches to food policy hamper the realization of a coherent and sustainable food policy. Food policy scholars hold that interactions between different types of actors (government agencies, civil society organizations and food supply actors) are critical in shaping food policy and in organizing policy integration.

The second proposal is to organize resistant governance, that is: to resist agro-industrial capitalist powers and neo-liberal thinking on food and agriculture by vesting powers over food systems in the hands of (movements of) small food producers and consumers. A specific proposal is to declare food sovereignty. Critical scholars on food regimes and private governance have developed such proposals or counter-frames. Their problem statement is that as long as food regimes remain dominated by corporate powers and private governance, another world characterized by sustainable agro-ecological practices, food democracy and respect to the human right to food is not possible. Scholars emphasize that food system governance is not so much about policy but power and rights.

The third proposal is to develop reflexive governance, that is: new policy spaces or 'spaces of deliberation' that can help stakeholders at different scales and stages of the food system to articulate, reflect on and reconcile different views and values on food. Scholars who see lack of deliberation and reflexivity as the main problem of food system governance have developed this proposal. Recognizing the complexity of food systems in terms of components and scales, their view is that traditional policy spaces located at one level, one office, one part of a food chain, or in one country will not do. Scholars emphasize that the aim of new food system governance is to cultivate new governance interactions between different stakeholders at different levels and from different places.

Appendix 2.1 Methodology: reference checking

Publication	*Backward (B) or forward (F) reference checking*	*Found via*
Thompson and Scoones (2009)	B	Challies et al. (2014)
Thornton et al. (2014)	F	Ericksen (2008)
Pereira (2013)	F	Ericksen (2008)
Yu et al. (2012)	F	Ericksen (2008)
Thornton et al. (2011)	F	Ericksen (2008)
Fresco (2009)	F	Ericksen (2008)
Herforth et al. (2014)	F	Vermeulen et al. (2012b)
Brinkley (2013)	F	Sundkvist et al. (2005)
Forster and Esceduro (2014)	F	Clancy (2014)
Hendrickson and Heffernan (2002)	B	Ericksen (2008)
Maxwell and Slater (2003)	B	Ingram (2011a)
Duit et al. (2010)	B	Challies et al. (2014)
Hammond and Dubé (2012)	F	Ericksen (2008)
Blay-Palmer (2010)	B	Blay-Palmer et al. (2013)
Anderson (2008)	B	Ingram et al. (2010)

Notes

1 Of the 41 journals, 21 are ISI indexed. For these journals the subject categories have been taken from the ISI Web of Knowledge *Journal Citations Report*. If multiple categories were mentioned, all categories were included. For the other 20 journals that are not ISI indexed, the general descriptions of the journals have been consulted and then classified under one of the best fitting ISI journal subject categories.

2 In one publication (Gillespie, 2010), the scale of the food system could not be specified.

References

Anderson, M. D. (2008). Rights-based food systems and the goal of food systems reform. *Agriculture and Human Values*, 593–608.

Barling, D., Lang, T. and Caraher, M. (2002). Joined-up food policy? The trials of governance, public policy and the food system. *Social Policy and Administration*, 36, 556–574.

Barungi, J. (2013). Agri-food system governance and service delivery in Uganda: A case study of Tororo District. *ACODE Policy Research Series*.

Bavorova, M., Hirschaeur, N. and Martino, G. (2014). Food safety and network governance structure of the agri-food system. *European Journal of Law and Economics*, 37, 1–11.

Biermann, F., Betsill, M. M., Gupta, J., Kanie, N., Lebel, L., Liverman, D., Schroeder, H. and Siebenhuner, B. (2009). Earth system governance: People, places and the planet. *Science and implementation plan of the Earth System Governance Project*. Retrieved from www.earthsystemgovernance.org/sites/default/files/publications/files/Earth-System-Governance_Science-Plan.pdf

Blanc, J. and Kledal, P. R. (2012). The brazilian organic food sector: Prospects and constraints of facilitating the inclusion of smallholders. *Journal of Rural Studies*, 28, 142–154.

Blay-Palmer, A. (2010). *Imagining Sustainable Food Systems: Theory and Practice.* Surrey: Ashgate.

Blay-Palmer, A. D., Knezevic, I., Andree, P., Ballamingie, P., Landman, K. E., Mount, P. A., Nelson, C. H., Nelson, E., Stahlbrand, L. M., Stroink, M. L. and Skinner, K. (2013). Future food system research priorities: A sustainable food systems perspective from Ontario, Canada. *Journal of Agriculture, Food Systems, and Community Development*, 3, 227–234.

Born, B. and Purcell, M. (2006). Avoiding the local trap: Scale and food systems in planning research. *Journal of Planning Education and Research*, 26, 195–207.

Brinkley, C. (2013). Avenues into food planning: A review of scholarly food system research. *International Planning Studies*, 18, 243–266.

Candel, J. J. L. (2014). Food security governance: A systematic literature review. *Food Security*, 6, 585–601.

Carpenter, S., Walker, B., Anderies, J. M. and Abel, N (2014). From metaphor to measurement: Resilience of what to what? *Ecosystems*, 4, 765–781.

Challies, E. (2012). The limits to voluntary private social standards in global agri-food system governance. *International Journal of Sociology of Agriculture and Food*, 20, 175–195.

Challies, E., Newig, J. and Lenschow, A. (2014). What role for social–ecological systems research in governing global teleconnections? *Global Environmental Change*, 27, 32–40.

Clancy, K. (2004). Potential contributions of planning to community food systems. *Journal of Planning Education and Research*, 23, 435–438.

Clancy, K. (2014). Digging deeper: Bringing a systems approach to food systems. *Journal of Agriculture, Food Systems, and Community Development*, 4, 3–6.

Clapp, J. and Cohen, M. J. (eds) (2009). *The Global Food Crisis: Governance Challenges and Opportunities.* Waterloo, ON: Wilfrid Laurier University Press.

Clapp, J. and Fuchs, D. (2009). Agrifood corporations, global governance, and sustainability: A framework for analysis. In: J. Clapp and D. Fuchs (eds.), *Corporate Power in Global Agrifood Governance.* Cambridge, MA: MIT Press.

Clark, P. (2010). Sowing the oil? the Chavez Government's policy framework for an alternative food system in Venezuela. *Humboldt Journal of Social Relations*, 33, 135–165.

Dubuisson-Quellier, S. and Lamine, C. (2008). Consumer involvement in fair trade and local food systems: Delegation and empowerment regimes. *GeoJournal*, 73, 55–65.

Duit, A., Galaz, V., Eckerberg, K. and Ebbesson, J. (2010). Governance, complexity and resilience. *Global Environmental Change*, 363–368.

Ericksen, P. J. (2008). Conceptualizing food systems for global environmental change research. *Global Environmental Change*, 18, 234–245.

European Science Foundation (2009). European food systems in a changing world. Retreived from www.esf.org/fileadmin/Public_documents/Publications/food.pdf

FAO (1996). World Food Summit: Rome Declaration on World Food Security. Retrieved from www.fao.org/docrep/003/w3613e/w3613e00.HTM

FAO (2011). Food, agriculture and cities: The challenges of food and nutrition security, agriculture and ecosystem management in an urbanizing world. Retrieved from www.fao.org/3/a-au725e.pdf

Folke, C. (2006). Resilience: The emergence of a perspective for social–ecological systems analyses. *Global Environmental Change*, 16, 253–267.

Forster, T. and Esceduro, A. G. (2014). *City Regions as Landscapes for People, Food and Nature*. Washington, DC: EcoAgriculture Partners.

Fresco, L. (2009). Challenges for food system adaptation today and tomorrow. *Environmental Science and Policy*, 378–385.

Fridman, J. and Lenters, L. (2013). Kitchen as food hub: Adaptive food systems governance in the City of Toronto. *Local Environment*, 18, 543–556.

Friedmann, H. (1995). The international political economy of food: A global crisis. *International Journal of Health Services*, 25, 511–538.

Gallopin, G. C. (2006). Linkages between vulnerability, resilience, and adaptive capacity. *Global environmental change*, 16, 293–303.

Ganry, J., Egal, F. and Taylor, M. (2011). Fruits and vegetables: A neglected wealth in developing countries. *Acta Horticulturae*, 921, 105–110.

Gereffi, G., Humphrey, J. and Sturgeon, T. (2005). The governance of global value chains. *Review of International Political Economy*, 12, 78–104.

Gerlach, S. C. and Loring, P. A. (2013). Rebuilding northern foodsheds, sustainable food systems, community well-being, and food security. *International Journal of Circumpolar Health*, 72.

Gillespie, G. W. J. (2010). 2009 AFHVS presidential address: The steering question: Challenges to achieving food system sustainability. *Agriculture and Human Values*, 27, 3–12.

Goldstein, J. (1999). Emergence as a construct: History and issues. *Emergence: Complexity and Organization*, 1, 49–72.

Hall, D. (2010). Food with a visible face: Traceability and the public promotion of private governance in the Japanese food system. *Geoforum*, 41, 826–835.

Hammond, R. A. and Dube, L. (2012). A systems science perspective and transdisciplinary models for food and nutrition security. *PNAS*, 109, 12356–12363.

Haysom, G. (2014). Food system governance for urban sustainability in the Global South. Unpublished Ph.D. thesis, University of Cape Town.

Hendrickson, M. K. and Heffernan, W. D. (2002). Opening spaces through relocalization: Locating potential resistance in the weaknesses of the global food system. *Sociologia Ruralis*, 42, 347–369.

Henson, S. (2011). Private agrifood governance: Conclusions, observations and provocations. *Agriculture and Human Values*, 28, 443–451.

Herforth, A., Frongillo, E. A., Sassi, F., Mclean, M. S., Arabi, M., Tirado, C., Remans, R., Mantilla, G., Thomson, M. and Pingali, P. (2014). Toward an integrated approach to nutritional quality, environmental sustainability, and economic viability: Research and measurement gaps. *Annals of the New York Academy of Sciences*, 1332, 1–21.

Hipel, K. W., Fang, L. and Heng, M. (2010). System of systems approach to policy development for global food security. *Journal of Systems Science and Systems Engineering*, 19, 1–21.

Hospes, O. (2014). Food sovereignty: the debate, the deadlock, and a suggested detour. *Agriculture and Human Values*, 31, 119–130.

Humphrey, J. and Schmitz, H. (2000). Governance and upgrading: Linking industrial cluster and global value chain research. *DS Working Paper 120*. Brighton: IDS.
Ingram, J. (2011a). A food systems approach to researching food security and its interactions with global environmental change. *Food Security*, 3, 417–431.
Ingram, J. (2011b). From food production to food security: Developing interdisciplinary, regional-level research. Unpublished Ph.D. thesis, Wageningen University.
Ingram, J., Ericksen, P. J. and Liverman, D. E. (2010). *Food Security and Global Environmental Change*. London and Washington, DC: Earthscan.
International Human Dimensions Programme (2009). Governance as a crosscutting theme in human dimensions science. Retrieved from www.ihdp.unu.edu/docs/Publications/Secretariat/Update-Dimensions/IHDP-Update-2009-3.pdf
Ison, R. L., Maiteny, P. T. and Carr, S. (1997). Systems methodologies for sustainable natural resources research and development. *Agricultural Systems*, 55, 257–272.
Johns, T., Powell, B., Maundu, P. and Eyzaguirre, P. B. (2013). Agricultural biodiversity as a link between traditional food systems and contemporary development, social integrity and ecological health. *Journal of the Science of Food and Agriculture*, 93, 3433–3442.
Kirwan, J. and Maye, D. (2013). Food security framings within the UK and the integration of local food systems. *Journal of Rural Studies*, 29, 91–100.
Konefal, J., Mascarenhas, M. and Hatanaka, M. (2005). Governance in the global agro-food system: Backlighting the role of transnational supermarket chains. *Agriculture and Human Values*, 22, 291–302.
La Vía Campesina (1996). Food sovereignty: A future without hunger. Statement by the NGO Forum to the Word Food Summit, 11–17 November. Retrieved from www.voiceoftheturtle.org/library/1996%20Declaration%20of%20Food%20Sovereignty.pdf
Lang, T. (2005a). What is food and farming for? – The (re) emergence of health as a key policy driver. *Research in Rural Sociology and Development*, 11, 123–144.
Lang, T. (2005b). Food control or food democracy? Re-engaging nutrition with society and the environment. *Public Health Nutrition*, 8, 730–737.
Lang, T., Barling, D. and Caraher, M. (2001). Food, social policy and the environment: Towards a new model. *Social Policy and Administration*, 35, 538–558.
Leach, M., Scoones, I. and Stirling, A. (2010). *Dynamic Sustainabilities: Technology, Environment, Social Justice*. London: Earthscan.
Lebel, L., Anderies, J. M., Campbell, B., Folke, C., Hatfield-Dodds, S., Hughes, T. P. and WIilson, J. (2006). Governance and the capacity to manage resilience in regional social–ecological systems. *Marine Sciences Faculty Scholarship*, Paper 52.
McMichael, P. (2011). Food system sustainability: Questions of environmental governance in the new world (dis)order. *Global Environmental Change*, 21, 804–812.
Macrae, R. (2011). A joined-up food policy for Canada. *Journal of Hunger and Environmental Nutrition*, 6, 424–457.
Macrae, R. and Donahue, K. (2013). Municipal food policy entrepreneurs: A preliminary analysis of how Canadian cities and regional districts are involved in food system change. Toronto: Toronto Food Policy Council and Canadian Agri-Food Policy Institute. Retrieved from http://capi-icpa.ca/pdfs/2013/Municipal_Food_Policy_Entrepreneurs_Final_Report.pdf

Mansfield, B. and Mendes, W. (2012). Municipal food strategies and integrated approaches to urban agriculture: Exploring three cases from the Global North. *International Planning Studies*, 18, 37–60.

Maxwell, S. and Slater, R. (2003). Food policy old and new. *Development Policy Review*, 21, 531–553.

Miller, M., Anderson, M., Francis, C. A., Kruger, C., Barford, C., Park, J. and McCown, B. H. (2013). Critical research needs for successful food systems adaptation to climate change. *Journal of Agriculture, Food Systems, and Community Development*, 3, 161–175.

Mount, P. (2012). Growing local food: Scale and local food systems governance. *Agriculture and Human Values*, 29, 107–121.

Nigh, R. and Gonzalez, Cabanas, A. A. (2014). Reflexive consumer markets as opportunities for new peasant farmers in Mexico: Constructing food sovereignty through alternative food networks. *Agroecology and Sustainable Food Systems* 39, 317–341.

Olson, J., Clay, P. M. and Pinto Da Silva, P. (2014). Putting the seafood in sustainable food systems. *Marine Policy*, 43, 104–111.

Pereira, L. M. (2013). The future of the food system: cases involving the private sector in South Africa. *Sustainability*, 1234–1255.

Pereira, L. M. (2014). The future of South Africa's food system: What is research telling us? SA Food Lab, South Africa. Retrieved from http://awsassets.wwf.org.za/downloads/safl_brochure_email.pdf

Pereira, L. M., Da Fontoura, Y. S. D. R. and Da Fontoura, C. F. V. T. (2013). Strategic CSR shifts towards adaptive food governance under environmental change: A comparison between South African and Brazilian retailers. *Revista de Gestao Social e Ambiental*, 7, 100–112.

Pereira, L. M. and Ruysenaar, S. (2012). Moving from traditional government to new adaptive governance: The changing face of food security responses in South Africa. *Food Security*, *4*, 41–58.

Pimbert, M. (2012). Putting citizens at the heart of food system governance. International Institute for Environment and Development. Retrieved from http://pubs.iied.org/17125IIED.html

Pol, J. L. V. (2014). The food commons transition: Collective actions for food and nutrition security. *Food sovereignty: A critical dialogue*. The Hague: International Institute of Social Studies.

Redman, C. L., Grove, J. M. and Kuby, L. H. (2004). Integrating social science into the Long-Term Ecological Research (LTER) network: Social dimensions of ecological change and ecological dimensions of social change. *Ecosystems*, 7, 161–171.

Rittel, H. W. J. and Webber, M. M. (1973). Dilemmas in a general theory of planning. *Policy Sciences*, 4, 155–169.

Rocha, C. and Lessa, I. (2009). Urban governance for food security: The alternative food system in Belo Horizonte, Brazil. *International Planning Studies*, 14, 389–400.

Schiff, R. (2008). The role of food policy councils in developing sustainable food systems. *Journal of Hunger and Environmental Nutrition*, 3, 206–228.

Schneider, D., Rodgers, Y. V. D. M. and Cheang, J. M. (2007). Local government coordination of community food systems in distressed urban areas. *Journal of Poverty*, 11, 45–69.

Seed, B., Lang, T., Caraher, M. and Ostry, A. (2013). Integrating food security into public health and provincial government departments in British Columbia, Canada. *Agriculture and Human Values*, 30, 457–470.

Sommerville, M., Essex, J. and Le Billon, P. (2014). The 'global food crisis' and the geopolitics of food security. *Geopolitics*, 19, 239–265.

Sonnino, R. (2013). Local foodscapes: Place and power in the agri-food system. *Acta Agriculturae Scandinavica Section B: Soil and Plant Science*, 63, 2–7.

Sonnino, R., Torres, C. L. and Schneider, S. (2014). Reflexive governance for food security: The example of school feeding in Brazil. *Journal of Rural Studies*, 36, 1–12.

Story, M., Hamm, M. W. and Wallinga, D. (2009). Research and action priorities for linking public health, food systems, and sustainable agriculture: Recommendations from the Airlie conference. *Journal of Hunger and Environmental Nutrition*, 4, 477–485.

Sundkvist, Å., Milestad, R. and Jansson, A. (2005). On the importance of tightening feedback loops for sustainable development of food systems. *Food Policy*, 30, 224–239.

Termeer, C. J. A. M., Dewulf, A. and Van Lieshout, M. (2010). Disentangling scale approaches in governance research: Comparing monocentric, multilevel, and adaptive governance. *Ecology and Society*, 15, 29.

Thompson, J. and Scoones, I. (2009). Addressing the dynamics of agri-food systems: An emerging agenda for social science research. *Environmental Science and Policy*, 12, 386–397.

Thornton, P. K., Ericksen, P. J., Herrero, M. and Challinor, A. J. (2014). Climate variability and vulnerability to climate change: a review. *Global Change Biology*, 20, 3313–3328.

Thornton, P. K., Jones, P. G., Ericksen, P. J. and Challinor, A. J. (2011). Agriculture and food systems in sub-Saharan Africa in a 4°C+ world. *Philosophical Transactions of the Royal Society A: Mathematical, Physical and Engineering Sciences*, 369, 117–136.

Treib, O., Bahr, H. and Falkner, G. (2007). Modes of governance: Towards a conceptual clarification. *Journal of European public policy*, 14, 1–20.

Vermeulen, S. J., Aggarwal, P. K., Ainslie, A., Angelone, C., Campbell, B. M., Challinor, A. J., Hansen, J. W., Ingram, J., Jarvis, A., Kristjanson, P., Lau, C., Nelson, G. C., Thornton, P. K. and Wollenberg, E. (2012a). Options for support to agriculture and food security under climate change. *Environmental Science and Policy*, 15, 136–144.

Vermeulen, S. J., Campbell, B. M. and Ingram, J. (2012b). Climate change and food systems. *Annual Review of Environment and Resources*, 37, 195–222.

Vervoort, J., Ingram, J., Ericksen, P., Chaudhury, M., Foerch, W., Thornton, P. and Kristjanson, P. (2012). Multi-actor scenarios to build capacity for food systems governance at the sub-continental level. *Earth System Governance*. Retrieved from www.earthsystemgovernance.org/lund2012/LC2012-paper332.pdf

Von Braun, J. and Islam, N. (2008). Toward a new global governance system for agriculture, food, and nutrition. *IFPRI Blogs*. International Food Policy Research Institute. Retrieved from www.ifpri.org/blog/toward-new-global-governance-system-agriculture-food-and-nutrition?print

Wahlqvist, M. L. and Lee, M. S. (2007). Regional food culture and development. *Asia Pacific Journal of Clinical Nutrition*, 16, 2–7.

Wegener, J., Raine, K. D. and Hanning, R. M. (2012). Insights into the government's role in food system policy making: Improving access to healthy, local food alongside other priorities. *International Journal of Environmental Research and Public Health*, 9, 4103–4121.

White, R., Stewart, B. and O'Neill, P. (2010). Access to food in a changing climate. Oxford Institute of Ageing and the Environmental Change Institute. Retrieved from www.ageing.ox.ac.uk/files/Access_to_food_in_a_changing_climate.pdf

WHO (2014). European food and nutrition action plan 2015–2020. Retrieved from www.euro.who.int/__data/assets/pdf_file/0008/253727/64wd14e_FoodNutAP_140426.pdf

WRR (2014). *Naar een voedselbeleid.* Amsterdam: Amsterdam University Press.

Yu, Q., Wu, W., Yang, P., Li, Z., Xiong, W. and Tang, H. (2012). Proposing an interdisciplinary and cross-scale framework for global change and food security researches. *Agriculture, Ecosystems and Environment*, 156, 57–71.

3 Food sovereignty

Governance and exclusion in an alternative social movement

Kristal Jones and John T. Eshleman

Introduction

Critical analysis of the contemporary dominant global food system often focuses on the economic arrangements that structure the system (Busch, 2010; Friedmann, 2005) and the power dynamics among actors that define certain linkages and paths (Bair and Werner, 2011; Gereffi et al., 2005). Questions about the political economy of food and agriculture have long focused on the inequalities inherent in these economic and power dynamics, and these questions have generated social movements to respond to a perceived injustice (for an overview of US agrarian political economy, see Buttel, 2001; for a global review, van der Ploeg, 2008). From fair trade and organic certification (see Busch and Bain, 2004; Guthman, 2004) to an emphasis on producing and buying local food (Hinrichs and Allen, 2008; Goodman and DuPuis, 2002) to a resistance toward genetically modified production systems (Schurman and Munro, 2010), individuals and communities have mobilized to create alternative food production and consumption systems as a way to deal with the negative externalities associated with the dominant global food system. Often termed "alternative agrifood movements" (AAMs), this range of movements each with their own particularistic goals "together reflect widening disenchantment with conventional corporatized agriculture and food" (Hinrichs and Eshleman, 2014, p. 139, see also Constance et al., 2014).

The inequalities and injustices that have sparked AAMs have been framed in a variety of ways, and these frames are then reflected in the institutions that support the alternative systems being created. The specific framing and institutionalization of social movement goals – diagnosing the problem, formulating a solution, and motivating social action – also affect the ultimate impacts of the movements (Benford and Snow 2000). Structural analysis of the role of social movements in generating alternative systems, like those emerging from political economy approaches, can provide a foundation for characterizing ideal and actual governance arrangements among systems (Evans, 2008; Brenner and Theodore, 2002). Holt-Giménez and Shattuck (2011), for example, analyze AAMs through the lens of modern political economy, and argue that the crises generated by the dominant food system have spawned the social movement responses to the dominant system. They pose the theoretical question of whether these social movements can in fact govern and change the dominant global food system, or whether the creation of alternative spaces actually supports the perpetuation of the dominant system with all its inequalities that AAMs are ostensibly mobilized against (see also Fairbairn, 2012).

Governance here focuses on questions of who holds rhetorical and political power, and "the *processes* by which power is exercised in society" (emphasis in original) (Tallontire, 2007, p. 776). How exactly abstract power is translated into impact, through institutionalization of governance relationships can be made further precise by drawing on social movements theory. Social movements theory provides conceptual tools for assessing the potential impact of specific movements and *why* and *how* actual impacts do or do not emerge by focusing on the movements' ability to both take advantage of political opportunities and mobilize formal and informal resources. In particular, exploring structural changes that have provided openings upon which food and seed sovereignty movements have capitalized for the good of their goals will be useful for clarifying the potential impacts of these movements (for a general review of political opportunity structure, see Tarrow, 2011; Meyer and Minkoff, 2004). Combining theoretical analysis of political economy and governance with social movement frameworks that focus on the rhetorical and structural characteristics of AAMs extends evaluations of the actual transformative potential for governance and justice in the food system.

This chapter presents an overview of the food sovereignty movement as a response to inequality and injustice identified in the dominant contemporary global food system. It explores the implications for governance and exclusion that emerge from investigating food sovereignty with a social movements framework. Historical and current trends of the food sovereignty movement within the broader global food system, and within the movement itself, are presented to elaborate the argument being made here: that the framing and governance structures of the food sovereignty movement have ambiguous potential to be both inclusive and exclusive. Using the specific example of seed sovereignty, we then present a short empirical case study that characterizes a potential seed sovereignty movement in West Africa, analyzing qualitative data for themes about which farmers choose to engage, which seed systems and why. The literature and history of food sovereignty, and empirical case of change seed systems in West Africa, suggest that any singular framing of how best to change the agrifood system is likely to exclude some individuals. Exclusion remains a challenge for AAMs and social movements focused on injustice and inequality, a challenge that can potentially be addressed through the same mechanisms of discourse and governance structures that define the social movements, if those mechanisms can shift to being inclusive and dynamic rather than reactive and static.

Food sovereignty as social movement and radical frame

Combining the governance and social movements theories of systemic change to evaluate the impact of AAMs requires characterizing the discursive process that translates abstract and rhetorical analysis into action (see Dryzek, 1990, for discussion of discourse and social change). Mooney and Hunt (2009) offer one example of a discursive approach to understanding and evaluating the emergence and impact of social movements that demand change in the food system. They draw on the sociological concepts of strategic frames and keys, and situate movements toward change through governance in the contemporary dominant food system within the broad frame of food security. Food security here is a colloquial 'consensus frame,' an articulation of the goals of the global food system that are broadly acceptable and shared by virtually all actors within and around the system. Identification of the actions necessary to achieve food security, as well as the deficiencies in the current system that must be addressed, then frames discourses that generate social movements motivated by keying concepts. Mooney and Hunt (2009) identify two frames within the goal of food security – risk and hunger – and two keys – sharp (radical) and flat (reformist) – that have generated movements, institutions and governance structures within and around the dominant contemporary global food system. The risk keys are addressed by other chapters in this book, with the sharp key focused on agricultural terrorism and conflicts, and the flat key focused on food safety (see Chapters 9 and 10, this volume).

The hunger keys are likely more familiar to readers interested in governance of global food systems than the risk keys. The flat key of hunger is food security in the United Nations' sense of "availability, accessibility, utilization and stability" (FAO, 2008). Mooney and Hunt's (2009) description of the flat key of food security echoes Holt-Giménez and Shattuck's (2011) and others' assessments that food security is a reformist movement within the existing food system (see also McMichael, 2005; Windhufr and Jonsen, 2005). The sharp key of hunger is food sovereignty, an AAM that emerged out of both structural and discursive analysis of inequalities in the dominant global food system, and arguments for food production and consumption as a basic human right (de Schutter, 2010; Borras et al., 2008; Desmarais, 2008; Windhufr and Jonsen, 2005). The framings of the flat and sharp keys of hunger have implications for the theoretical and structural analysis that provide a foundation for related AAMs, and thereby influence the types of governance structures that these social movements generate and their ultimate impacts. The flat key food security movement is reformist, in that it neither challenges the neoliberal underpinnings of the dominant global food system, nor engages radical challenges of the national and international governance institutions, instead working for reform within these systems. In contrast, the sharp key of food sovereignty demands both resistance to and autonomy from the economic systems that shape the dominant global food system working to create alternative policy and governance structures that function outside of the dominant system.

Food sovereignty as a social movement to govern inequalities in the food system

The food sovereignty movement is today discussed as a relatively unified social movement, with an origin story, key organizational leaders and a consistent presence, both participating and protesting at major international fora. As an AAM, food sovereignty is generally framed as a transnational agrarian movement (Borras et al., 2008; Desmarais, 2008), a description that situates the theoretical and material goals both spatially and substantively. The food sovereignty movement emerged in the early 1990s, and began not as a single transnational movement but as a collection of disparate localized reactions to the disembedding and disenfranchising effects of neoliberal economic and trade policies (see Desmarais, 2002, for a history of the emergence of the food sovereignty movement). As agricultural producers in specific places began to identify common patterns in their experiences of inequality in the global food regime (see Friedmann, 2005), a structural analysis and framing of the issues began to emerge. Academics and advocacy organizations provided language to help unify the patterns in experience, solidifying the social movement in a frame of resistance, 'rebellion,' and ultimately self-determination (Vía Campesina, 2009; Borras et al., 2008; Holt-Giménez and Peabody, 2008). McMichael (2008, p. 43) defines the food sovereignty frame quite succinctly: "food embodies a broader set of relations, becoming a window on the social, demographic and ecological catastrophe of neoliberalism."

As this frame was articulated by activists and academics to give language to agrarian experiences of the 1990s, and as personal and organizational connections were established, the peasant organization the Vía Campesina ('Peasants' Way' in Spanish) became the face of the food sovereignty movement globally. Desmarais (2002, p. 2014) charts the emergence of the Vía Campesina as both a confederation of local and regional peasant and farmer organizations, and a composite organization that consolidated the social movement framed in resistance to neoliberalism. As many observers have noted, the food sovereignty movement in general and the Vía Campesina in particular have had success in generating and framing global conversations about governance and power in the food system (Holt-Giménez and Shattuck, 2011; Borras et al., 2008; Friedmann, 2005). From a broader social movements perspective, however, analyzing the actual impacts of the food sovereignty movement requires unpacking the political opportunities and resource mobilization upon which the movement has been able to build. The Vía Campesina has struggled with these questions from the beginning, with especially intense focus on questions of which types of political opportunities are appropriate and acceptable given the movement's framing. For example, as the organizational head of the transnational food sovereignty movement, the Vía Campesina has consistently struggled with whether or not to engage with dominant global governance systems like the World Trade Organization (which they have consistently opposed) and the United Nations agencies and conventions on food security (with which they collaborate) (Borras et al., 2008). At the same time, the food sovereignty movement has allied itself with transnational social movements like the World Social Forum, which are working to articulate alternatives to the global governance structures like those mentioned above that dominate the neoliberal era (Desmarais, 2008).

The food sovereignty movement and the Vía Campesina currently exist in an ambiguous space, where the framing of the social movement demands one approach to governance and change in the food system, while the pragmatic political reality suggests that opportunities for compromise and reform are more likely to generate hybrid governance than commitment to radical change (see Higgins and Lockie, 2002; Stenson and Watt, 1999 for discussion of hybrid governance). From a structural perspective, the food sovereignty movement has been framed as one of resistance to neoliberalism, and in part because the academic and theoretical discourse has defined neoliberalism as a monolithic, global force, resistance is defined as similarly absolute (Kloppenburg, 2010; McMichael, 2008; Harvey, 2006; Shiva, 2002). However, the experiences lived by the diverse actors within the food sovereignty movement have generated a range of political opportunities upon which the movement can and has capitalized. These opportunities range from participating in the United Nations Committee on World Food Security to working with states to incorporate food sovereignty principles into national constitutions (Vía Campesina, 2014; Pimbert et al., 2010; Windhufr and Jonsen, 2005).

The seed sovereignty movement provides a specific example of the potential conflict that exists between the framing of the food sovereignty movement and contemporary political and material opportunities. Seed sovereignty has been championed by some in the movement, as an ultimate right for farmers, and one that can only exist outside of modern plant breeding techniques and the proprietary systems that enable the commodification of the genetic material contained in seeds (Vía Campesina, 2014; Shiva, 2002). This vision of seed sovereignty, which is based on seed saving and sharing and the non-monetized use of genetic resources, is consistent with the broader frame of food sovereignty as resisting the commodification of food and the means of producing it. Kloppenburg (2010) and the Open Source Seed Initiative,[1] however, offer a vision of seed sovereignty that tries to operationalize the discourse of the food sovereignty movement while building on contemporary political opportunities to ensure free use of genetic resources. Kloppenburg's (2010) vision of seed sovereignty is predicated on the notion of a public commons that is protected by hybrid governance structures rather than through the creation of a separate, similarly exclusive seed system based on saving and sharing (see also McCarthy, 2005, for discussion of commons as 'counter-hegemonic' governance). The tensions that exist between the framing and actions of the food sovereignty movement are captured in debates about seed sovereignty as well, and provide a window into questions about equity and inclusion in the food sovereignty movement as a whole.

Who is included and who is excluded in the food sovereignty frame?

The framing of the food sovereignty movement as being anti-neoliberal, anti-colonial, and self-deterministic has implications for how the movement relates to other AAMs, as well as to organizations and institutions that constitute the dominant global food system. Tensions between the abstract framing of food sovereignty as resistance to a monolithic modern agriculture and the material realities of individual farmers and communities also play out within the food sovereignty movement itself. In a paper for the recent conference, Food Sovereignty: A Critical Dialogue,[2] Bernstein (2013) poses several questions that highlight these tensions and the potential for exclusion and injustice within the food sovereignty movement that they raise. Who is considered a peasant for the purposes of food sovereignty? Are all peasants the same in their interests, production practices, and market actions? And, finally, how do the material realities of individuals and communities relate to the structural analysis that frames the food sovereignty movement in resistance to the absolutism of contemporary globalization of the food systems? Bernstein's (2013) ultimate critique of the rhetoric of the food sovereignty movement follows this last point. "An abstract and unitary conception of 'peasants' is actualized in the food sovereignty discourse through farming practices that exemplify their virtues as capital's other: the 'emblematic instance' of agroecological principles at work" (Bernstein, 2013, p. 22).

Essentialism within the food sovereignty frame has the potential to generate the same type of exclusion from the proposed alternative as that identified and resisted in neoliberalism. In the latter, the market system is taken as a given, and those who cannot or will not accept market principles, including the commodification of nature, are excluded from participating on their own terms. In the food sovereignty frame, agroecology, resistance to commodification of the inputs and outputs of agriculture, and the primacy of local institutions are foundational. What place is there then for a medium-size farmer in North America, who shares the structural critiques of the food sovereignty frames and yet lives wholly in a market society (Desmarais and Wittman, 2015)? What about a smallholder, labor-constrained farmer in sub-Saharan Africa who relies on herbicide rather than hand-weeding to increase yields? And what if local priorities fall somewhere in the complex middle between complete independence from or acceptance of the dominant global food system?

Desmarais (2008) identifies these and other long-standing tensions within the food sovereignty movement, and argues that the movement had remained inclusive through its discursive and democratic approach to articulating a unified frame. Holt-Giménez and Shattuck (2011) argue that this frame consolidation will be necessary for the food sovereignty movement to counter hegemonic globalization, and maintain that the inclusion of self-determination as foundational to goals of the movement will mitigate potential exclusion. Claeys (2013) notes as well that engagement with the human rights frame has helped the food sovereignty movement to define a new type of discursive space that emphasizes collective over individual claims, and asks questions about self-determination at multiple scales. The framing process in social movements is dynamic, so questions about inclusion and exclusion through boundary setting persist. Frame disputes regarding the movement's goals, strategies, and targets can create fissures within the collective effort (Benford, 1993), giving way to challenges in frame alignment, processes intended to bolster intra-movement solidarity and increase potential impacts (Snow et al., 1986). Recent critiques include Park, White, and Julia (2013), who note the lack of critical gender analysis within food sovereignty goals and priorities, and Bernstein (2013), who questions whether the production goals of the food sovereignty movement are in fact realistic for the majority of the world's producers.

These and other contemporary critiques of the food sovereignty movement continue to note that peasants' self-determination and ideal governance structures have the potential to be essentialized within the food sovereignty frame, a problem that is not unique to the food sovereignty movement as an example of either an AAM or a social movement more generally. Guthman (2004) charts a similar trajectory in the organics movement in the United States, where initial radical goals for agricultural production systems and the social relationships within those systems have moved toward a more reformist orientation over time. Radical framings in social movements and the symbols generated to mobilize support can be polarizing and therefore exclusionary, fostering disengagement among participants (Snow and Soule, 2010). The upside to this exclusion is a purity in mission and the ability to focus on building governance structures that can push alternative prescriptions into dominant political and social spaces. In the case of organics, however, the third-party certification system that has emerged as the major governance mechanism has had to be negotiated within the dominant food system, thereby broadening the tent of organic producers and diluting some key features of the original organic AAM (Guthman, 2004; Goodman and DuPuis, 2002).

Efforts toward seed sovereignty present a similar, emerging example from within the food sovereignty movement. Seed sovereignty as articulated by Vía Campesina (2014) and others working within the food sovereignty frame focuses on the rights of farmers to save seeds, and on how proprietary governance structures and modern plant breeding are antithetical to seed sovereignty (see also Shiva's Navdanya movement).[3] Another vision for seed sovereignty reframes the conversation to focus on the contemporary governance mechanisms that can be used to protect seeds, a type of commons (Chapter 8, this volume; Kloppenburg, 2010; McCarthy, 2005). Ongoing framing and mobilization work by the Open Source Seed Initiative engages with the contemporary political and economic governance structures, and works to creatively adapt these structures and create seeds systems that respond to the social and political demands of seed sovereignty. Seed sovereignty in this altered frame also brings modern plant science into the conversation with peasant farmer needs through adaptive approaches like participatory plant breeding

(Badstue et al., 2012; Kloppenburg, 2010). The short case study that follows uses the example of emerging seed systems in West Africa to illustrate the exclusionary potential of engaging with only a single frame for food (and seed) systems, and identifies governance structures that have the potential to construct an inclusive seed sovereignty in the region.

Case study: reframing seed systems in West Africa

Seed systems are one small component of agricultural production systems, and of the food system overall. At the same time, seed systems are a useful, manageable microcosm within which to ground discussions about governance, sovereignty, and framing. Seed systems "are comprised of a set of market and non-market institutions that govern farmers' access to and use of seeds, and of the genetic resources held therein" (Lipper et al., 2010, p. 5). Although using the language of systems and networks, seed systems are often characterized in the literature as dichotomously either formal or informal. Formal seed systems consist of institutions that use modern scientific plant breeding techniques to produce and disseminate seeds that can be certified as distinct, uniform and stable (Louwaars and de Boef, 2012; Desclaux et al., 2008). These institutions include public and private research centers and scientists, third-party certifiers and the regulatory regimes that they enforce, intellectual property rights (patents) law, and market actors to reproduce and disseminate seeds via seed sales. Informal seed systems, in the literature, are often defined in contrast to these specific types of institutions and processes. Informal seed systems are 'everything else' – seeds that have been saved and managed by farmers for any length of time, genetic combinations that are not standard or static, and methods of producing, reproducing, and disseminating seeds that do not utilize modern science and formal markets (see Louwaars and de Boef, 2012; Sperling and McGuire, 2010 for extensive discussion of seed system characteristics). In the characterization of seed systems, we see corollaries to the definitions and dichotomies present in the definitions of the dominant food system and the food sovereignty alternative.

Seed systems for local grain crops (sorghum and pearl millet) in the Sahelian West African countries of Mali, Burkina Faso, and Niger have historically been informal, with little emphasis from public or private plant scientists on breeding improved varieties and virtually no development of a formal market (Lynam, 2011). The lack of engagement by the formal system with seed systems for local grain crops does not mean, however, that the informal seed systems were static or insulated. Agricultural production systems in the region are characterized by a high degree of variability in micro-ecosystems, which means that farmers are both innovative and diversified in their management of production systems (Moseley, 2008). Farmer experimentation and management of genetic resources is integral to these informal seed systems, even if this management occurs at a phenotypic (based on observable traits) rather than genotypic (genetic) level (Haussmann and Kapran, 2007; Omanya et al., 2007). And similarly, farmers and other actors have a range of institutional arrangements that facilitate access to the seeds, including seeds sales, seed exchanges, and in-kind gifts. In many ways, seed systems in the region can be characterized less in dichotomous terms and more as increasingly integrating formal and informal institutions and designations into a single, inclusive seed system. One important component of Sahelian seed systems that has remained relatively inflexible, however, is the injunction against selling sorghum or pearl millet seeds. This is because seeds are seen to be a historical birthright and function as social currency outside of the monetary system (Smale et al., 2008). This economic conviction is reminiscent of food and seed sovereignty's adamant stance against the commodification of nature and the means of agricultural production, although it has not to date been explicitly mobilized to this end.

Beginning in 2009, one of the authors of this chapter conducted dissertation research in conjunction with an international agricultural research center based in Sahelian West Africa, documenting the social impacts of participatory plant breeding (PPB) and seed system development activities. During this time, there were many changes in the framing of seed system challenges and appropriate responses to them, as well as the opportunity structures upon which potential AAMs could build. Discussion about the introduction of genetically modified cotton began in the early 2000s, and it was this issue that catalyzed the emergent food sovereignty movement in West Africa. In 2006, a series of farmer 'citizen juries' was held in Mali to evaluate the framing and impact of agricultural research in the region. The results of these juries provided a frame for a new AAM in the region, and demanded of research a focus on agroecology and the development of seed varieties that could be saved by farmers (SWAC, 2007; Pimbert et al., 2010). In 2007, there was an international meeting of the food sovereignty movement held in Nyéléyni, Mali, which helped to expand the West African Peasant Organisations and Producers (ROPPA) regional food sovereignty movement (Nyéléni, 2007; SWAC, 2007). In 2009, at the regional policy level, a law was passed that established a framework for harmonizing the seed certification laws of the Economic Community of West African States (ECOWAS). Part of this law made it illegal to sell seeds that had not been formally certified in a laboratory, and these regulations now guide the activities of the international and national public research centers working on seed system development (INSAH, 2009). And at the level of research-for-development actors, the PPB project had been under way for five years, funded initially by a small, US-based philanthropic organization that focuses funding on agroecological research for development. In 2009, however, the research organization received a large, multi-year, tens-of-millions-of-dollars project from the Bill & Melinda Gates Foundation to fund the downstream work of seed diffusion and the development of commercial (formal) seed systems.

Farmers in Sahelian West Africa began to work with plant breeders and agronomists on modern or formal varietal development projects just a few years before the citizens' juries began (vom Brocke et al., 2010; Pimbert et al., 2010; Weltzien et al., 2008). On the upstream side, PPB approaches are both pragmatic and inclusive, seeking to bring all actors in the seed system together to set priorities for the types of characteristics and varieties demanded by specific ecological and social settings (for extensive discussion of the PPB process, see Ceccarelli et al., 2009). The commitment to incorporating all actors' perspectives is foundational to participatory approaches and broadly means that the public-sector plant breeders leading the PPB process have identified farmer engagement and empowerment as possible solutions to the challenges of increasing access to quality seed. These commitments clearly drove the conceptualization and implementation of the PPB project with which one of the authors works – the plant breeders were dedicated to spending time in the field with farmers, incorporating their feedback, and working toward empowering outcomes (Jones et al., 2014). The framing in the upstream phase of this project, by funders, researchers, and farmers was that solutions to the problem of vulnerability and unimproved seeds included incorporating both farmer and scientist knowledge, acknowledging the particularities of the social and ecological contexts, and working toward a 'development-oriented' seed system (Badstue et al., 2012; Desclaux et al., 2008).

The second phase of the seed system development project followed the PPB process and focused on reproduction and diffusion of seeds of new varieties of sorghum and pearl millet that were generated out of the PPB process. Although initially conceptualized as participatory seed diffusion (Bishaw and Turner, 2008), the seed system development project's goals and framing of problems and solutions shifted with the influx of the Gates Foundation money. The local categorization of seeds as something not to be sold was already a challenging element of the social context for PPB activities to incorporate into their downstream seed dissemination activities. With the Gates Foundation rhetoric about public–private partnerships and the importance of agrodealers and seed companies, however, any discussion of non-market-based seed reproduction and diffusion ceased (for discussion of the Gates Foundation in international development, see Scoones and Thompson, 2011; Brooks et al., 2009). The convergence of policy changes (toward seed laws that legitimate only the formal seed system) and funding priorities have led to the dominant agricultural research and development organizations to frame seed system challenges in terms of lack of improved varieties, especially hybrid varieties, of sorghum and pearl millet, and lack of functioning formal markets. In contrast, the emerging seed sovereignty movement has framed their demands in terms of local knowledge and rights to genetic resources, much like the sharp key food sovereignty frame. This frame takes issue with trade liberalization, and the privatization of agricultural research and knowledge (Pimbert et al., 2010; SWAC, 2007).

The food and seed sovereignty movement in West Africa is led by the Network of West African Peasant Organisations and Producers (ROPPA), of which many local farmer organizations are a part. Interviews conducted by one of the authors with over 500 farmers who are members of some of these farmer organizations over the past several years have identified both a consistent frame for understanding seed access issues in the region, as well as some ambiguities in the solutions identified by either the dominant or the alternative narratives about seed system development. These interviews were conducted over four years in five sites across Mali, Burkina Faso, and Niger, in areas where local farmer organizations have participated in the PPB and seed system projects to develop and disseminate improved, open-pollinated, and hybrid varieties of sorghum (in the former two countries) and pearl millet (in the latter). These farmer organizations are also members of ROPPA, although none of them explicitly participated in the citizen juries or the Nyéléni meeting described above. Instead, these farmer organizations and the individual farmers who interact with them exemplify the tensions within and around the food and seed sovereignty movement in Sahelian West Africa.

When asked about their perceptions and experiences of the shift from informal seed systems, in which there is an injunction against selling local grain seeds, toward a formal, market-based seed system, many farmers expressed appreciation for the certainty that comes with seed sales. "When you ask another farmer [for seeds], maybe they will not give you what you ask for. But when you buy, you know that what you want is what you bought," one farmer in Mali explained. The formal seed system, with its networks of agrodealers and packaged, labelled seeds, increases access by standardizing both the information and the process for acquiring seeds. The vagaries of interpersonal relationship that support seed access in information seed systems are replaced by consistent market mechanisms. However, this standardization also means that access to improved variety seeds in the formal system is only available through monetary transactions. Therefore, anyone without cash is inherently excluded. One woman in Burkina Faso summed it up, saying that "before, there was solidarity. People gave seeds, and others exchanged. But now you have to pay."

The reality that different types of people will require different types of system to access seeds means that the distinct dominant, formal seed system and alternative, sovereign seed system frameworks will always leave out some more inclusive, in-between space. Most farmers in West Africa do in action what some academics and activists are calling for in theory: integrating formal and informal seed systems through localized institutions and conventions (Louwaars and de Boef, 2012; Kloppenburg, 2010; Sperling and McGuire, 2010). From the point of view of research and technology, the formal seed system frame focuses on generating distinct, uniform and stable improved varieties that by definition cannot be saved from year to year. The emphasis on not saving seeds entering the PPB and seed system projects overviewed above in large part is based on donor and policy priorities. In reaction, some regional and international AAMs associated with some of the food sovereignty movement in the region began a publicity campaign against 'new' seeds, highlighting their inability to be saved. The scientific truth is somewhere in the middle, since many of the new varieties of sorghum and pearl millet generated by the PPB project are open-pollinated, and so can be saved but will have increasing genetic heterogeneity over subsequent generations. In Mali, however, the word chosen for both 'new' seeds and 'genetically engineered (GE)' seeds in Bambara translates to 'seeds that cannot be saved,' and so information specific to GE seeds was attributed to all new seeds. Many farmers, having received conflicting messages about the desirability of relinquishing seed saving, have instead continued to experiment and make decisions that fit into their own contexts. As one man in Niger explained, he "replants the seeds one time, after the second use, for [an improved variety], if he plants the first generation, after the following year, he replants, and then he will no longer use them."

The formal seed system frame also emphasizes the need for certification and market structures for seed dissemination, two institutional forms fundamentally opposed by the sharp key seed sovereignty frame. Many farmers who have access to the formal market as seed producers identify the tension that exists between these two frames within their communities. One farmer in Mali explained that "since I produce seeds, and then I sell them, [people] think that they are my own seeds [local varieties] that I'm selling. And they want to have them as a gift." To deal with this tension, seed producers and farmers who want to share the benefits of improved varieties have adapted a range of institutions that are compatible with their social context. In terms of standardization, some farmers simply sell or exchange seeds that could otherwise be certified outside of the formal markets. In addition, in some places socially embedded certification systems, based on familiarity and trust rather than a third party, are also beginning to emerge (see Sperling and McGuire, 2010, for discussion of social certification). The terms for accessing seeds also continue to evolve away from the singular formal market but continuing to include some type of valuation and exchange basis. For example, one seed producer in Burkina Faso who functions very much within the formal seed system explained how kinship ties mediate market structures: "When it's family, it's among us, sometimes we do exchanges ... because people don't have the money to buy. If your brother comes and says, I want that variety, you have to exchange." Exchange institutions have begun to emerge more generally in the region, as farmers have "adopted a system of exchange: one measure of improved variety seeds for two measures of local seeds."

Discussion

This case study can be analyzed from a social movements perspective to identify the framing choices made by actors working to build support for the dominant and alternative food systems, as well as some key moments of political opportunity that have created the possibility for change in specific context of seed systems in Sahelian West Africa. Most individual farmers who are members of farmer organizations that participate in regional food sovereignty discussions do not explicitly make use of either the dominant (flat) or alternative (sharp) frames to describe their desires for seed system development. However, farmer organizations, particularly those connected to international social movements and organizations, are increasingly drawing on the language and framing of global AAMs (Desmarais, 2014). The sharp key of seed sovereignty in West Africa warns against modern genetic combinations, scientific certification, and market institutions to facilitate access to seeds. This response is largely a reaction to global and regional pressures from trade and science policy, international development donors (and in this specific context the frame provided by the Gates Foundation's vision for seed system development) and contextual scientific research.

The confluence of discussions about the introduction of GE crops and the influx of philanthropic and donor money focused on developing formal seeds systems have created political opportunities upon which a small but emerging food and seed sovereignty movement has capitalized through activities like the citizen juries and Nyéléni meetings (Pimbert et al., 2010; Nyéléni, 2007). With an influx of resources (and by extension influence) from the Gates Foundation in service to the flat key of creating food security through increased production and economic efficiency, food and seed sovereignty movements have an opportunity to mobilize for local knowledge and control of genetic resources. In other words, attempts by the international development community to move the seed system toward formality have created openings for the sharper frame of food and sovereignty to challenge the motivations and meanings of that push, while advocating and pressuring for a more inclusive and just seed system rather than the dominant one. Specifically, farmer organizations seized the opportunity afforded them via the donor and policy push for formal seed systems by framing such initiatives as attempts to limit community embedded seed saving practices and exchange patterns common in Sahalian West Africa. Certification policies present food and seed sovereignty adherents as an additional opportunity, as the 2009 law requiring formal certification for all sellable seeds suggests. Policies such as these create opportunities for movements to respond and mobilize, particularly when they can frame these policy changes as problems that require action from food and seed sovereignty advocates.

Farmer organizations in Sahelian West Africa and the AAMs of which they are a part are employing the food sovereignty frame to act on political opportunities to resist the encroachment of the dominant seed system in the region. However, individual farmers' descriptions of how and why they choose to access seeds express less of an either/or orientation toward potential changes in seed systems, and more of an interest in governing the exclusionary effects of any single system. Many farmers in the region have substantial experience with PPB and other adaptive forms of agricultural research for development. This long-term familiarity with iterative innovation processes has the potential to build capacity and empower farmers to generate new framings of problems and solutions (Ashby et al., 2009). In the Sahelian West African context, farmers are beginning to develop some adaptive approaches to facilitating access to a wide range of seed types (including improved varieties being produced and sold in the formal seed system) and governing the exclusionary effects of the market-oriented approach to seed dissemination (Jones et al., 2014). Generating non-monetary exchange rates of seed for seed and sharing information with other farmers about the phenotypic changes that come from saving new seed varieties, are two examples of adaptive governance to generate an integrated, rather than alternative, seed system (see Louwaars and de Boef, 2012).

Food sovereignty as a type of AAM has been largely framed as resistance to the exclusionary impacts of the dominant global food system. Busch (2010) argues that the singular focus on resistance of the dominant global food and economic system has generated creative conversations and actions that work to implement the resistance and alternative frames through new institutions and governance arrangements (see also Wright and Middendorf, 2008). However, the sharp key of food sovereignty can become a homogeneous alternative frame, and then has the potential to exclude individuals and organizations who want to broaden options and opportunities within the food system by governing the dominant/alternative dichotomy. McCarthy (2005) identifies the contemporary notion of the commons as a 'counterhegemonic' category that offers a new frame for governance of natural (and virtual) resources. In the context of agricultural production (as a subsystem within the global food system), seeds are a useful example of a commons, and are acknowledged as such by the singular, sharp key food sovereignty frame as well as by governance-oriented seed sovereignty movements like the Open Source Seed Initiative (Kloppenburg, 2010). Individual farmers' actions also often reflect a notion to explore the framings and governance structures that could catalyze activities oriented toward integrated, rather than singular, systems.

Notes

1 For full description of the project, see www.osseeds.org
2 All conference papers available at www.yale.edu/agrarianstudies/foodsovereignty
3 For full description of the project, see www.navdanya.org

References

Ashby, J. A, Braun, A, Gracia, T., Guerrero, M. D. P., Hernández, L. A., Quirós, C. A. and Roa, J. I. (2009). *Investing in Farmers as Researchers*. Cali, Colombia: International Center for Tropical Agriculture.

Badstue, A. L. B., Hellin, J. and Berthaud, J. (2012). Re-orienting participatory plant breeding for wider impact. *African Journal of Agricultural Research*, 7(4), 523–533.

Bair, J. and Werner, M. (2011). Commodity chains and the uneven geographies of global capitalism: A disarticulations perspective. *Environment and Planning A*, 43(5), 988–997.

Benford, R. D. (1993). Frame disputes within the nuclear disarmament movement. *Social Forces*, 71(3), 677–701.

Benford. R. D. and Snow, D. A. (2000). Framing processes and social movements: An overview and assessment. *Annual Review of Sociology*, 26, 611–639.

Bernstein, H. (2013). Food sovereignty: A skeptical view. Paper presented at the Food Sovereignty: A Critical Dialogue Conference. New Haven, CT, Sept. 14–15, www.yale.edu/agrarianstudies/foodsovereignty/papers.html

Bishaw, Z. and Turner, M. (2008). Linking participatory plant breeding to the seed supply system. *Euphytica*, 163(1), 31–44.

Borras, S. M., Edelman, M. and Kay, C. (Eds.). (2008). *Transnational Agrarian Movements Confronting Globalization*. Malden, MA: Wiley-Blackwell.

Brenner, N. and Theodore, N. (2002). Cities and the geographies of "actually existing neoliberalism." *Antipode*, 34(4), 351–379.

Brooks, S., Leach, M., Lucas, H. and Millstone, E. (2009). *Silver Bullets, Grand Challenges and the New Philanthropy*. STEPS Working Paper. Brighton, UK: STEPS Centre.

Busch, L. (2010). Can fairy tales come true?: The surprising story of neoliberalism and world agriculture. *Sociologia Ruralis*, 50(4), 331–351.

Busch, L, and Bain, C. (2004). New! Improved? The transformation of the global agrifood system. *Rural Sociology,* 69(3), 321–346.

Buttel, F. (2001). Some reflections on late 20th century agrarian political economy. *Sociologia Ruralis*, 41(2), 165–181.

Ceccarelli, S., Guimaraes, E. P. and Weltzien, E. (2009). *Plant Breeding and Farmer Participation*. Rome: United Nations Food and Agriculture Organization.

Claeys, P. (2013). From food sovereignty to peasants' rights: An overview of La Vía Campesina's rights-based claims over the last 20 years. Paper presented at the Food Sovereignty: A Critical Dialogue Conference. New Haven, CT, Sept. 14–15, www.yale.edu/agrarianstudies/foodsovereignty/papers.html.

Constance, D. H., Renard, M., and Rivera-Ferre, M. G. (eds.) (2014). *Alternative Agrifood Movements: Patterns of Convergence and Divergence*. Research in Rural Sociology and Development 21. London, UK: Emerald.

de Schutter, O. (2010). *Report by the Special Rapporteur on the Right to Food*. Geneva: United Nations General Assembly.

Desclaux, D., Nolot, J. M., Chiffoleau, Y., Gozé, E. and Leclerc, C. (2008). Changes in the concept of genotypes x environment interactions to fit agriculture diversification and decentralized participatory plant breeding: Pluridisciplinary point of view. *Euphytica*, 163(3), 533–546.

Desmarais, A. A. (2002). The Vía Campesina: Consolidating an international peasant and farm movement. *Journal of Peasant Studies*, 29(2), 91–124.

Desmarais, A. A. (2008). The power of peasants: Reflections on the meaning of La Vía Campesina. *Journal of Rural Studies*, 24(2), 138–149.

Desmarias, A. A. (2014). Building alliances for food sovereignty: La Vía Campesina, NGOs, and social movements. *Research in Rural Sociology and Development*, 21, 89–110.

Desmarais, A. A. and Wittman, H. (2015). Farmers, foodies and First Nations: getting to food sovereignty in Canada? In A. Trauger (ed.), *Food Sovereignty in International Context*. New York: Routledge.

Dryzek, J. (2005). *The Politics of the Earth* (2nd edn). New York: Oxford University Press.

Evans, P. (2008). Is an alternative globalization possible? *Politics and* Society, 36(2), 271–305.

Fairbairn, M. (2012). Framing transformation: The counter-hegemonic potential of food sovereignty in the US context. *Agriculture and Human Values*, 29(2), 217–230.

FAO (2008). An introduction to the basic concepts of food security. *Food Security Information for Action Practical Guides*. Rome: United Nations Food and Agriculture Organization.

Friedmann, H. (2005). From colonialism to green capitalism: Social movements and the emergence of food regimes. *Research in Rural Sociology and Development*, 11, 227–264.

Gereffi. G., Humphrey, J. and Sturgeon, T. (2005). The governance of global value chains. *Review of International Political Economy*, 12(1), 78–104.

Goodman, D. and DuPuis, E. M. (2002). Knowing food and growing food: Beyond the production–consumption debate in the sociology of agriculture. *Sociologia Ruralis*, 42(1), 5–22.

Guthman, J. (2004). *Agrarian Dreams: The Paradox of Organic Farming in California.* Berkeley, CA: University of California Press.

Harvey, D. (2006) Neo-liberalism as creative destruction. *Geografiska Annaler*, 88(2), 148–158.

Haussmann, B. I. G. and Kapran, I. (2007). *Farmer-participatory Improvement of Sorghum and Millet Genetic Resources for Increased Adaptation to Diverse Production Environments in West Africa.* Niamey: International Crops Research Institute for the Semi-Arid Tropics.

Higgins, V. and Lockie, S. (2002) Re-discovering the social: Neo-liberalism and hybrid practices of governing in rural natural resource management. *Journal of Rural Studies*, 18(4), 419–428.

Hinrichs, C. and Allen, P. (2008). Selective patronage and social justice: Local food consumer campaigns in historical context. *Journal of Agricultural and Environmental Ethics*, 21(4), 329–352.

Hinrichs, C. and Eshleman, J. (2014). Agrifood movements: Diversity, aims, and limits. In C. Bailey, L. Jensen, and E. Ransom (eds.), *Rural America in a Globalizing World.* Morgantown, WV: West Virginia University Press.

Holt-Giménez, E. and Peabody, L. (2008). From food rebellions to food sovereignty: Urgent call to fix a broken food system. *Food First Backgrounder.* Oakland: Institute for Food and Development Policy.

Holt-Giménez, E. and Shattuck, A. (2011). Food crises, food regimes and food movements: Rumblings of reform or tides of transformation? *Journal of Peasant Studies*, 38(1), 109–144.

INSAH (2009). Regulation c/reg.4/05/2008 on the Harmonization of Rules Governing Quality Control, Certification and Marketing of Plant Seeds and Seedlings in the ECOWAS Region. Bamako: Institute du Sahel.

Jones, K., Glenna, L. L. and Weltzien, E. (2014). Assessing participatory processes and outcomes in agricultural research for development from participants' perspectives. *Journal of Rural Studies*, 35, 91–100.

Kloppenburg, J. (2010). Impeding dispossession, enabling repossession: Biological open source and the recovery of seed sovereignty. *Journal of Agrarian Change*, 10(3), 367–388.

Lipper, L., Dalton, T., Anderson, C. L. and Keleman, A. (2010). Agricultural markets and the sustainable use of crop genetic resources. In L. Lipper, C. L. Anderson and T. Dalton, (eds.), *Seed Trade in Rural Markets: Implications for Crop Diversity and Agricultural Development.* Sterling, VA: Earthscan.

Louwaars, N. and de Boef, W. S. (2012). Integrated seed sector development in Africa: A conceptual framework for creating coherence between practices, programs, and policies. *Journal of Crop Improvement*, 26(1), 39–59.

Lynam, J. (2011). Plant breeding in sub-Saharan Africa in an era of donor dependence. *Institute of Development Studies Bulletin*, 42(4), 36–47.

McCarthy, J. (2005). Commons as counterhegemonic projects. *Capitalism, Nature, Socialism*, 16(1), 9–24.

McMichael, P. (2005). Global development and the corporate food regime. In F. Buttel and P. McMichael (eds.), *New Directions in the Sociology of Global Development*. Oxford: Elsevier.

McMichael, P. (2008). Peasant make their own history, but not just as they please … In S. M. Borras, M. Edelman and C. Kay (eds.), *Transnational Agrarian Movements Confronting Globalization*. Malden, MA: Wiley-Blackwell.

Meyer, D. S. and Minkoff, D. C. (2004). Conceptualizing political opportunity. *Social Forces*, 82(4), 1457–1492.

Mooney, P. and Hunt, S. (2009). Food security: The elaboration of contested claims to a consensus frame. *Rural Sociology*, 4(4), 469–497.

Moseley, W. G. (2008) Strengthening livelihoods in Sahelian West Africa: The geography of development and underdevelopment in a peripheral region. *Geographische Rundschau*, 4(4), 44–50.

Nyéléni. (2007). *Declaration of Nyéléni*. Declaration of the Forum for Food Sovereignty. Nyéléni, Mali, Feb. 27.

Omanya, G. O., Weltzien, E., Sogodogo, D. Sanogo, M., Hanssens, N., Guero, Y., and Zangre, R. (2007). Participatory varietal selection with improved pearl millet in West Africa. *Experimental Agriculture*, 43(1), 5–19.

Park, C. M. Y., White, B. and Julie (2013). We are not all the same: Taking gender seriously in food sovereignty discourse. Paper presented at the Food Sovereignty: A Critical Dialogue Conference. New Haven, CT, Sept. 14–15, www.iss.nl/fileadmin/ASSETS/iss/Research_and_projects/Research_networks/ICAS/17_Park_et_al_2013_APPROVEBIO-1.pdf

Pimbert, M., Barry, B., Berson, A. and Tran-Thanh, K. (2010). *Democratising Agricultural Research for Food Sovereignty in West Africa*. London: International Institute for Environment and Development.

Schurman, R. and Munro, W. A. (2010). *Fighting for the Future of Food*. Minneapolis, MN: University of Minnesota Press.

Scoones, I. and Thompson, J. (2011). The politics of seed in Africa's Green Revolution: Alternative narratives and competing pathways. *Institute of Development Studies Bulletin*, 42(2), 1–23.

Shiva, V. (2002). Globalisation and food security. In V. Shiva and G. Bedi (eds.), *Sustainable Agriculture and Food Security: The Impact of Globalisation*. Thousand Oaks, CA: Sage.

Smale, M., Dembélé, B., Traor'e, I. S., Guindo, O. and Konta, B. (2008). *Trading Millet and Sorghum Genetic Resources: Women Vendors in the Village Fairs of San and Douentza, Mali*. IFPRI Discussion Paper Series, No. 746. Washington, DC: International Food Policy Research Institute.

Snow, D. A., Rochford, E. B., Worden, S. K., and Benford, R. D. (1986). Frame alignment processes, micromobilization and movement participation. *American Sociological Review*, 51, 464–481.

Snow, D. A. and Soule, S. A. (2010). *A Primer on Social Movements*. New York, NY: Norton.

Sperling, L. and McGuire, S. (2010). Understanding and strengthening informal seed markets. *Experimental Agriculture*, 46(2), 119–136.

Stenson, K. and Watt, P. (1999). Governmentality and 'the death of the social'?: A discourse analysis of local government texts in south-east England. *Urban Studies*, 36(1), 189–201.

SWAC (2007). *Food Sovereignty in West Africa: From Principles to Reality*. Report for the Network of West African Peasant Organisations and Producers. Issy-les-Moulineux, France: Sahel and West Africa Club.

Tallontire, A. (2007). CSR and regulation: Towards a framework for understanding private standards initiatives in the agri-food chain. *Third World Quarterly*, 28(4), 775–791.

Tarrow, S. G. (2011). *The Power in Movement: Social Movements and Contentious Politics* (3rd edn). New York, NY: Cambridge University Press.

Van der Ploeg, J. D. (2008). *The New Peasantries: Struggles for Autonomy and Sustainability in an Era of Empire and Globalization*. Sterling, VA: Earthscan.

Vía Campesina (2009). *Declaration of Rights of Peasants – Women and Men*. Seoul: Vía Campesina International Coordinating Committee. Retrieved from www.isa-sociology.org/publ/sociopedia-isa_harvard-style-guidelines.pdf

Vía Campesina (2013). Gaining support for the peasant's way – La Vía Campesina at UN's leading food security institutions. *Food Sovereignty and Trade*. Vía Campesina Main Issues. Retrieved from http://viacampesina.org/en/index.php/main-issues-mainmenu-27/food-sovereignty-and-trade-mainmenu-38/1501-gaining-support-for-the-peasant-s-way-la-via-campesina-at-un-s-leading-food-security-institutions

Vía Campesina (2014). Open letter to the secretary of ITPGRFA on farmers' rights. *Biodiveristy and Genetic Resources*. Vía Campesina Main Issues. Retrieved from http://viacampesina.org/en/index.php/main-issues-mainmenu-27/biodiversity-and-genetic-resources-mainmenu-37/1669-open-letter-to-the-secretary-of-the-international-treaty-on-plant-genetic-resources-for-food-and-agriculture-on-farmers-rights

Vom Brocke, K., Trouche, G., Weltzien, E., Barro-Kondombo, C. P., Gozé, E. and Chantereau, J. (2010). Participatory variety development for sorghum in Burkina Faso: Farmers' selection and farmers' criteria. *Field Crops Research*, 119(1), 183–194.

Weltizen, E., vom Brocke, K., Touré, A., Rattunde, F. and Chantereau, J. (2008). Review and outlook for participatory plant breeding in West Africa. *Cahiers Agricultures*, 17(2), 165–171.

Windhufr, M. and Jonsen, J. (2005). *Food Sovereignty: Towards Democracy in Localized Food Systems*. Bourton-on-Dunsmore, UK: Intermediate Technology Development Group.

Wright, W. and Middendorf, G. (2008). *The Fight over Food: Producers, Consumers, and Activities Challenge the Global Food System*. University Park: Pennsylvania State University Press.

4 Seed sovereignty and inequality

An analysis of seed systems and their impacts on small-scale farmers

Elise Wach[1]

> Who controls the seed gains a substantial measure of control over the shape of the entire food system.
>
> (Kloppenburg, 2008)

Introduction

Seeds are vital. Seeds are the basis for food production, determining above all what is grown and consumed, and in some cases dictating the agricultural methods used for growing. For some crops such as maize, seeds serve as food itself. Seeds are also sold and purchased as a commodity, generating income for individuals or businesses that produce and sell them. In many communities, seeds have great cultural or spiritual significance (Gonzales, 1996). Seeds also serve as a source of genetic material, which is relevant to discussions of property rights and genetic modification.

Aid donors and governments have worked towards the formalization of the seed system over the past several decades, typically pursuing a linear approach in moving from the 'traditional' towards the formal, based on a series of stages which culminate in a strengthened commercial seed sector providing high yielding varieties (Louwaars, 2007, analysing Douglas, 1980). Formalization, that is, putting the seed breeding in the hands of public research institutes and private companies rather than with farmers and their informal networks, has been implemented in the name of benefiting small-scale farmers through increasing their incomes and contributing to overall food security through increasing yields. Many national seed policies include targets for replacing the informal with a formal seed sector (Louwaars and Engels, 2002). More recently, emphasis has been on the development of crop varieties with additional micronutrients to address problems of malnutrition in society.

While 'it was believed that the formal seed sector would steadily replace traditional methods of seed provision once farmers realized the benefits of improved seed' (FAO, 2006), the formalization of seed systems has been met with resistance from farmers' and civil society organizations which claim that the informal seed systems hold the key to food security and are most beneficial to farmers. Many organizations focus their critiques of the formal seed system primarily on private seed companies and on the institutionalization of intellectual property rights.

'Seed Sovereignty', as a component of food sovereignty, could be conceptualized as the right of people to define their own seed systems (Kloppenburg, 2008; UN Human Rights Council, 2015). La Vía Campesina's Declaration of Rights of Peasants (2009a) includes the right for peasants to 'determine the varieties of the seeds they want to plant', 'to choose their own products, varieties, amount, quality and the ways of farming', 'the right to grow and develop their varieties and to exchange, to give or to sell their seeds'.

While the concept of seed sovereignty has the potential to go beyond rigid ideas about formal or informal seed systems, it is typically misused or misinterpreted as romanticizing farmer-led systems or eschewing any role for the public or private sectors (Bernstein, 2014). To date, those advocating seed sovereignty have typically focused on resisting intellectual property right systems and the use of genetic modification (Kloppenburg, 2008, drawing on La Vía Campesina position papers), with little consideration of the other ways in which different seed systems affect the rights and outcomes for small-scale farmers, or how changes in seed systems could result in improvements in these areas.

This chapter will aim to evaluate the specific advantages and disadvantages of different seed systems for small-scale farmers. Specifically, it will analyse the extent to which various aspects of formal and informal seed systems impact on the livelihoods, food security, nutrition and above all the agency of small-scale farmers, and the ways in which concepts of seed sovereignty could lead to improvements for these populations and for overall food systems.

The chapter is organized as follows. The following section discusses why small-scale farmers and consumers need to be the primary concern for seed systems in the interest of reducing inequalities. Next, a detailed overview of different forms of formal and informal seed systems, considering the ways in which breeding, production and distribution affect the accessibility and appropriateness of seeds for small-scale farmers is undertaken. This leads into an analysis of the ways in which formal and informal seed systems affect the livelihoods, food security and nutrition of small-scale farmers. The final section discusses the implications of these seed systems on the ability of farmers to exercise their right to use, save and exchange seed and to define their own seed systems.

Small-scale farmers as stakeholders

While concepts of sovereignty have traditionally pertained to the nation state, when used in food sovereignty and the right-to-food movements, the focus is on the right of the 'people' to decide. La Vía Campesina (2009a) defines food sovereignty as 'the right of peoples to healthy and culturally appropriate food produced through socially just and ecologically sensitive methods and their right to define their own food and agriculture systems'. The UN Human Rights Council shares this definition but also adds that 'it entails people's rights to participate in decision-making, and to define their own food and agriculture systems' (UNHRC, 2015). Given the essential role of seeds in food systems, seed sovereignty is a critical aspect of food sovereignty (Kloppenburg, 2008).

But which 'peoples' specifically get to define these systems? There are a number of different stakeholders in seed systems: governments, private breeding companies, seed traders, agro-dealers and farmers. Farmers are the primary users of seed and are directly dependent on seed for their livelihoods. For some farmers, particularly small-scale farmers, seeds also directly impact on their food security and nutrition, and may also have cultural or spiritual value that cannot be commoditized. The term 'farmer' encompasses a wide range, including family farmers, small landholders, farm labourers, contract farmers and farm owners. A 'farmer' can be a person producing agricultural products on less than one acre for their own subsistence, or a person(s) cultivating upwards of 10,000 hectares.

We argue that in the interest of reducing inequalities, the governance of seed systems needs to focus primarily on the needs and preferences of small-scale[2] farmers in particular. We focus on small-scale farmers for three main reasons. The first is sheer numbers: there are 2.2 billion small-scale farmers, which makes them the largest of any farmer group (Singh, 2012). Second, most small-scale farmers live near (above or under) the poverty line (IAASTD, 20) and also make up the majority of food insecure people in the world (Bailey, 2011). Third, small-scale farmers produce the majority of the world's food, particularly that consumed by people living in poverty (Nwanze, 2011; IFAD, 2013), and do so with more efficiency than large-scale farmers. A number of studies have demonstrated that small-scale farms are more productive per hectare than larger ones (Assuncao and Braido, 2007; Altieri, 2009) and it is estimated that if all farms had the productivity levels of small-scale farms, food production would increase by a factor of 2 to 6, depending on the country (Grain, 2014). In summary, focusing on the needs and preferences of small-scale farmers will help to curb inequalities and increase food security.

It is also important to consider the impact of different seed systems on small-scale farmers as *consumers*. Despite the general conception that small-scale farmers produce for their 'subsistence', up to 50 per cent of these farmers are net purchasers of food (Wegner and Zwart, 2011, in Vorley et al., 2012). Thus, analysing the effects of seed systems on food security and nutrition of small-scale farmers will also provide some insight into how they affect consumers, the population of 7 billion people who depend on seeds for food and particularly those who are resource poor.

While small-scale farmers and consumers are the groups most affected by decisions about seed systems, they are the least included stakeholders in formal decision making processes. Top-down policy processes, such as the conferences leading up to the founding of the International Union for the Protection of New Varieties of Plants (UPOV), and the Convention of Biological Diversity, which significantly affect the ways in which seed systems are governed, have excluded farmers in general and small-scale resource-poor farmers in particular from attending (Louwaars, 2007; La Vía Campesina, 2009b). However, as will be discussed, there are a number of other touch points and levels in seed systems in which the abilities of small-scale farmers to determine what they plant, their ways of farming and ultimately their seed systems are limited.

Overview of formal and informal seed systems

Seed systems are defined as the 'flows of seed and other planting materials through the production system, and the roles of both formal and informal sector institutions and farmers in these flows' (Hodgkin et al., 2007, p. 78, drawing on Almekinders et al., 1994). Seed systems are often characterized as either formal or informal, the separation based on the key actors involved. Formal seed systems are associated with the public and commercial sectors, and informal seed systems primarily with farmers and informal traders (Louwaars, 2007). The distinction is not always clear, and there can be many combinations of varying levels of formality. For example, formally bred seeds can be exchanged through informal farmer-to-farmer networks (Almekinders, 2000), and farmer-bred seeds can be incorporated into the formal seed regulation system, i.e. FAO's Quality Declared Seed System (FAO, 2006). Thus, it is often unhelpful to generalize about formal or informal seed systems.

In this section, we will describe the breeding, production, distribution and quality assurance of seeds, and their implications on the access and appropriateness of current seed systems for small-scale farmers. Analysing the different aspects of seed systems in this manner is intended to provide an understanding of seed systems that goes beyond an overall dichotomy of 'formal' vs. 'informal'. The next section will then discuss the ways in which different aspects of formal and informal seed systems affect the livelihoods, food security and nutrition of small-scale farmers, as both producers and consumers.

Formal seed systems

Formal seed systems include seeds of varieties that have been registered or certified by a national governmental body (often but not necessarily members of UPOV) or organizations such as the UN Food and Agriculture Organization (FAO). The system of formalization was initially developed in countries such as the UK in order to protect farmers from rogue seed traders. The aims of the Seeds Act of 1920 was quality control and to ensure protection was offered if purchased seeds did not germinate or were not free from pathogens. Regulations were later added to certify varieties to ensure seeds remained 'true to variety': seeds could only be traded if they were on the official list of varieties. This occurred at a national level (e.g. the UK Plant Varieties and Seeds Act 1964) and an international level (UPOV – various acts between 1961 and 1991) (Kloppenburg, 1998; UK Food Group, 2010). In 1995, the World Trade Organization institutionalized intellectual property protection, allowing the patenting of living organisms, including seeds (Dutfield, 2008).

Formal seed breeding

In theory, any seed variety can be registered and therefore integrated into the formal system. However, in practice, the majority of formally registered seeds have been developed by professional breeders, rather than by farmers or through natural selection. Professional breeders include seed companies (e.g. Syngenta); International Agricultural Research Centres (IARCs) created under the World Bank-created Consultative Group on International Agricultural Research (CGIAR) (e.g. the International Crops Research Institute for the Semi-Arid Tropics, ICRISAT); governmental breeding institutes (e.g. under the Ministry of Agriculture); or universities which typically receive a mix of public and private funding (e.g. University of California at Berkeley). Over the last several decades, public funding for agriculture and plant breeding has declined, leaving private companies to dominate this sector, in line with the progression towards a formalized and commercially led seed sector (Douglas, 1980). Seed varieties developed by professional breeders are often referred to as 'improved', 'quality' or 'conventional' seeds, both reflecting and influencing judgements about their value.

Breeding techniques are often based on molecular biology and can include the use of molecular markers (in order to identify genes responsible for certain traits), reverse breeding or controlled pollination. The latter is used in the development of hybrids and can include simple techniques conducted on farms, such as detassling corn or removing anthers from an ear of wheat and then allowing the wind to pollinate. More complicated techniques for the development of hybrid varieties might include the use of chemical agents which inhibit the synthesis of viable pollen, or induce cytoplasmic male sterility (CMS), in which male sterility is transferred by protoplast fusion between different crops (e.g. radish and cabbage) (European Seed Association, 2013). Finally, genetic modification (GM) is used in order to transfer genes from one species into another.

Production and distribution of formally bred seeds

The production of seed for reuse, sale or distribution depends in part on the level of technicality of the breeding process. For varieties which have been developed through relatively straightforward methods, seeds can be produced by growing out varieties and saving seed (e.g. by farmers, governments or enterprises).[3] In the case of some hybrid and GM varieties, seed of the same variety is produced through the replication of the same technical processes which led to their development (e.g. by public agencies or private companies with technical expertise and equipment). While many have opposed 'F1' hybrids on the grounds that their seeds cannot be saved and reused and that the varieties cannot be built upon, this isn't entirely accurate. It is important to distinguish between producing seeds of the exact same variety and producing seeds that are of different varieties. When the seeds from an F1 hybrid are planted out, the next generation (F2) will be a mixture of many varieties. From the F2 and subsequent (F3 and so on) generations, varieties can be selected by farmers to arrive at one or more new varieties in a process called 'dehybridisation' (Deppe, 2000). However, this process requires time (e.g. six to 10 seasons for crops such as tomatoes) (Deppe, 2000). During this period, if there is a preference for uniformity or specific characteristics, the subsequent generations of a hybrid variety (before a stable variety is achieved) will be much less profitable than a single uniform variety.

In addition to the breeding processes, methods for ensuring commercial viability may limit the production of seeds to formal breeders. Varieties can be regulated in their use through protection of intellectual property rights (IPRs), in which case licences (usually purchased), are required to produce and/or sell them (exceptions such as India will be discussed later). In the UK, farmers must 'declare' any seed saved which has been registered with the British Society of Plant Breeders (BSPB), pay fees for the use of farm-saved seed of certain varieties, and are unable to transfer saved seed to other farmers (BSPB, 2015). Companies have also developed and patented varieties with traits that prevent plants from producing viable seed for reuse (sometimes referred to as GURTS, genetic use restriction technologies). Seeds from these varieties (or for inputs which activate their expression) need to be continually re-purchased through the seed company (Shi, 2006). However, these technologies have been widely opposed (Shi, 2006) and at the time of writing, it appears they have not yet been commercialized.

Thus the seeds of formally bred varieties are typically purchased through formal market suppliers, such as agro-dealers that are linked to seed companies. Governmental bodies can also distribute formally bred seeds (either directly or through private sector partnerships), and this occurs in developing countries such as Malawi (e.g. the Malawi Input Subsidy Programme). In such countries, seeds are distributed either for free or at subsidized prices. The costs of such initiatives however has meant that they have been reduced or halted in some countries, e.g. Zambia in 1994–95 (Rusike et al., 1997).

Accessibility of formally bred seeds for small-scale farmers

Access to seeds within the formal seed system largely depends on the ability of small-scale farmers to purchase seeds. This relates in large part to the ability to afford the seeds or the ability to access and repay loans. Formally bred seeds are almost always more expensive than informally bred seeds. Rubyogo et al. (2007), for example, reports that formally bred bean seeds in East Africa can be three times the price of informal seeds. The difference in price between formally bred, and informally bred seeds, is largely due to the intensive technical and regulatory processes involved in the development and production of seeds in the formal system. It is likely also due, in part, to the small number of seed companies which dominate the formal seed market (Paul and Steinbrecher, 2003; Kloppenburg, 2008). Legislation which has been developed to protect breeders' rights also contributes to higher costs in the formal system. In the UK, for example, farmers are required to pay a fee in order to save and reuse seeds that have been registered with the British Society of Plant Breeders (BSPB, 2015).

The proximity of retailers and the availability of appropriate seed quantities also determine the accessibility of seed for small-scale farmers. In recognition of the fact that private seed companies were not adequately servicing small-scale farmers, particularly those living in poverty, a number of public (governmental and non-governmental) initiatives have been implemented in recent years, such as the Alliance for a Green Revolution in Africa (AGRA) and Making Markets Work for the Poor (M4P) initiatives (DFID and SDC, 2008). These programmes often include support to agro-dealer networks, which provide small-scale farmers in remote areas with information about the formally bred seed varieties which are available, as well as the agri-chemical inputs that are required when they plant these varieties. Access to formal seeds has been part of a broader agenda for 'improved' agriculture and 'farmer education'. Offering support to seed and input companies to better enable them to 'reach' small-scale farmers, providing subsidies and microcredit for inputs, setting up demonstration plots and linking small-scale farmers to formal value chains are examples of initiatives of this broader agenda. While these initiatives often increase the accessibility of formally developed seeds among small-scale farmers, they often exclude the poorest and hardest to reach farmers (Vorley et al., 2012). Further, if small-scale farmer use of formally bred seeds is not financially viable once public support is withdrawn, companies are likely to subsequently shift away from marginalized farmers, making these seeds once again unavailable to small-scale farmers.

Appropriateness of formally bred seeds to small-scale farmer needs and preferences

In addition to considering whether small-scale farmers have access to seeds, it is essential to explore whether formally bred seeds are appropriate for small-scale farmers. This entails considering the ecological conditions in which small-scale farmers are working, the farming methods they use and a wider set of farmer preferences.

Ecological conditions

The resources required for the development of formally bred varieties (including both the breeding and the certification processes) means that breeders typically aim to develop varieties that will work in 'most' environments (Almekinders and Louwaars, 2002; Louwaars, 2007). This is the case both for public breeding, which aims to increase the impact of their seeds (e.g. related to aggregate measures of food security, economic growth or nutritional benefits), and for private companies, which aim to maximize profits (Friedman, 1970). Thus, the varieties developed are typically suitable to areas with homogenous environments (e.g. wheat in the Punjab or corn in Nebraska). However, many small-scale farmers, particularly those living on marginal lands, farm in areas with unique micro-ecologies, and formal varieties are not appropriate. It is not feasible for the formal system to develop unique varieties for each micro user group (Weltzien and Christinck, 2009). Some formal varieties of seeds, however, function when conditions are 'made homogenous' through the use of agri-chemical inputs or irrigation (Louwaars 2007).

Farming methods

Many formally bred varieties depend on the use of certain agri-chemical inputs in order to achieve their yield potential. For example, the high yields from the variety of wheat introduced to India's Punjab state in the 1960s resulted in large part from the irrigation and fertilizer use associated with it (Byerlee and Siddiq, 1994). The development of new varieties which depend on agri-chemical inputs continues today. Without such chemical inputs, the yields achieved can be the same (or even lower) as the informal varieties of seed already in use. In Kenya, farmers using improved maize varieties without fertilizers experienced no difference or even a reduction in yields, when compared to those using local varieties without inputs (Nyangena and Juma, 2014). Formally bred wheat varieties are also found to have decreased competitiveness against weeds and robustness against mechanical weed control, thereby increasing reliance on herbicides (Lammerts van Bueren et al., 2011). Given the increasing convergence of seed and agrichemical companies through mergers, acquisitions and alliances (Tansey, 2008), there is incentive within the commercial seed sector to continue to develop varieties that require agri-chemical use. The use of such agri-chemicals may not be feasible or desirable for small-scale farmers, as will be discussed later in this chapter.

Farmer preferences

Formally bred seeds are typically developed based on ideas about what will be most appropriate and suitable for farmers. Again, because of commercial interests, the preferences of large-scale farmers, who have larger purchasing power, may be advanced over the preferences of small-scale farmers. Even when formal seeds are bred with the intention of meeting the wide-ranging needs of small-scale farmers, the qualities deemed valuable by plant breeders are often out of sync with those valued by this type of farmer. Small-scale farmers' preferences may relate to disease and pest resistance, taste and texture, cooking times, water use, marketability, ecological services (such as ground cover to retain moisture) and a myriad of other factors (Rubyogo et al., 2007). However, the vast majority of governmental and non-governmental initiatives which aims to expand the use of formally bred seeds by small-scale farmers, focuses almost exclusively on increasing yields or on promoting uniformity for entry into high-value supply chains (e.g. supermarkets, global food traders) and for the mechanization of agriculture (Almekinders and Louwaars, 2002; Louwaars and de Boef, 2012).

Participatory breeding

In order to address the disconnect between breeder and farmer preferences for varietal traits in formal seed systems, participatory plant breeding (PPB) initiatives have attempted to involve farmers in the breeding process. Participatory breeding initiatives typically entail a process by which farmers identify the traits that they prefer in a crop, and breeders then develop or distribute varieties with those qualities (Almekinders et al., 2007; Rubyogo et al., 2007). This approach represents a significant improvement over the typical pathway of identifying desirable qualities based on market demands (often largely tailored towards large-scale farms) or breeders' interpretations of small-scale farmer needs. It offers opportunities for the development of new varieties that have traits which could benefit small-scale farmers, but which might be difficult to develop through local breeding techniques.

However, participatory breeding approaches face limitations given the unique farming ecosystems of many small-scale farmers. Reporting on a collaborative initiative implemented by the Centre for Tropical Agriculture (CIAT) and National Agricultural Research Systems (NARS) in east, central and southern Africa, Rubyogo et al. (2007) found that some of the varieties developed had potential for wider adaptation while others were suitable for particular micro-environments. In addition, such initiatives need to ensure they do not result in the transfer of agency from farmers to 'expert' breeders.

Quality assurance of formally bred seeds for small-scale farmers

In formal seed systems, quality is assured through the certification of seed varieties. According to Almekinders and Louwaars (1999) there are four main aspects of seed quality: physiological quality (germination, vigour), sanitary quality (related to seed-borne disease), analytical quality (amount of seed vs. rocks or weeds) and genetic quality (variety type and purity). While seed regulation was initially developed in the interest of farmers to address the first three aspects (Kloppenburg, 1998; UK Food Group, 2010), it is the last aspect, genetic quality, which is the current primary focus of certification and regulation.

While the certification standards vary across countries, almost all countries follow the UPOV convention of specifying the criteria of a formal variety as being: distinct, uniform and stable (DUS). Initial certification requires:

- carrying out field inspections during multiplication processes to ensure the variety is true to type and that there is little contamination;

- growing samples in control plots to ensure the progeny conform to the characteristics of the variety; and
- seed quality testing in laboratories.

(OECD, 2012)

While farmer-developed varieties can also be certified, the certification process favours professional breeders in terms of process and varieties. Few farmers have the time or money to go through the multi-step process required to certify a variety. In the UK, the process can take one to four years depending on the crop, and costs range from £100 for 'amateurs' (vegetables only) to £2,300 for field peas (DEFRA, 2012). In addition, the requirement of uniformity means that the formal system favours varieties that have low genetic diversity, whereas farmer-developed varieties often favour high diversity, in part because they diminish risks (Almekinders and Louwaars, 2002).

In formal seed systems, ensuring that seeds sold in markets under a certified name or label breed true to type is the responsibility of national quality control schemes. In situations where enforcement capacity is low, as is common in developing countries such as Uganda, counterfeiting of labelled seeds can be widespread and this has negative impacts on farmers who purchase the fake seeds (FAO 2006; Joughin 2014). Sperling and McGuire (2010, p. 125) state that the enforcement of formal certification is 'of little direct value to farmers purchasing sub-standard seed. [It] lies within a complicated web of expensive and often far-removed regulators.'

Box 4.1 Basic plant breeding definitions

Self-pollinating: plants reproduce via transfer of pollen to stigma on the same plant. Examples include rice, wheat, oats, peanuts, tomatoes, apricots, etc. Many plants capable of self-pollinating can also be cross-pollinated.

Cross-pollinating: plants reproduce by crossing of different plants of the same species (through transfer of pollen from one flower to stigma of another). These plants resist self-pollination. Examples include maize, spinach, apples, pumpkins, etc.

Clonally propagated: plants reproduce asexually, as in the case of tubers, roots and stem cuttings. Examples include potatoes, bananas and tree crops, such as apples and avocados, which can be grafted.

F1 hybrids: the result of a cross between two different varieties, each of which is genetically uniform. They do not 'breed true' and produce plants like themselves. If seeds from an F1 plant are saved and replanted, they will produce a range of different varieties. With selection over a number of generations, a new variety can be developed.

Open-pollinated varieties (OPVs): a term which refers to self- or cross-pollinating plants which reproduce normally, and do not have for example male sterility. OPV is often used to refer to plants that are not F1 hybrids (e.g. open pollinated wheat). Plants 'breed true', producing plants, which are fairly consistent to the parents, though are less uniform than F1 hybrids.

Informal seed systems

Informal seeds can include informally bred (i.e. 'landraces' or 'local') varieties as well as the informal reproduction of formal (i.e. registered) varieties. Informally bred seed varieties are developed by farmers or through natural selection processes and are not formally registered or certified. Technically, a public breeding programme could also develop a new variety and not register it, though incentives in the formal seed system mean that this is not common practice.

Informal seed breeding

The development of varieties by farmers can range from basic to highly sophisticated. It can entail:

- simply selecting the best plants or seeds at the time of harvest or before planting based on visual inspection;
- selecting seeds from plants with specific traits; or
- actively isolating and crossing plants in order to develop new varieties with desirable characteristics, a process which can take up to 10 years for some crops.

(Deppe, 2000)

In addition to selection and crossing practices, some new varieties can be developed through naturally occurring genetic mutations. This is rare in pollinated crops and typically only seen in clonally propagated crops.

While the number of distinct informal varieties is difficult to estimate (Hodgkin et al., 2007), numbers far exceed formally bred varieties and crop species. For example, in the CIMMYT (the International Maize and Wheat Improvement Center) gene bank collection, 24,463 of the 27,500 varieties are 'landraces' or informal varieties, and only 10 are primarily commercial (Germinate 3 SeeD Maize database, 2014; Hellin et al., 2014). For crop species, it is estimated that there are 80,000 plant species that can be consumed (de Schutter, 2010), and only 200 certified crop varieties (OECD, 2012). Given these numbers and the fact that informal varieties have been developed over thousands of years (Ceccarelli et al., 2009), the 'conservation' or 'maintenance' of existing varieties could be considered at least as crucial for crop diversity as the development of new varieties. While in formal seed systems, variety maintenance may occur through genebanks (*ex situ*), in informal seed systems, maintenance occurs *in situ*: in the locations where it is currently found and within the communities to which it belongs (Maxted et al., 1997).

The roles that farmers need to play in the maintenance of varieties and their traits largely depend on the reproduction processes of a crop (see Box 4.1) and considerations of cross-breeding, seed production and saving. For clonally propagated plants such as potatoes and bananas, seeds are rarely produced and little variation within varieties occurs; thus minimal effort is needed to maintain varieties and their traits. Self-pollinated crops such as rice and wheat also require little effort to maintain varieties and their properties. Cross-pollination can still occur among some (mostly) self-pollinated crops such as sorghum and fava beans, however, and these require more care (Hodgkin et al., 2007). Varieties of cross-pollinated crops such as maize and onions are more difficult to maintain, as genes can flow naturally between different varieties (within farms and across different farms e.g. via insects, wind or birds).[4] Therefore, active selection by farmers (as often as each season) is normally required in order to maintain varieties and their traits. Seed saving practices depend in part on the type of breeding system: seeds which double as food (e.g. maize) can be saved without extra effort (though can be consumed during times of food insecurity), whereas for crops such as parsnips, the farmer must deliberately leave some of the plants to go to seed rather than harvest them.

Systems of variety maintenance are often organized at the community level (e.g. with individual households maintaining separate populations), however this varies depending on the geographic scale at which the crop is viable. Those crops with specific varieties which are only appropriate for small local areas would be maintained locally. Other crops which can be grown across large regions may be maintained by regional networks of farmers or by farms that produce specific varieties for seed (Louette et al., 1997; Hodgkin et al., 2007; Sperling and McGuire, 2010). The implications for this on the conservation of varieties and the availability of seed are discussed later in this chapter.

The size of a population (both on individual farms and the aggregate of multiple farms) is a significant factor in the maintenance of varieties. Small population sizes can lead to genetic instability of local varieties, and the loss of rare alleles. Thus, if the number of farmers cultivating or the area planted of a variety decreases, even for one year, a bottleneck effect can be created resulting in the loss of valuable traits and genetic diversity (Louette, 2005; Hodgkin et al., 2007). In other words, if farmers stop using local varieties because they have adopted formal seeds, the availability and diversity of local varieties could irreversibly decrease. This will be discussed in more detail later in the chapter.

Production and distribution of informally bred seeds

In terms of production and distribution, informal seed can be saved and used on the same farm, exchanged through farmer networks (neighbours, relatives, cooperatives, etc.), or purchased through informal markets. While the rates vary, the majority of seed used by small-scale farmers is produced on their own farms. Cromwell (1996) reported that 60 to 70 per cent of seed used by smallholders in Africa was saved on-farm. In Tanzania, Rubyogo et al. (2007) found that 82 per cent of farmers reported home saved seed as their most important source of seed. Approximately 70 per cent of seeds planted in India are supplied by farmers (Rangnekar, 2013). Again, rates vary across crops: Sperling and McGuire (2010) note that in northern Mali, on-farm production provides more than 80 per cent of seeds used by farmers for major crops, but that for groundnuts and cowpeas, most farmers source seed from informal markets.

Complementing on-farm seed sourcing, informal markets can be an important source of seed for small-scale farmers, particularly during years when crop production is low. Traders have been shown to respond to demands for different qualities and help to mitigate high stress periods. For example, in Ethiopia a local trader had maintained a specific variety of pearl millet seed in storage houses throughout the year, which served as a backup for local communities following the 2003 drought (Sperling and McGuire, 2010).

Accessibility of informally bred seeds for small-scale farmers

Given that the majority of informally bred seed is produced on-farm, the size of the previous season's harvest largely determines availability of seed. This means that seed is almost always available for these farmers, and often at low or no cost. However, in the event of a low harvest or an emergency (e.g. drought or flood), farmers may travel to other villages with similar environmental conditions to exchange or buy seed, or procure them from informal markets. Farmers in remote areas far from markets have been found to be more vulnerable to seed insecurity (Hodgkin et al., 2007). In addition, studies have shown that some farmers living in poverty may rely more on off-farm sources of seed when their production is below the level of subsistence (in the case of seeds that double as food, they can be consumed rather than saved for planting) or when they urgently need their crops to provide some income (Almekinders, 2000). When purchased from another farmer or through an informal market, farmers will have to pay for such seeds, though the cost is often many times less than formal seeds (Rubyogo et al., 2007).

In many areas, seed is exchanged primarily through social networks rather than sold and purchased. The ways in which these exchanges are structured varies. In Yucatan, Mexico, for example, the ability to exchange depends on social ties or kin networks, which can serve to exclude or disadvantage some farmers. Depending on the location and culture, exchange can be gendered, with men exchanging some crops and women others, such as in Yucatan. However, in Nepal, exchange of seeds is not affected by gender or wealth categories (Hodgkin et al., 2007, drawing on Lope, 2004 and Subedi and Garforth, 1996).

Studies have shown that social networks that underpin informal seed exchange are in decline due to a number of factors including commercialization, labour migration and livelihood diversification (Bellon 2004). With increasing efforts to formalize seeds and their trade, e.g. through agro-dealer network initiatives, it could be expected that as farmers switch to formal seed dealers, informal seed markets may also be in decline, although there has been little research to investigate this.

Appropriateness of informally bred seeds to farmer needs and preferences

The varieties of informal seeds developed for self-supply or community exchange are typically well suited to the ecosystems they are grown in, especially where farmers have the knowledge and capacity to develop niche varieties. Informal markets also have a high capacity to cater to the specialized needs of farmers, with markets carrying both niche seed varieties (e.g. for use in a radius of 10 km or less) and those developed by large-scale breeders suitable for use across wide geographic areas (Sperling and McGuire, 2010).

The level of knowledge and skill of farmers in seed variety development and maintenance is reported as widely varying. Some authors, such as Hodgkin et al. (2007), highlight a myriad of examples which demonstrate sophisticated levels of farmer knowledge and skill. Others, such as Louwaars (2007) discuss instances in which farmers are ignorant of basic knowledge, for example, the ways in which diseases are the result of seed-transmitted bacteria. These differences likely reflect variances across communities and countries. The loss of skills in countries such as the US has been attributed to the introduction of formal varieties, particularly those that are not selected and saved from year to year. Fitzgerald (1993) argues that the introduction of hybrid corn into the US was 'perhaps more profoundly deskilling than any mechanical implement' (p. 327, cited in Rangnekar, 2013). In the UK, new initiatives are attempting to develop the skills of small-scale farmers in seed selection and saving (LWA, 2015).

Appropriateness of seeds does not only relate to plant traits. In some cultures, varieties and/or seeds are associated with distinctive cultural and spiritual values, which cannot be improved upon in a laboratory. For example, Perales et al. (2005) indicate that maize seeds (and the knowledge associated with them) are often closely associated with community identity in Chiapas, Mexico. Gonzales et al. (1999) discuss the ways in which seed plays a significant role in wider spiritual beliefs in the Andes. Development and maintenance of these varieties by farmers on farms is thus the only culturally appropriate way for these seeds to be preserved.

The disadvantage of informal seed systems is that the characteristics of informal varieties might not match demand in high-value markets (though organic markets are often an exception to this), which favour uniformity, size and other traits. Thus, the price received by farmers for informal varieties can be lower than those obtained by farmers selling into high-value commercial markets.

Quality assurance of informally bred seeds for small-scale farmers

In informal seed systems, quality is assured through both farmer inspection of the seeds (relying on colour, shape and size characteristics) as well as through assessing the attributes of the person providing the seed, which could be referred to as 'social certification' (Sperling and McGuire, 2010, p. 125) or 'neighbourhood certification' (Thiele, 1999, p. 87). This is the case for seeds acquired through farmer networks, neighbours and informal traders. Sperling and McGuire (2010) highlight that as people who have been known to supply poor-quality seed risk losing clients and jeopardizing their relationships and status among neighbours and relatives, such social certification mechanisms can be powerful, particularly for farmers, which may otherwise have no redress.

Again, farmer skill and knowledge play an important role in quality assurance in the informal system, both for seed produced on farm and acquired from other sources. If skills and knowledge are eroded, the ability for farmers to ascertain the quality of and appropriately store seed will be compromised.

Implications on livelihoods, food security and nutrition for small-scale farmers

This section analyses the implications of different aspects of the formal and informal seed systems on the livelihood, food security and nutrition of small-scale farmers.

Livelihood

Today, most efforts to promote the use of formally bred seeds or to formalize seed systems are aimed at increasing incomes for small-scale farmers. Formally bred seeds, such as those introduced during the Green Revolution, have resulted in significant increases in aggregate yields (FAO, 2005). However, small-scale farmers continue to be one of the poorest and also most food insecure populations. This is in part because formal varieties do not always yield higher for small-scale farmer conditions, and because higher yields do not directly correlate with an increase in income. Income received depends on input costs (i.e. seeds, agri-chemicals, labour) as well as the marketability (price and risk) of the harvested products.

As noted above, informally bred seeds are almost always less expensive than formally bred seeds. In addition, many formally developed seeds require the use of agri-chemical inputs in order to produce their potential yields or properties. Taking into account the costs of both the seeds and the inputs, even higher yielding formal seeds can be less profitable for small-scale farmers than informal seeds (David, 2006). In developing countries, resource-poor small-scale farmers are often unable to afford or access the pesticides, herbicides, fertilizers or irrigation required to attain the maximum potential yields of modern varieties and thus yields (and profitability) can be even lower. Government subsidies might enable farmers to purchase these inputs initially, though once subsidies end, cultivation of formally bred varieties can become less profitable or may not be viable at all if they rely on inputs or irrigation.

Labour costs can either increase or decrease with the use of formally bred seeds. Given that seeds from the formal sector are commonly used in conjunction with agri-chemical inputs, requirements for agricultural labour can, at times, be reduced for farmers using such seeds. For example, instead of manually weeding, farmers may apply herbicides, particularly if the variety they are cultivating is herbicide resistant. However, for some crops, the modern formal varieties can require more labour, as in the case of hybrid rice in the Philippines which needs to be transplanted from seedling rather than sown directly into fields (David, 2006). The extent to which changes in labour requirements impact the livelihoods of small-scale farmers depends on several factors, including the requirement and cost of agri-chemical inputs, the alternative income-generating activities available to farmers, and the extent to which additional labour is provided by traditional forms of social obligations. A reduction in labour required is not a simple way to determine whether changes in income for small scale farmers occur. A myriad of factors such as gendered roles (which may not be paid) and community beliefs about job creation (i.e. replacing human labour with inputs when job opportunities are scarce can be socially unacceptable) (Comte, 1994), must be considered.

The marketability of products from the farm (i.e. price and certainty of a buyer) is the other key factor determining farmers' incomes. Many development initiatives have promoted formally bred seeds to small-scale farmers on the assumption that this will enable them to link with higher value supply chains and will therefore increase incomes. Farmers producing for formal value chains (e.g. for supermarkets or global value chains) often need to produce particular varieties (almost always formally bred) and need to ensure uniformity of their product (often through the use of agri-chemical inputs). These farmers, however, only represent 2–10 per cent of small-scale farmers, and are often the wealthiest (Vorley et al., 2012).

It is essential to consider not just the short-term change in farm income but the level of resilience (i.e. risk and adaptability) of the cropping systems over time. Minimizing risk is particularly key for people living at or near the poverty line, as even small disruptions can push an already asset-poor household into further poverty, or drive a household on the cusp, below the poverty line (Hoogeveen et al., 2001). The preference of qualities such as drought tolerance is a clear indication of farmer concerns and the need to avert risk (Aw-Hassan et al., 2008).

In informal seed systems the higher level of genetic and crop diversity can often translate to lower vulnerability to disease epidemics (Adams et al., 1971) and to climate-related changes (e.g. temperature, rainfall) (Ho, et al., 2008; IAASTD, 2009; UK Food Group, 2010). The growing practices that can accompany such seeds (i.e. agroecological practices) have also been shown to be more resilient in the face of climate change than those practices which rely on agri-chemical inputs (Holt-Giménez, 2002). However, there may be a potential for formal breeders to introduce a greater *degree* of diversity to assist in resilience (Mba et al., 2012) or respond to crises (Almekinders and Louwaars, 2002).

The ability to build on and adapt varieties also contributes to farmer resilience. This may be limited within some formal seed systems (e.g. through the use of IPRs or through GURTs), though some countries such as India have taken measures to ensure that farmers have the right to save, re-sow and continue to develop formal seed varieties (de Schutter, 2009; Rangnekar, 2013), at least in legal terms. However, as will be discussed in the final section of this chapter, there are other factors that may affect the ability of farmers to build on and adapt varieties.

Food security and nutrition

This section discusses the implications of different aspects of informal and formal seed systems on the food security and nutrition of small-scale farmers, bearing in mind that 50 per cent are net consumers of food – that is, they purchase more than they produce, be it by weight, calories or financial value (Seville et al., 2011). This analysis could also provide insights into the ways in which seed systems affect consumers more generally.

From the 1950s and 1960s, formally bred varieties were developed to curb food insecurity and famine, as part of what was termed the 'Green Revolution'. Primarily, the Green Revolution focused on improving yields of basic staples such as wheat and rice, and was largely successful in achieving this: per capita world food production (in calories) increased by 23 per cent from 1965 to 2010 (FAO, 2015), despite a rise in population. Although global agriculture currently produces an amount of food equivalent to more than 2,790 kilocalories per person per day (FAO, 2015) – more than enough to meet global caloric requirements – more than 800 million people are chronically hungry (FAO, 2012), with small-scale farmers making up majority of these food insecure people (Bailey, 2011). The nutrient densities of many formal varieties are less than those of the seeds from which they were derived. The micronutrient content of mainstream crop varieties has also declined. In a study of 43 foods, Davis et al. (2004) found that today's varieties overall have lower levels of protein, calcium, phosphorus, iron, riboflavin and ascorbic acid than the varieties consumed just 50 years ago. The study attributed these declines to the trade-offs that occurred in formal breeding programmes, for example, selecting for particular qualities such as yield or chemical resistance, while neglecting others such as nutrient content.

While recent efforts have been made to develop and promote varieties that have a higher content of a particular micronutrient through 'biofortification', such as rice with pro-vitamin A ('Golden Rice') (Stein et al., 2008), overall, the rise of formal breeding efforts has occurred alongside significant declines in the aggregate nutritional value of agricultural crops. The nature of the formal breeding process means that a relatively limited number of varieties can be developed and released each year, for a relatively limited number of crops (again, only 200 of the 80,000 available plant species for consumption have been certified) (de Schutter, 2010; OECD, 2012). Combined with other factors such as retailer or consumer preferences, this has led to an overall decline in diversity of dietary crops, and a reduction in the nutrient densities of widely consumed crops. According to the FAO, approximately 75 per cent of the world's food is generated from 12 plant and five animal species (FAO, 2004).

This decline in dietary diversity reduces the ability of consumers to attain essential nutrients. Both changing patterns of cultivation and consumer demand have largely shifted commercial farmers from growing higher to lower nutrient crops. In sub-Saharan Africa, for example, cultivation and collection of African indigenous vegetables such as jute mallow and Ethiopian mustard has declined dramatically as farmers have switched to the cultivation of 'exotic' vegetable cash crops, such as tomato and onion (Virchow, 2008).

Implications for choice and agency of small-scale farmers

The above analysis indicates that different aspects of formal and informal seed systems can have both advantages and disadvantages for small-scale farmers and consumers. These largely depend on the type of crop, and vary with the location and needs of small-scale farmers. However, formal seed systems as they typically operate have many disadvantages for small-scale farmers in terms of access to seeds, appropriateness of varieties, and the ability to achieve sustainable livelihoods, food security and nutritional outcomes.

Efforts to mitigate the disadvantages of formal seed systems are often primarily focused on addressing the legislation (i.e. related to IPRs) or technologies (i.e. related to whether seeds breed true), which restrict farmers' rights to save and reuse seeds (La Vía Campesina and Grain, 2015; Kloppenburg, 2008, 2014). India's seed laws, for example, have been heralded as a model for protecting the rights of small-scale farmers to save and exchange seeds, regardless of property protection. While these are absolutely critical issues, they are not the only factors that inhibit the ability of farmers to exercise choice and agency in seed systems. The ability of farmers to choose the varieties and seed systems which are appropriate to their needs can actually be undermined by efforts to increase the use of formally bred seeds. These efforts affect farmer access to balanced information and have the potential to create a path dependency on formal seed systems.

Farmer choice and access to information

Many policies and programmes related to seed systems are based on the premise that farmers will make a rational choices based on 'perfect information' about the economic viability of the seeds they will grow. In other words, there is an implicit 'free market' assumption that farmers have the ability of choice and that if they choose formally or informally bred seeds, they are exercising their own autonomy.

There are several problems with this assumption. One is that farmers, like any consumer, rarely have access to 'perfect information'. Information provided to farmers about the advantages and disadvantages of different varieties has long been influenced by the dominant paradigm that formally bred varieties are 'improved' or of 'high quality', which inherently indicates that traditional varieties are inferior, even though this may not be true. As public funding for agricultural extension services decreases or is funnelled through private channels, the imbalance in information transfer could worsen.

Many development initiatives, aimed at increasing farmer incomes or reducing poverty, attempt to strengthen agro-dealer networks in order to increase farmer access to formally bred seeds and agri-chemical inputs. Demonstration plots are often planted to exhibit the benefits of formally bred varieties. However, there are no comparisons with alternative cultivation practices which could improve the production of informal varieties. These initiatives are essentially marketing one type of seed and production system, rather than providing balanced information that enables farmers to make informed choices. In addition, these plots are often cultivated using agri-chemical inputs and irrigation, which, as discussed, may not be financially viable for small-scale farmers. Therefore such programmes can either exclude resource-poor small-scale farmers, or worse, mislead them into using seeds that are actually not helpful for them. The mandate of private seed companies to maximize profits often conflicts with the interests of small-scale, resource-poor farmers. Working through such companies in order to reduce poverty therefore comes with significant limitations.

Second, the number of possible scenarios for cultivars, their inputs and market values can be enormous. As Vanloqueren and Baret (2008, p. 441) state

> it seems rather unlikely that a farmer could, without the appropriate information and tools, analyse the results from 20 to 70 cultivars and compare the results of three different cropping systems (low, moderate and high-input).

There are instances in which small-scale farmers are unaware of the fact that some informally bred varieties are more profitable when the costs of inputs are taken into account than formal seeds. In Belgium, disease resistant barley seeds are rarely grown by farmers despite the fact that they would be more economically viable than formally bred varieties (Vanloqueren and Baret, 2008).

Path dependency and lock-in

The promotion of formal seed systems has lead to the erosion of informal systems to the point where undesirable 'path dependencies' have emerged. According to Liebowitz and Margolis (1995), path-dependent processes are self-reinforcing and can lead to a 'lock-in' situation, where a dominant technology excludes potentially superior alternatives.

The purchase of formally bred seed can undermine informal seed systems when it comes to the expense of saving seeds or maintaining crop varieties. As mentioned above, crop varieties can be quickly lost when not maintained or when the population size of a certain variety decreases, even if just for one season (Hodgkin et al., 2007). Thus the promotion of formal seeds, through initiatives which ostensibly aim to 'reach poor smallholder farmers' by market linkages (e.g. supply chain strengthening or Making Markets Work for the Poor initiatives supported by agencies such as USAID and DFID), or which distribute free or subsidized seeds to farmers in the name of food security and income generation (e.g. Malawi's Farm Input Subsidy Programme) pose a significant risk to varietal diversity in the informal sector.

Farmers' loss of the necessary skills and knowledge required to save and store seed, and most importantly about variety maintenance and development, is even more detrimental to the maintenance of current and development of new varieties. Those losses have occurred in countries such as the UK where seed breeding has been highly formalized for the past 50 years. Given that in 2009 the average age of 'landrace' growers in the UK was 66 years and less than half of these growers had successors (Vetelainen et al., 2009), loss of genetic variety would be expected to continue. The loss of such varieties is often irreversible, despite the efforts to preserve diversity through gene banks (Vetelainen et al., 2009). In developing countries, participatory plant breeding initiatives can also undermine informal systems when they result in a transfer of agency in varietal development from farmers to professional breeders and farmers collectively lose skills and knowledge over time.

The loss of genetic and crop diversity, and skills required to develop new varieties, has reduced the resilience of small-scale farmers in the face of climatic changes, pests or other shock events, and in turn has increased farmers' reliance on formally bred seeds. In addition, the loss of skills related to seed selection can increase farmers' vulnerabilities to counterfeit seeds. It also makes farmers susceptible to the volatility in prices and supplies of formal seeds and agri-chemical inputs, which are often tailored to wealthier or large-scale farmers. The costs of these inputs are especially high for farmers who are poorly served by the transport and distribution system.

Path-dependent lock-in situations are also a consequence of the methods of farming used, which are largely dependent on seed varieties. The yields, and even the fertility or other functions of formally bred varieties may be regulated or induced by the application of chemicals. The use of pesticides and other agro-chemicals has been shown to induce path dependencies (Wilson and Tisdell, 2001; Cowan and Gunby, 1996). Once a farmer begins to use such inputs, they continue to require them as the ecosystem changes (e.g. in the emergence of superweeds in the US) and as agroecological knowledge and skills are lost (e.g. on integrated pest management). This can sometimes occur as a gradual process. For example, herbicides have been promoted for zero-tillage cropping systems in Central America and are often hailed as an example of a sustainable agricultural practice due to the minimal disturbance of soil (Khan et al., 2009), However, once farmers have regularly used herbicides, the planting of herbicide-resistant varieties becomes increasingly inevitable (Paul and Steinbrecher 2003).

Similarly, path dependencies have occurred with respect to nutrition. Many nutrient-rich crops, such as traditional African vegetables, are no longer cultivated by farmers (Virchow, 2008), and subsequently, dietary diversity and micronutrient intake has diminished. Rather than examining pathways for increasing the cultivation and consumption of a wider diversity of nutrient-rich vegetables, a progressively dominant pathway has focused on the introduction of a genetically engineered individual micronutrient into one staple crop (i.e. 'golden rice'). However, given the challenges of access and appropriateness (e.g. especially for hard to reach and/or niche environments) inherent in the contemporary formal seed system, it could be anticipated that such initiative may have limited impact on small-scale farmers living in poverty or in remote areas.

Finally, the increased reliance on formal seed systems and the resulting decrease in knowledge about the benefits of and skills to undertake seed saving, variety maintenance and development can reduce the demand for such processes to be considered in the regulation of seed systems. This means that even when small-scale farmers are actually included in decision-making, they may not necessarily advocate the protection or promotion of seed systems that would directly benefit them.

Moving towards seed sovereignty

In summary, the promotion of formally bred seeds and development of the formal seed sector has occurred without the protection or support of the informal seed sector, and has therefore led to path-dependent lock-in situations which negatively impact small-scale farmer livelihoods, food security and nutrition. These path dependencies have been misinterpreted as farmer choice and have also led to a reduced ability for farmers to exercise agency. This creates a positive feedback loop, which reduces farmers to passive recipients of formally bred seed. Thus, even changes to UPOV or national legislation to explicitly give farmers the 'right' to save, develop and exchange seeds will be of little consequence if the knowledge, skills, networks and varieties in the informal seed sector have been undermined to the point where exercising these rights is not actually feasible or viable.

These challenges of farmer agency and path dependency must be mitigated in order to reach a situation in which small-scale farmers define their own seed systems and these systems serve to enhance their livelihoods, food security and nutrition. There have been some general recommendations for ways to ensure that informal and formal systems become mutually supportive systems, rather than the current arrangement in which the formal system undermines and disrupts informal systems (Almekinders and Louwaars, 2002; Louwaars, 2007). However, it is ultimately small-scale farmers who need to be at the heart of the decision-making processes, which determine how seed systems are structured and function.

The establishment of ongoing deliberative processes (Fearon, 1998) in which small-scale farmers provide, receive and exchange information in order to analyse and debate the different aspects of seed systems could serve as one way for this to happen. Such processes could go beyond an analysis of formal vs. informal to explicitly consider the current implications of different aspects of existing seed systems, and identify new pathways to reclaim their agency and ensure that seed systems serve their needs and preferences.

This chapter has indicated that many of the ways in which different aspects of seed systems have an impact on the livelihoods, food security and nutrition of small-scale farmers and producers are highly nuanced. What may benefit one type of small-scale farmer or function in a certain geographical location may be detrimental for others. Thus, it is essential that small-scale farmer participation goes beyond high-level policy development. Small-scale farmers must be included as active participants of decision-making processes related to seed systems at all levels, from local-level projects aiming to 'benefit' them to national policies and international agreements. Given the current lack of small-scale farmer participation in shaping the programmes and policies that are ostensibly aimed at giving them an advantage, there is a need for significant and sweeping change in the way these initiatives are designed and implemented.

Notes

1 With contributions from Santiago Ripoll, Ph.D. researcher at the University of Sussex.
2 The definition of 'small-scale' varies between countries and by type of farm (e.g. livestock and tree crops generally require more space). In developing countries, a farm with fewer than 2 hectares is generally considered 'small' (Vorley et al., 2012); while in the UK, a small farm would be fewer than 20 hectares (Laughton, 2015).
3 Seed companies often contract seed growers in order to produce seeds.
4 Birds distribute seed to other areas, and once these mature, they can cross with other varieties through pollen or wind.

References

Adams, M., Ellingboe, A., and Rossman, E. (1971). Biological uniformity and disease epidemics, *BioScience*, 21(21), 1067–1070.

Almekinders, C. (2000). The importance of informal seed sector and its relation with the legislative framework GTZ (2000 jul. 4–5: Eschborn).

Almekinders, C. and Louwaars, N. (1999). *Farmers' Seed Production. New Approaches and Practices*. London: IT Publications.

Almekinders, C. and Louwaars, N. (2002). The importance of the farmers' seed systems in a functional national seed sector. *Journal of New Seeds*, 4(1–2), 15–33. http://dx.doi.org/10.1300/J153v04n01_02

Almekinders, C., Louwaars, N. and Bruijn, G. (1994). Local seed systems and their importance for an improve seed supply in developing countries. *Euphytica*, 207–216.

Almekinders, C. J. M., Thiele, G. and Danial, D. (2007). Can cultivars from participatory plant breeding improve seed provision to small scale farmers? *Euphytica*, 153, 363–372.

Altieri, M. A. (2009). Agroecology, small farms and food sovereignty. *Monthly Review – An Independent Socialist Magazine*, 61, 102–111.

Assuncao, J. and Braido, L. (2007). Testing household-specific explanations for the inverse productivity relationship. *American Journal of Agricultural Economics*, 89(4), 980–990.

Aw-Hassan, A., Mazid, A. and Salahieh, H. (2008). The role of informal farmer-to-farmer seed distribution in diffusion of new barley varieties in Syria. *Experimental Agriculture*, 44, 413–431.

Bailey, R. (2011). Growing a Better Future: Food justice in a resource-constrained world. Oxfam. Retrieved from www.oxfam.org/sites/www.oxfam.org/files/growing-a-better-future-010611-en.pdf

Bellon, M. R. (2004). Conceptualizing interventions to support on-farm genetic resource conservation. *World Development*, 32, 159–172.

Bernstein, H. (2014). Food sovereignty via the 'peasant way': a sceptical view. *Journal of Peasant Studies*. http://dx.doi.org/10.1080/03066150.2013.852082

BSPB (British Society of Plant Breeders) (2015). Farm Saved Seed. Retrieved from www.bspb.co.uk/farmsavedseed/index.php

Byerlee, D. and Siddiq, A. (1994). Has the green revolution been sustained? The quantitative impact of the seed-fertilizer revolution in Pakistan revisited. *World Development*, 22(9), 1345–1361.

Ceccarelli, S., Guimaraes, E. P. and Weltzien, E. (2009). *Plant Breeding and Farmer Participation*. Food and Agriculture Organization of the United Nations.

Comte, M. C. (1994). Labour in low-input systems: A bibliography. In FAO *Working out the Kinks: Labor in Sustainable Agriculture*, Ceres No. 148, Rome: FAO.

Cowan, R. and Gunby, P. (1996). Sprayed to death: path dependence, lock-in and pest control strategies. *Economic Journal*, 106, 521–542.

Cromwell, E. (ed.) (1990). Seed diffusion mechanisms in small farmer communities: Lessons from Asia, Africa and Latin America. *Agricultural Administration Network. Network Paper 21*. London, UK: Overseas Development Administration

Cromwell, E. (1996). *Governments, Farmers and Seeds in a Changing Africa*. Wallingford: CAB International.

David, C. (2006). The Philippine Hybrid Rice Program: A case for redesign and scaling down. Philippine Institute for Development Studies (PIDS) Research Paper 2006–03. Makati City, Philippines: PIDS

Davis, D., Melvin, D. and Riordan, H. (2004). Changes in USDA food composition data for 43 garden crops, 1950–1999. *Journal of the American College of Nutrition*, 23(6) 669–682.

DEFRA (UK Department for Environmental and Rural Affairs) (2012). Farm saved seed rules, eligible species for payment and how to declare and make payments online. Retrieved from www.gov.uk/farm-saved-seed

Deppe, C. (2000). Breed your own vegetable varieties. *The Gardener's and Farmer's Guide to Plant Breeding and Saving*. Totnes, England: Chelsea Green Publishing.

de Schutter, O. (2009). Seed policies and the right to food: Enhancing agrobiodiversity and encouraging innovation. Background document to the report (A/64/170) presented by Prof. Olivier de Schutter, Special Rapporteur on the right to food, at the 64th session of the UN General Assembly.

de Schutter, O. (2010). Report submitted by the Special Rapporteur on the right to food, Human Rights Council 16th Session, New York: United Nations General Assembly, United Nations. Retrieved from www2.ohchr.org/english/issues/food/docs/A-HRC-16–49.pdf

DFID (UK Department for International Development) and SDC (Swiss Development Cooperation) (2008). A synthesis of the Making Markets Work for the Poor (M4P) approach. Bern, Switzerland: SDC. Donor Committee on Enterprise Development. Retrieved from www.enterprise-development.org/page/m4p

Douglas, J. (1980). *Successful Seed Programs: A Planning and Management Guide*. Boulder, CO: Westview Press.

Dutfield, G. (2008). Turning plant varieties into intellectual property: the UPOV Convention. In G. Tansey, and T. Rajotte (eds.), *The Future Control of Food: a guide to international negotiations and rules on intellectual property, biodiversity and food security*. London: Earthscan.

European Seed Association (2013). Hybridisation and male sterility (MS) in plant breeding: history, current use and legal status. Retrieved from www.sementi.it/informazione/download/materiali/ESA_13_0834_3.pdf

FAO (2004). What is agrobiodiversity? *Building on Gender, Agrobiodiversity and Local Knowledge*. Rome: FAO.

FAO (2006). Quality declared seed system, Plan Production and Protection Paper 185. Rome: FAO.

FAO (2012). *FAO Statistical Yearbook 2012*. Rome: FAO. Retrieved from www.fao.org/3/a-i2490e/index.html. FAO. (2015). *FAOSTAT*. Retrieved from http://faostat3.fao.org

Fearon, J. D. (1998). Deliberation as Discussion. In J. Elster (ed.), *Deliberative Democracy*. Cambridge: Cambridge University Press.

Fitzgerald, D. (1993). Farmers deskilled: Hybrid corn and farmers' work. *Technology and Culture*, 34, 324–343.

Friedman, M. (1970, September 13). The social responsibility of business to increase its profits. *New York Times Magazine*.

Germinate 3 SeeD Maize database (2014). Retrieved from http://germinate.seedsofdiscovery.org/maize

Gonzales, T. (1996). Political ecology of peasantry, the seed and non-governmental organisations in Latin America. Unpublished Ph.D. thesis, University of Wisconsin, Madison.

Gonzales, T., Chambi, N. and Machaca, M. (1999). Agricultures and cosmovision in contemporary Andes. *Cultural and Spiritual Values of Biodiversity*. London: Intermediate Technology.

Grain (2014). *Hungry for Land*. Grain report. Retrieved from www.grain.org/article/entries/4929-hungry-for-land-small-farmers-feed-the-world-with-less-than-a-quarter-of-all-farmland

Hellin, J., Bellon, M. and Hearne, S. (2014). Maize landraces and adaptation to climate change in Mexico. *Journal of Crop Improvement*, 28(4), 484–501.

Ho, M. W., Burcher, S. and Ching, L. L. (2008). *Food Futures Now*. London and Penang: Institute of Science and Society and Third World Network.

Hodgkin, T. R., Rana, J., Tuxill, D., Balma, A., Subedi, I., Mar, D., Karamura, R., Valdivia, L., Collado, L., Latournerie, M., Dadiki, M., Sawadogo, A. H. D., Brown, and Jarvis, D. (2007). Seed systems and crop genetic diversity in agroecosystems. In D. Jarvis, C. Padoch and H. D. Cooper (eds.), *Managing Biodiversity in Agricultural Ecosystems*. Chichester, West Sussex: Bioversity International, Columbia University Press.

Holt-Giménez, E. (2002). Measuring farmers' agroecological resistance after Hurricane Mitch in Nicaragua: A case study in participatory, sustainable land management impact monitoring. *Agriculture, ecosystems and environment*, 93(1–3), 87–105. http://dx.doi.org/10.1016/S0167-8809(02)00006-3

Hoogeveen, J, Tesliuc, E., Vakos, R. and Dercon, S. (2001). *A Guide to the Analysis of Risk, Vulnerability and Vulnerable Groups*. Washington, DC: World Bank.

Retrieved from http://siteresources.worldbank.org/INTSRM/Publications/20316319/RVA.pdf

IAASTD (2009). *Agriculture at a Crossroads: Global Report.* Retrieved from http://apps.unep.org/publications/pmtdocuments/Agriculture_at_a_Crossroads_Global_Report.pdf

IFAD (2013). *Smallholders, Food Security and the Environment.* Rome: International Fund for Agricultural Development.

Joughin, J. (2014). The political economy of seed reform in Uganda: Promoting a regional seed trade market. Africa Trade Practice Working Paper Series, Number 3, World Bank.

Khan, S., Khan, M., Hanjra, M. and Mu, J. (2009). Pathways to reduce the environmental footprints of water and energy inputs in food production. *Food Policy*, 34(2), 141–49.

Kloppenburg, J. (1988). *First the Seed: The Political Economy of Plant Biotechnology.* New York, NY: Cambridge University Press.

Kloppenburg, J. (2008). Seeds, sovereignty, and the Vía Campesina: Plants, property, and the promise of open source biology. Paper prepared for the Workshop on Food Sovereignty: Theory, Praxis and Power, St. Andrews College, University of Saskatchewan, Saskatoon, Saskatchewan.

Kloppenburg, J. (2014). Re-purposing the master's tools: The open source seed initiative and the struggle for seed sovereignty. *Journal of Peasant Studies.* http://dx.doi.org/10.1080/03066150.2013.875897

Lammerts van Bueren, E. T., Jones, S., Tamm, L., Murphy, K., Myers, J. Leifert, C. and Messmer, M. (2011). The need to breed crop varieties suitable for organic farming, using wheat, tomato and broccoli as examples: A review. *Wageningen Journal of Life Sciences*, 58, 193–205.

Laughton (2015). Personal communication, email dated 7 April 2015.

Liebowitz, S. and Margolis, S. (1995). Path dependence, lock-in, and history. *Journal of Law, Economics and Organization*, 11(1), 205–226.

Lope, D. (2004). Gender relations as a basis for varietal selection in production spaces in Yucatan, Mexico. Unpublished master's thesis, Wageningen University.

Louette, D. (2005). Management of maize varieties in a traditional agricultural system of Mexico. In D. Jarvis, R. Sevilla-Panizo, L. Chavez-Servia, and T. Hodgkin (eds.), *Seed Systems and Crop Genetic Diversity On-farm.* Proceedings of a workshop, 16–20 September 2003, Pucullpa, Peru. Rome: IPGRI.

Louwaars, N. (2007). Seeds of confusion: The impact of policies on seed systems. Unpublished Ph.D. thesis, Wageningen University, the Netherlands.

Louwaars, N. and de Boef, W. (2012). Integrated seed sector development in Africa: A conceptual framework of creating coherence between practices, programs, and policies. *Journal of Crop Improvement*, 26, 39–59.

Louwaars, N. and Engels, J. M. (2002). Seed policies: Enabling support to informal seed systems. In M. H. Thijssen, Z. Bishaw, A. Beshir, and W. S. de Boef, *Farmers, Seeds and Varieties: Supporting Informal Seed Supply in Ethiopia.* Wageningen: Wageningen International.

LWA (Land Workers' Alliance) (2015). South West Seed Savers' Coop. Retrieved from www.landworkersalliance.org

Maxted, N., Ford-Lloyd, B. V. and Hawkes, J. G. (1997). *Plant Genetic Conservation: The in Situ Approach.* London: Chapman & Hall.

Mba, C., Guimaraes, E. and Ghosh, K. (2012). Re-orienting crop improvement for the changing climatic conditions of the 21st century. *Agriculture and Food Security*, 1(7).

Nwanze, K. (2011). Smallholders can feed the world. International Fund for Agricultural Development (IFAD) Viewpoint 1. Rome: IFAD.

Nyangena, W. and Juma, O. M. (2014). Impact of improved farm technologies on yields: The case of improved maize varieties and inorganic fertilizer in Kenya. *Environment for Development*, Discussion Paper Series 14–02.

OECD (2012). OECD Seed Schemes: A synthesis of international regulatory aspects that affect seed trade, Organisation for Economic Cooperation and Development. Retrieved from www.oecd.org/tad/code/internationalregulatoryaspectsseedtrade.pdf

Paul, H. and Steinbrecher, R. (2003), *Hungry Corporations: Transnational Biotech Companies Colonise the Food Chain*. New York: Zed Books.

Perales, H., Benz, B. and Brush, S. (2005). Maize diversity and ethnolinguistic diversity in Chiapas, Mexico. Proceedings of the National Academy of Sciences of the USA 102(3).

Rangnekar, D. (2013). The cunning state of farmers' rights in India: Aligning with global law or emancipating farmers? A paper presented at Food Sovereignty: A Critical Dialogue International Conference, Yale University, 14–15 September, conference paper 73.

Rubyogo, J. C., Sperling, L., Nasirumbi, L., and Kasambala, S. (2007, December). Developing seed systems with and for the marginalized: Case of common beans (Phaseolus vulgaris L.) in East, Central and Southern Africa. In *Proceedings of Farmer First Revisited Conference, Sussex, UK* (vol. 1214).

Rusike, J., Howard, J. and Maredia, M. (1997). Seed sector evolution in Zambia and Zimbabwe: Has farmer access improved following economic reforms? *Policy Synthesis for USAID Bureau for Africa Office of Sustainable Development, No. 31.*

Seville, D., Buxton, A. and Vorley, B. (2011). Under what conditions are value chains effective tools for pro-poor development? London: Sustainable Food laboratory. Retrieved from http://pubs.iied. org/16029iied

Shi, G. (2006). Intellectual property rights, Genetic Use Restriction Technologies (GURTs) and strategic behaviour. Paper for presentation at the American Agricultural Economics Association Annual Meeting, Long Beach California, July 2006. University of Wisconsin, Paper No. 156058.

Singh, S. (2012). The woes of rural labour. *Capcity.org*, 44(8–9).

Sperling, L. and McGuire, S. (2010). Understanding and strengthening informal seed markets, *Experimental Agriculture*, 46. http://dx.doi.org/10.1017/S0014479709991074

Stein, A.J., Sachdev, H. P. S. and Qaim, M. (2008). Genetic engineering for the poor: Golden rice and public health in India. *World Development*, 36(1) 144–158. http://dx.doi.org/10.1016/j.worlddev.2007.02.013

Subedi, A. and Garforth, C. (1996). Gender information and communication networks: implications for extension. *European Journal of Agricultural Education and Extension*, 3(2), 63–74.

Tansey, G. (2008). Farming, food and global rules. In G. Tansey and T. Rajotte (eds.), *The Future Control of Food: A Guide to International Negotiations and Rules on Intellectual Property, Biodiversity and Food Security*. London: Earthscan.

Thiele, G. (1999). Informal potato seed systems in the Andes: Why they are important and what should we do with them? *World Development*, 27(1), 83–99.

UK Food Group (2010). Securing future food: Towards ecological food provision. UK Food group briefing. London: UKFG.

United Nations Human Rights Council (2015). Draft UN Declaration on the Rights of Peasants and Other People Working in Rural Areas. Advanced Version 27/01/2015, Second session of the open-ended intergovernmental working group on a United Nations declaration on the rights of peasants and other people working in rural areas. Retrieved from www.ohchr.org/EN/HRBodies/HRC/RuralAreas/Pages/2ndSession.aspx

Vanloqueren, G. and Baret, P. (2008). Why are ecological, low-input, multi-resistant wheat cultivars slow to develop commercially? A Belgian agricultural 'lock-in' case study, *Ecological Economics*, 66(2–3), 436–446. Retrieved fromwww.sciencedirect.com/science/article/pii/S0921800907005083#bib12

Vetelainen, M., Negri, V. and Maxted, N. (2009). European Landraces: On-farm conservation, Management and Use. Technical Bulletin 15. Bioversity International, Rome, Italy.

Vía Campesina (2009a) Declaration of Rights of Peasants – Women and Men, adopted by the Vía Campesina International Coordinating Committee in Seoul, March 2009.

Vía Campesina (2009b) UPOV denies participation to farmers' and civil society organizations. Press release, retrieved from www.viacampesina.org

Vía Campesina and Grain (2015). Seed laws that criminalize farmers: Resistance and fightback. Retrieved from http://viacampesina.org/en/index.php/main-issues-mainmenu-27/biodiversity-and-genetic-resources-mainmenu-37/1783-new-publication-seed-laws-that-criminalise-farmers-resistance-and-fightback

Virchow, D. (2008). Indigenous vegetables in East Africa: Sorted out, forgotten, revitalised and successful. In J. Smartt and N. Haq (eds.). *New Crops and Uses: Their Role in a Rapidly Changing World.* Chichester: Centre for Underutilised Crops, University of Southampton.

Vorley, B., Pozo-Vergnes, E. and Barnett, A. (2012). *Small Producer Agency in the Globalised Market: Making Choices in a Changing World.* London: IIED.

Wegner, L. and Zwart, G. (2011). Who will feed the world: The production challenge. Oxfam Research Report. Retrieved from www.oxfam.org/sites/www.oxfam.org/files/who-will-feed-the-world-rr260411-en.pdf

Weltzien, E. and Christinck, A. (2009). Methodologies for priority setting in plant breeding programs. In S. Ceccarelli, E. P. Guimaraes, and E. Weltzien (eds.), *Plant Breeding and Farmer Participation.* Rome: FAO.

Wilson, C. and Tisdell, C. (2001) Why farmers continue to use pesticides despite environmental, health and sustainability costs. *Ecological Economies*, 39, 449–462.

5 Transnational legal processes of the right to food

Lessons learned from Papua, Indonesia

Irene I. Hadiprayitno

Introduction

Human rights movements go hand in hand with globalization. As networks increase, practices are exchanged and human rights ideas are spread. Where relationships between actors become more complex, transnational legal process is a common phenomenon. The borders of national and international contexts tend to blur, as both laws of the nation states and communities, from the bottom, and international regulations, from the top, interact, so as to give shape to the meaning of human rights and the ways its principles are realized.

The internationally declared human right to food has increasingly been advocated to address one of the most crucial global phenomenon of the twenty-first century: agricultural modernization. Executed through large-scale land acquisitions, it is argued that agricultural modernization is one of the effects of rising food prices in 2008. While the data varies, its scope and speed are vast. GRAIN (2012) reports that 416 large-scale land acquisitions that cover nearly 35 million hectares in 66 countries have occurred. The International Land Coalition says that 80 million hectares have been acquiesced since 2001. One common aspect of agricultural modernization projects is that they are undertaken by wealth funds and multinational corporations based in wealthier countries or the developed world, on a permanent or temporary basis, with the purpose of exporting agricultural products, biofuel production or foresting for carbon litigations. While some argue a win-win solution resulting from the development opportunity, i.e. the injection of much-needed investment into agriculture and rural development in poor developing countries, these projects have raised concerns about their impacts on local people who risk losing access to and control over the land on which their livelihood depends.

The global land grab is to a large extent the result of the liberalization of land markets, which became a major policy goal in the course of the 1990s and has contributed to the commoditization of land and other natural resources (Zoomers, 2010, p. 431). Local people are often forced to either endure enclosure or move to more isolated and marginal locations. These negative impacts of agricultural modernization are arguably connected to, in many cases, the question of inequality and injustice.

It is frequently suggested that the right to food contributes important ethical guidelines to address injustice and inequality resulting from agricultural modernization. The right is defined in international law as constituting, first, 'the availability of food in a quantity and quality sufficient to satisfy the dietary needs of individuals, free from adverse substances, and acceptable within a given culture',[1] and second 'the accessibility of such food in ways that are sustainable and that do not interfere with the enjoyment of other human rights'.[2] The basis for the use of the right-to-food principle to address impacts of agricultural modernization is found in paragraph 13 of the General Comment No. 12. The paragraph asserts, 'special attention must be paid to socially vulnerable groups such as landless persons or indigenous people' and 'indigenous population groups whose access to their ancestral lands may be threatened'.[3] In the Special Rapporteur on the Right to Food (2009), Olivier de Schutter, further elaborates that:

> the human right to food would be violated if people depending on land for their livelihoods, including pastoralists, were cut off from access to land, without suitable alternatives; if local incomes were insufficient to compensate for the price effects resulting from the shift towards the production of food for exports; or if the revenues of local smallholders were to fall following the arrival on domestic markets of cheaply priced food, produced on the more competitive large-scale plantations developed thanks to the arrival of the investor.
>
> (p. 3)

Activists, human rights advocates, international and national non-governmental organizations move beyond national and legal borders as they invoke the ideas and principles of the right to food to address the question of injustice and inequality. As part of international human rights law, the right to food may serve as both legal resources and political instruments for framing the local struggles aimed at securing access to and control of food and land. However, the question remains as to what extent such transnational legal processes delivers political change, in the sense that they challenge the order of power in the society.

This chapter seeks to answer the above question by discussing transnational legal processes with regard to the right to food that occur in Merauke, Papua, Indonesia. In 2010, the Indonesian government launched the Merauke Integrated Food and Energy Estate (MIFEE), a national agricultural modernization project that aims at achieving food security by increasing food production and safeguarding food availability. The programme has been met with resistance. The Marind – the Indigenous peoples of Merauke – together with civil society organizations have been increasingly applying human rights discourses to frame their struggles and to secure their access to and control of land. Several reports and letters of requests have been published and submitted not only to the government of Indonesia, but also to international organizations.

In 2011 and 2012, three requests for consideration were sent to the UN Special Rapporteur on the Right to Food, the UN Committee on the Elimination of Racial Discrimination and Human Rights Council.

The structure of this chapter is as follows. A theoretical framework will first be provided to explain the meaning of transnational legal process in globalized legal spaces of food, land and human rights. Second, the chapter will explain the political economy context of land acquisitions in Merauke, Indonesia, in which the concerns of injustice and inequality will be addressed. The negotiations of the right to food in the Merauke case will be presented in the third section to illustrate the transnational legal processes in Merauke. Concluding remarks reflect and deliberate on the significance of the case in Merauke to the ongoing academic discussion on the modern challenges in realizing human rights in global food and land governance.

Transnational legal process in globalized legal spaces of food, land and human rights

Transnational legal process is broadly defined by Harold Hongju Koh as 'a process whereby public and private actors, including nation states, corporations, international organizations, non-governmental organizations, and individuals interact in a variety of fora to interpret, enforce, and ultimately internalize rules of international law' (1996, p. 183). Transnational legal process has four distinctive features. First, it is non-traditional, as it breaks down two traditional dichotomies: domestic and international, public and private. Second, it is non-statist, as the actors in this process are not just, or even primarily, nation states, but include non-state actors as well. Third, transnational legal process is dynamic, not static. Transnational law transforms, mutates and percolates up and down, from the public to the private, from the domestic to the international level and back down again. Fourth, and finally, it is normative. From this process of interaction, new rules of law emerge, which are interpreted, internalized and enforced, thus beginning the process all over again (Koh, 1996, p. 184).

Koh's analysis implies that it is becoming difficult to distinguish the respective remits of domestic and international law. As non-state actors are active contributors in shaping human right norms, movement of norms from the national and the international level operate in both directions (Topid and Fielder, 2013, pp. 1–2). In this regard, further analysis is required to assess whether transnational legal processes produce laws that require states to comply with, or at least changes the ways states operate in international communities or towards citizens.

Different terminologies are proposed to describe the ways in which actors engage in transnational legal processes. One is the internalization of norms, which occurs either horizontally or vertically (Topid and Fielder, 2013, p. 2). Horizontal internalization consists of intergovernmental forums such as conferences or summits that aim to promote compliance with international law. Vertical internalization happens when state or non-state actors interact with a violating state nationally or internationally to induce compliance. This terminology highlights international law as the main focus. It emphasizes the global spaces taking place particularly at the international level. The complexity of globalization however has reinvented the geographical boundaries as to what global spaces constitute. In 'local forums', such as seminars, human rights training or meetings or other deliberation meetings, one can observe interactions between global actors as well as how local problems are being reproduced into global concerns and global discourses are invoked in local struggles. What comprise horizontal internalization would thus entail forums, or specifically spaces of negotiations, that aim to promote, diffuse and negotiate international norms.

In this context, Sally Engle Merry (2006, p. 39) uses the term 'vernacularization' to identify the ways actors, particularly middle actors or non-governmental organizations, are translating international norms in local domains as they connect victims' grievances into internationally accepted human rights languages. Originally employed to describe how language is being translated, vernacularization is comparable with the term internalization in approaching the activation of international norms in local and nation contexts. The emphasis is placed however on the epistemological aspects of the norms adoption. Here, Merry (2006) categorizes vernacularization into replication and hybridization. Replication refers to a process where human rights claims are implanted in a cultural context with very little attempt at modification, or in other words, sources are relatively dominant. Replication retains the basic structure of the imported institution (Merry, 2006, p. 44). In hybridization, on the other hand, targets are more powerful. Hybridization merges local structures, such as councils with imported human rights ideas (Merry, 2006, p. 46). Merry further argues that the positioning (of all actors in the open conceptual space between global and local), the loyalties and commitments as well as the knowledge of both sides (right-holders and duty-bearers), shapes the vernacularization processes.

The position of actors in globalized legal spaces is observed as a crucial factor in determining the process and the impacts of transnational legal processes. It is increasingly clear that human rights in their normative sense do not constitute a coherent and static system, but are contingent, fragmented and unevenly supported in general. An articulation of rights guarantees no performance (Hathaway, 2002). Nonetheless, universal human rights are also political instruments (De Gaay Fortman, 2006), in the sense that they serve as a source of inspiration for framing grievances into actions. As a political means, invoking rights would imply making political claims, which therefore connects with an actors' position in society, in the sense of both how actors position themselves, as well as how society perceives their positions, in the context of power. Actors with stronger political positions (either individuals or organizations) are observed to adopt culturally legitimate adaptation (in this regard of human rights norms) early on by customizing them (Levitt and Merry, 2009, p. 444). In contrast, marginal actors are likely to adopt innovations that are uncompromising, as they can afford to do so. The compatibility between actors, structurally and institutionally, also allows coercive, mimetic or normative isomorphism, which eventually encourages adoptions.

In the global debates pertaining to food and land, as mentioned before, the right to food is often referred to as the global space to facilitate participation in transnational legal processes. Substantively, the normative content of the right to food asserts the protection of physical and economic access to food. Procedurally, its realization is to be acquired: (a) by earning incomes from employment or self-employment; (b) through social transfers; or (c) by producing their own food, for those who have access to land and other productive resources.[4] Furthermore, Olivier de Schutter, the UN Special Rapporteur of the Right to Food, argues the potentiality of the right to food to provide normative guidelines for complex political actions which require a combination of (1) empowering local communities, (2) implementing supportive policies at the national level, and (3) creating an enabling international environment that can affect the ability of countries to guarantee the right to food. The first point especially relies on the argument of the transformative role of human rights. Moreover de Schutter[5] also proposes to use the human right to food in designing a coherence agricultural governance which comprises 'supportive policies at the national level that ensure the right sequencing between the various policy reforms that are needed, across all relevant sectors, including agriculture, rural development, health, education and social protection'. Empowered by these normative points and the growing body of international human rights law, transnational actors are advocating human rights based legal and political solutions in various forums, including tribal states and international tribunals as well as legislatures, agencies and other organs in civil society. As observed by Carpenter and Riley (2014, p. 177), in their studies on Indigenous peoples, actors are participating beyond borders and influencing the law around and outside their communities all the way up to state and international arenas.

The aspect of transnational legal process is important to understanding the diffusion and invocation of international norms, and their relevance to agricultural governance. Nowadays movements of actors and capital have multiple consequences not only for the accumulation of wealth but also for the production of inequality and injustice. The protections of physical and economic access to food have therefore become part of the development portfolio, which is frequently invoked by transnational actors to combat marginalization and impoverishment. In the following sections this subject will be discussed in detail by studying the case of MIFEE in Merauke, Indonesia.

Positioning MIFEE in the agricultural modernization debates in Indonesia

In order to establish the political economy context of the transnational legal process in the Merauke case study, this section will explain the position of

MIFEE in the specific context of agricultural debates in Papua, Indonesia, which include concerns pertaining to decentralization and economic development policies in this region.

Food and agricultural policies in Indonesia are often linked to the economic and political situation of the country. The Indonesian state regulates food and agriculture, which therefore requires the state's full control based entirely on government decisions. To many, this approach would imply that the government would keep the issue of food availability and food accessibility under control. However competitors are favourable as well, especially pertaining to the role of corporations in agricultural policies (Hadiprayitno, 2010).

In August 2010, MIFEE was launched with a view to developing a plantation of 1.2 million hectares for a cash crop and biofuel plantation in Merauke. The government foresees by 2020 that the region will produce 1.95 million tonnes of rice, 64, 000 cows, 2.5 million tonnes of sugar, 167, 000 tonnes of soybean, 2.02 million tonnes of maize and 937, 000 tonnes of crude palm oil annually. The project will be developed in stages from 2010 to 2014, 2015 to 2019 and 2020 to 2030. According to government estimates, the project will also create 44,900 jobs in the agricultural sector for both Indigenous people and trans-migrants, and increase income by up to US$13,500 per household per year (Government of Indonesia, 2010).

MIFEE is an integral part of the Master Plan for Acceleration and Expansion of Indonesian Economic Development formally launched by President Susilo Bambang Yudhoyono through the adoption of the Presidential Decree No. 32 of 2011 (Government of Indonesia, 2010). The Master Plan (MP3EI), sees Indonesia become one of the top ten major economies in 2025. It centres around three main strategies: to develop six national economic corridors,[6] to speed up the capacity of human resources and to stimulate innovation through national science and technology, which will feed into the long-term support of such accelerated economic development.

The government has pinpointed specific development themes for each economic corridor. Sumatra will be the centre for production and processing of natural resources and the nation's energy reserves. Java will continue to act as the driver of national industry and service provisions. Kalimantan is identified as the centre for production and processing of national mining and energy. Sulawesi has the potential to be the home for the production and processing of the product derived from the nation's agriculture, plantations, fisheries, oil, gas and mining industries. Bali and Nusa Tenggara will remain the gateway for tourism and national food support. This is particularly connected to the plan intended for Moluccas and Papua, which are to be the centre for food, fisheries as well as energy and mining. The corridor is an ideal space of arable land, divided into eight economic centres. To investors, the Moluccas and Papua economy presents an opportunity for agricultural expansion. The corridor has an abundance of economic resources, with a high GRDP of 7 per cent in 2006 to 2009.

Specifically, Merauke is a designated area for food and energy reserves in East Indonesia, due to its flat geographical terrain and fertile land. As mentioned, the MIFEE programme is located in an area of 1.2 million hectares and it will consist of 10 clusters of Agricultural Production Centres[7] and at least 36 companies will be involved in their implementation. The aim is to establish a central production area for food and horticultural crops, livestock, fisheries and plantations in the Nakias and Selil clusters by 2030. Agricultural plans for MIFEE will include rice, corn, soybeans, sorghum, wheat, vegetables and fruits; and livestock will include chicken, cow, goat and rabbits. As for non-food crops, the programme will include sugar cane, rubber and palm oil.

As in other economic corridors, the state is playing an active and decisive role in the execution of the MIFEE programme. This is because investment (both foreign and domestic) is the core of the argument for the expansion and the acceleration of economic development.[8] The Indonesian government has limited funds to finance development through its State Budget (APBN). Therefore, according to the MP3EI, 44 per cent of the total investment needed is expected to come from private centres and industries. Hence, it is intended that all existing regulatory frameworks must be evaluated, and strategic steps must be taken to revise and change regulations in order to attract such support from investors. Furthermore, more incentives will be implemented on tariffs, taxes, import duties, labour regulations, licensing, permits and land procurements.

To achieve this the government has issued Law No. 41 of 2009 on the Protection of Sustainable Agricultural Land and the Government Regulations No. 18 of 2010 on Cultivation with Special Attention to MIFEE. Particularly, Law No. 41 of 2009 allows local and foreign private investors to actively participate in the production and trade of agriculture products both for the domestic and export markets.[9] Most recently, Law No. 2 on Land Acquisition for Development was emanated in January 2012. Many observed that Law No. 2 of 2012 was motivated to provide more security for investors regarding land acquisitions (Sumardjono, 2012). These legal sources increase the flexibility and provide the facilities for foreign capital to secure contracts and concessions pertaining to land and natural resources in Indonesia.

There is a wide-ranging debate surrounding the agricultural modernization and MIFEE in Merauke Papua. From the decentralization perspective, the expansion of the agricultural production to Papua is explained by how finance is organized in this region compared with other regions. In Indonesia, decentralized regional governments are under financial pressure to fund the daily organization of their regions. The status of special autonomy of Papua, granted for 25 years, ending in 2026, provides the financial support for economic development. However, changes are observably meagre in Papua. Intervention in the form of development funds coming from the Special Autonomy Status has not significantly improved the quality of public services and infrastructure. In fact many have observed that decentralization has led to political contests between elites over autonomy contestations (Hadiz, 2004).

LIPI observes that the most striking change since Special Autonomy Status came into effect has only been the increase in the amount of development funds coming into Papua, rather than actual autonomy. Finance drawn from Special Autonomy has merely been used to finance facilities for the bureaucracy in the new agencies. The central government maintains its opinion that granting independence in terms of political and economy autonomy would provide a larger space for the hidden agendas of the separatists (Chauvel and Bhakti, 2004). In reality a new paradigm has been acquired for development processes that would genuinely empower people in Papua, and that can hold the bureaucrats in Papua accountable. Yet, despite the dominant capital flows for development, the people of Papua, both in rural and urban areas, are still just spectators, particularly as there isn't as yet any policy that is truly directed at the interests of Indigenous communities (Widjojo, 2010, p. 94). In this context, the idea of promoting a massive expansion of agricultural enterprises into Papua has been argued as a logical process. Profits arising from agricultural investment are said to be securing the finance for the development process.

Nevertheless, income sustainability remains questionable. There are various calculations as to how much local government earnings from MIFEE will be. If the profits of such agricultural modernization will be organized according to the provision regarding the distribution of benefits from exploitation natural resources, such as forest or peat land, in Law No. 21 of 2001, Papua will roughly receive 80 per cent of the funds. If it includes the distribution of export revenue based on the RSPO scheme, it means at least 1 million hectares (for the purpose of calculation) could produce $US 166 million in annual revenue for the Indonesian government over the first seven years, and Merauke District's share of these financial resources would be $US 62 million annually over the same period. In subsequent years, the total revenue would decline sharply to $US 7 million annually and Merauke's share of this would be $US 2 million (Obidzinski et al., 2013).Based on progress observed so far, many fear disaster may follow the removal of financial support from Jakarta and MIFEE. Massive development projects that involve a considerable appropriation of traditional land lead to significant social and economic challenges, especially for Indigenous peoples. Based on a qualitative research conducted in two villages in Merauke, Zakaria et al. (2010) argues that the sociocultural gap, demographic revolutions, economic marginalization and political marginalization will be the detrimental effects of MIFEE.[10]

The emphasis on investment relies heavily on private actors and industries that have the potential to reshape and redefine the governance of access to food and land resources. As new actors, in particular private ones, are being introduced, negotiations of rights and obligations of both right-holders and duty-bearers would thus have different strategies and goals, as well as substance. Responses to this situation take place through the active role of civil society organizations – international and national non-governmental organizations, which will be discussed in the next paragraphs.

Transnational legal process in the struggles against MIFEE

As mentioned previously, transnational legal process is a process whereby public and private actors, including nation states, corporations, international organizations, non-governmental organizations, and individuals interact in order to interpret, enforce and ultimately internalize international norms. In the context of human rights, it implies challenging, if not changing, the relationships between individuals and the state. With regard to the right to food, the concern is argued to be too complex for the internalization of norms as they need to account for the complexity of the food systems and the needs of the community, in order to ensure the formulation of accountable policies and an enabling environment.

In Indonesia, the governance of food system and agricultural modernization is arranged within the myriad of at least three legal frameworks. The first is the human rights legal framework. The ratification of the two human rights covenants and the adoption of the Law No. 39 of 1999 by the Indonesian government implies that the right to food has a legal standing in the court of law. However, assessing their actual impact on the right-holders' position to acquire the right to food, the judicial system is not straightforward and has to be read in conjunction with Law No. 26 of 2000 on Human Rights Courts. This law asserts the jurisdiction of the ad hoc Human Rights Court to hear only cases of gross violation of human rights, i.e. genocide and crimes against humanity. This discrepancy creates an area of uncertainty on the promotion and protection of the right to food in the governance of the food system.

The MIFFE legal framework requires one to at least make a reference to Law No. 41 of 2009 on the Protection of Sustainable Agricultural Land, the Presidential Decree No. 32 of 2011 on the Acceleration and the Expansion of Economic Growth and Law No. 2 on Land Acquisition for Development. As argued before, these legal sources have been predominantly defined in the governance of land acquisition in Merauke, Papua, and their purpose is to secure private investment.[11]

Customary claims pertaining to land tenure are arranged under the Ministry of Agraria Regulation No. 5 of 1999, which instructs regional governments to research claims of the recognition of customary communal land and record their findings in a regional regulation. Under the 1945 Constitution, Article 18B(2) recognizes and respects individual customary law communities, in as far as they are 'still alive' and 'in line with the evolution of society and the unitary state' and national law. Article 28i(3) offers protection of the cultural identity and rights of traditional communities in accordance with changing times and culture. The limitation to the Indigenous rights to land is however found in Article 67(1) of the Law No. 21 of 2001 on Special Autonomy of Papua, which asserts that claims regarding control over lands and property based on customary law can only be established if they are found to be 'still relevant' and not 'conflicting with national interests'.[12]

While internalization of norms in its strictest legal sense might be challenging, it does not mean the human right to food is of little relevance. In Merauke, Papua, human right norms and principles have acquired a dominant position in the struggles for land rights. The right to food and human rights discourse, particularly as part of international legal norms and discourses, are employed by about 22 civil society organizations which are currently involved in the MIFEE network by providing a wider range of advocacy works. Workshops and training courses are the common advocacy methods, and they are therefore the key sites for transnational legal processes for at least two reasons. 'Horizontally', a transfer of knowledge pertaining to human rights norms and principles can occur from the human rights activists to the constituents. It also provides an opportunity to share experiences and grievances. Workshop and training courses consequently allow a mutual exchange of discourses and practices, a model of communication required for both parties to frame their own understanding of human rights. In these events, actors formulate claims and plans for actions, which can take the forms of human rights reports. With regard to MIFEE, at least three human rights reports and requests have been written and submitted to the international community.

In August 2011, a Request for Urgent Assistance to Address the Imminent Threat to the Right to Food of the Indigenous Peoples in Merauke, Papua Province, Indonesia was also sent to the UN Special Rapporteur on the Right to Food.[13] The letter emphasizes the acts and omissions committed by the government of Indonesia that have negative impacts on people's access to food and their ability to feed themselves. Paragraph 9 of the letter reads as follows:

> To date, indigenous Papuans (to which the Malind and other Merauke indigenous peoples belong) already have lost a considerable area of their traditional territories due to logging, mining, oil palm plantations and population transfers. They have received few benefits and suffered severe negative impacts, which, in many cases, amount to irreparable harm. These operations have the full support of the State in Indonesia, at all levels, and frequently enjoy the protection of the Indonesian Army. The MIFEE Project is in direct contradiction to the affirmation by the UN Committee on Economic, Social and Cultural Rights that (i) when it comes to the Right to Food '[s]ocially vulnerable groups such as landless persons and other particularly impoverished segments of the population may need attention through special programmes' and (ii) a 'particular vulnerability [to the exercise of the right to food] is that of many indigenous population groups whose access to their ancestral lands may be threatened'.

A slightly different wording is observed in the Request for Consideration of the Situation of Indigenous Peoples in Merauke, Papua Province, Indonesia, submitted to the Committee on Elimination of Racial Discrimination in September 2011, which makes reference to Indigenous rights and self-determination principles to describe the gravity of the situation.[14]

> Agro-industry in Indonesia, such as the MIFEE project, is highly detrimental to indigenous peoples and this has been widely acknowledged. Indonesia, however, continues to disregard its obligations and is now massively expanding agro-industry operations into Papua, the territories of the most vulnerable and discriminated against indigenous peoples in that country. The subject of this request, the MIFEE project, is emblematic of this expansion and the drastic and extreme impacts on the affected indigenous peoples, whose survival as distinct cultural and territorial entities is gravely and imminently threatened. Without urgent and sustained international scrutiny and attention, they may cease to exist as collective entities altogether in the coming years.

A group of civil society organizations whose concerns relate to the impact of cash crops and biofuel plantations to Indigenous rights to land also raised the issue of MIFEE in their Stakeholders' Submission to the 13th session of the Human Rights Council's Universal Periodic Review in November 2012.[15] The report presents evidence on the continued neglect of the right to land, territory and natural resources by rural communities and particularly Indigenous peoples by the government of Indonesia. Derived from several cases in Kalimantan, Sulawesi, Sumatera and Papua, it was observed that such neglect has increasingly worsened in the implementation of policies and practices of natural resource exploitation and climate change impact mitigation in the last four years. On the case of MIFEE in Merauke, Papua, paragraph 21 of the report states:

> The documented negative impacts of MIFEE include coercion and manipulative practices to obtain certification that indigenous peoples have relinquished their land; increased inter-ethnic conflict and violence; and the clearance of the forests on which the Malind and other indigenous communities depend on directly and almost entirely for their subsistence, in order to make way for monocrop plantations under long-term leasehold contracts between the state and private companies. Violations associated with the MIFEE project also include the violation of rights of free assembly, speech and the right of freedom from threats to one's physical integrity.

From the three comparable reports, one could conclude that human rights discourses have obtained a privileged position in the formulation of claims. While the reports also make a reference to the national law and regulations that are unfavourable to protect people from the impact of MIFEE,[16] human rights law, particularly international human rights principles and norms are invoked prominently to explain the infringements conducted by the State. The excerpts from the reports above reveal the focus towards Indigenous identity, and the attributes surrounding that identity. In these reports the core of the problem is beyond the question of law enforcement, rather it is about justice making, for what is understood by the civil society organizations as a particular problem embedded within the Indigenous identity of the victims and the right-holders.

The connection to Indigenous identity provides a rooted elucidation of the impact as well as a contextualization necessary to elevate the negotiation of the right to food from the local to the global arena. In this regard, the transnational legal process happens not in a translation or a linguistic logic, in the sense that it expands or reinterprets the content of the right to food. Rather, it occurs in the prudent demonstration pertaining to the complexity in securing access to food and the ability for one to feed themselves in the context of Indigenous rights. This in turn provides a prescription as to what efforts are required for progressive realization. Moreover, recognition of the distinct cultural and territorial entities, for example, in combination with a reference to international norms on the right to food, can reconcile the contentions that might occur in the process of defining the power relationship.

The latter is observably arduous when one examines the actual struggles at the grass roots. In such domains, numerous actors are involved, and the state, in this regard represented by the local and district government, is recurrently underrepresented in the negotiations, as they are only involved as an initial facilitator. Moreover, anchoring claims to formal sources such as international human rights norms and principles is identifiably more of a choice than a necessity in such sites.

The negotiation regarding financial compensation for the exploitation of Indigenous land rights in the Zanegi village by Selaras Inti Persada Inc. can provide a specific illustration. In this village, initial negotiations started in 2007.[17] In the beginning, meetings between the company and head of Marga (clans) were facilitated by the Head of District Animha, Merauke, whose authoritative influences could forestall resistance. The outcome of the negotiations was what the population called 'a dowry' of 300 million IDR (down from the initial demand of 1.2 billion IDR)[18] to be given to each of the Margas in exchange for 'the permission' given to the company to exploit the forest surrounding the village. Another financial note is that during its operation the company will consider 'buying' the original timber they extracted from the forest, which according to the villagers remains their 'traditional property'.

When asked why financial compensation for land acquisition took place in the form of a 'dowry', the representative of the company claimed it as a constitutive part of their commitment to 'corporate social responsibility'. In addition to the rights acquired to exploit the forest, the company employed the terms 'tali asih' (compassionate agreement), 'piagam penghargaan' (appraisement plaque) to describe other arbitrary outputs of negotiations. These terms are claimed to express their extraordinary appreciation of their relationship with the Zanegi villagers. This form was chosen to symbolize the company's highest appreciation of people's cooperation and to euphemize the inability to balance the spiritual value of Indigenous lands. Materially, such an agreement is manifested in the company's commitments to develop infrastructure and social facilities in the village, such as building schools, churches, a village office, cultural centres, electricity generators, water provider facilities and connecting roads. In many cases, these agreements come with other assurances such as providing a salary for schoolteachers or employing local population in the company's activity, through a plasma model of land tenure.

Companies are very aware of human rights, the right to food and their advocates. Negotiations are therefore arranged in order to fulfil what they understood as the 'free, prior and informed consent' principle. Obviously, Indigenous rights, ideals and discourses are alive in shaping and providing 'the direction' for negotiations. The emphasis on Indigenous identity, however, is chosen to clarify the distribution of compensation. In response, claims made by Indigenous peoples are made to achieve compensatory arrangements, which essentially comprise the pursuit of securing necessary (and access to) resources for Indigenous peoples to sustain their daily livelihoods. In the context of the Zanegis' struggles against MIFEE, recognition towards Indigenous identity and rights, however, has not benefited the right-holder in getting fair and equal compensation for their claims.

The concern is that such interpretations of Indigenous identity have led to several confusions and blunders. First is the status of their Indigenousness, in that which groups they belong to and the borders of rights for each Indigenous community and/or persons are contentious. Second is the procedure for distributing the financial compensation, which is practised arbitrarily outside the formal system of the state. These issues arise because of the invocation of the right to food engaged by the company at the grass roots is premised on the ambition to secure investment through arbitrary financial compensation. Rather than a discursive practice, the invocation of human rights norms becomes a utilitarian activity in the sense that it serves the company's interests. This is extremely dicey terrain, and a venture in translating human rights discourses into avaricious calculations as such tend to push both Indigenous peoples and human rights activists into defending customary practices of negotiations and the appropriateness of technical methods to control borders of Indigenous territory, such as mapping Indigenous land for acquiring formal land titles.

Notably in the case of Merauke, public and private actors (e.g. corporations, non-governmental organizations, individual and communities) have interpreted the substantive and procedural contents in various ways. This represents the non-static and dynamic characters of the transnational legal process of the right to food. Assessing its contribution in transforming practices and rules from up and down, and vice versa, would imply a more complex scrutiny. As observed, while framing grievances into human rights language has contributed to the political legitimacy of claims in the international arena, and at the grass-roots level it has created an adventurous way of negotiating land rights, financial compensation and basic facilities. However, it remains problematic to conclude whether it has challenged the order of power in society.

This is not a novel strategy of private actors involved in agricultural or natural resources projects. The powerful position of corporations in the design and implementation of MIFEE might contribute to the puzzle. The strong emphasis of the acceleration of economic development expands the roles of the companies with regard to how the MIFEE project is implemented. The plurality of legal sources, yet the lack of clarity pertaining to the scope of companies' interventions, adds to the situation. Rules and regulations have been forged as an instrument that defines the relationships between companies, Indigenous communities and the state. Companies are observed as having the ability and competence to replicate human rights norms in their actions and to culturally legitimatize their adoption of human rights norms. In many aspects, providing arbitrary compensation on the ground could be seen as mimicking, if not replacing the role of the state.

As a result, justice and equality are persistently challenged and in this respect it becomes more crucial to investigate how actors are involved in the struggles. Specific here is the configuration of private and state actors in contrast with the position non-governmental organizations. Human rights activists and Indigenous communities have to dispute the sociocultural manifestations of power relations in everyday life. Moreover, vertical actions need to aim at answering the radical, yet basic, questions with regard to democratization and citizenship. In this vein, one might need to examine the conditions pertaining to the representative agencies accountability, which can shift national and regional political discourses regarding agricultural modernization.

Concluding remarks

This chapter was written in order to critically assess the invocation of the right to food ideals and norms in the transnational legal process to address injustice and inequality resulting from agricultural modernization projects, such as the one implemented by the government of Indonesia in Merauke Papua. In the foregoing sections the complex challenges of inequality and injustice resulted from the project and the ways different actors and factors invoke the right to food have been explained.

Theoretical arguments on transnational legal process assert the non-traditional, dynamic, non-static and normative attributes. In the age of globalization these imply that interpreting how rights should be and could be realized is no longer the domain of public actors. In answering the question as to what extent transnational legal processes deliver political changes necessary for combating injustice and inequality, it was shown that the right to food as an international norm has compelled actors to engage in the process of negotiations. However, as revealed in the case of Merauke, the issues of access, land tenure, and compensation are open for flexible interpretation.

The nature of transnational legal process may be a source of inspiration for actors to engage in negotiation processes, but the politics of an agreement may not always be desirable, given the rise in its strategic implications. As companies focus on the questions of land tenure and compensation becomes typically larger, they have been able to acquire the aptitude to culturally adopt universal human rights norms. An emphasis on these concerns has provided them with a competitive position pertaining to the process and the result of negotiations. In the case of Merauke this process has provided leeway for the state to be absolved from carrying out its obligation to protect and provide people access to food and feed themselves.

Moreover 'vertical' processes of negotiations from the local to the global arena need to account for the horizontal and vertical politics at the local level. The actors, non-governmental organizations, the state and corporations, all have their own agenda in invoking the human rights norms, and these interests can be to the detriment of the Indigenous community. The emphasis on the legality of actions and the rigidity of the human rights norms may also deliver similar consequences as the approach on indigeneity taken by the corporations.

The case discussed in this chapter reflects the complexity of the 'global legal space' at the local arenas and the contemporary challenges in realizing human rights in global food and land governance. Notably invocations of norms through transnational legal processes can result in various ways depending on the interest and the political position of public and private actors in society. In this vein, changing the societal order vis-à-vis addressing injustice and inequality may demand more active roles by public actors to move beyond legalism, and address the unattended and enhanced power and entitlements of private actors.

Notes

1 Committee on Economic, Social and Cultural Rights, General Comment 12, Right to adequate food (Twentieth session, 1999), UN Doc. E/C.12/1999/5 (1999), paragraph 8.
2 Committee on Economic, Social and Cultural Rights, General Comment 12, Right to adequate food (Twentieth session, 1999), UN Doc. E/C.12/1999/5 (1999), paragraph 8.
3 Committee on Economic, Social and Cultural Rights, General Comment 12, Right to adequate food (Twentieth session, 1999), UN Doc. E/C.12/1999/5 (1999), paragraph 13.
4 Human Rights Council, Report submitted by the Special Rapporteur on the right to food, Olivier de Schutter, Women's rights and the right to food, A/HRC/25/57 (2014), paragraph 2.
5 Human Rights Council, Report submitted by the Special Rapporteur on the right to food, Olivier de Schutter, Women's rights and the right to food, A/HRC/25/57 (2014), paragraph 50.
6 These economic corridors are – Sumatera, Java, Kalimantan, Sulawesi, Bali – Nusa Tenggara and Papua – Mollucs.
7 The short-term development priority of MIFEE (2011–14) is to develop clusters I to IV, covering an area of 228,023 ha. The four KSPP clusters being developed are: Greater Merauke, Kali Kumb, Yeinan, and Bian located in the Merauke Regency. The medium-term (2015–19) development will be directed at developing areas of agricultural production centres for food crops, horticulture, animal husbandry, plantation, and aquaculture in Clusters Okaba, Ilwayab, Tubang and Tabonji.
8 The total investment required for the six corridors is IDR 4,012 trillion. From this total, it is expected that the Sumatra Corridor will receive IDR 714 trillion (18 per cent of total investment), the Kalimantan Corridor will receive IDR 945 (24 per cent of total investment), the Java Corridor will receive IDR 1,290 trillion (32 per cent of total investment), the Sulawesi Corridor will receive IDR 309 trillion (8 per cent of total investment), the Bali-Nusa Tenggara Corridor will receive IDR 133 trillion (3

per cent of total investment) and lastly the Papua–Kepulauan Maluku Corridor will receive IDR 622 trillion (15 per cent of total investment).

9 Before 2009, the government has issued several laws and regulations that support privatization of agricultural modernization. For instance, the Law No. 41 of 1999 on Forestry; Law No. 18 of 2004 on Plantation; Law No. 7 of 2004 on Water Resource; 2005 Agricultural Revitalization; Law No. 25 of 2007 on Investment; Law No. 4 of 2009 on Mineral and Coal (Minerba).

10 Zakaria et al. (2010) argues that these impacts include the low level of education of Papuans, and their hunting and gathering mode of production, will exclude them in the transformation from household farming to corporate–mechanization farming (the sociocultural gap), the labour demand of corporate farming is calculated to absorb about 4.8 million new migrants from outside Papua, which will leave Papuans as only 5 per cent of the total residents. This demographic change will displace Papuans from access to economic power, as experienced by the Papuans during a transmigration programme in the 1980s (demographic revolution), agricultural modernization that provides no space for Papuans will further the socio-economic polarization, leaving Papuans on the lowest level of the economic ladder (economic marginalization), and the greater economic power that will be better accessed by migrants than native Papuans may also bring migrants better access to political power as well in government offices and other forms of political leadership (political marginalization).

11 Other legal sources for legitimating land acquisitions in Indonesia are Law No. 41/1999 on Forestry Law, Law No. 26/2007 on Spatial Planning; Government Regulation No. 26/2008 on National Territory Spatial Planning. The Law No. 41 of 1999 on Forestry especially allows the state to create a massive system of publicly – and privately – held forestry concessions in the forests traditionally owned by Indigenous peoples without any regard for their rights or existence.

12 In this regard, the Forestry Department claims that the state has jurisdiction over 72 per cent of land (Bakker and Moniaga 2010, p. 189).

13 Submitted by Sawit Watch and Forest People Program, 9 August 2011.

14 Submitted to United Nations Committee on the Elimination of Racial Discrimination, 79th session, 8 August–2 September 2011.

15 Stakeholders' Submission to the 13th session of the UPR Working Group (21 May–1 June 2012). Joint report submitted on 21 November 2011 by HUMA, Pontianak Institute, Down to Earth, Pusaka, Walhi, AMAN, Forest People Program, KKI Warsi, YMP, and RFN. The submission of a stakeholders' report aims at providing information related to the level of compliance of the government of Indonesia to those UPR recommendations that are listed in Section II of the Report of the Working Group A/HRC/8/23. It pertains especially to paragraphs 77 (5) and (7), to which the government of Indonesia declared its support, and paragraph 78 of the same report and paragraph 77 (5) of the UPR Working Group report recommends that the government of Indonesia continues measures to promote and protect the human rights of all components of the Indonesian people.

16 See Request for Consideration of the Situation of Indigenous Peoples in Merauke, Papua Province, Indonesia, under the United Nations Committee on the Elimination of Racial Discrimination's Urgent Action and Early Warning Procedures, United Nations Committee on the Elimination of Racial Discrimination, 79th session, 8 August–2 September 2011, paras. 18–23.

17 The first finalization of the negotiation took place in 2010. At the time when the field study was conducted in July 2011 and during the time writing this chapter, there are still many unresolved issues.

18 The currency rate at that time was 1 US$ = 12.500 IDR (Indonesian rupiah).

References

Bakker, L. and Moniaga, S. (2010). The Space Between: Land Claims and the Law in Indonesia. *Asian Journal of Social Science*, 38.

Baxi, U. (2002). *The Future of Human Rights*. New Delhi: Oxford University Press.

Brown, W. (1995). *States of Injury: Power and Freedom in Late Modernity*. Princeton: Princeton University Press

Carpenter, K. A. and Riley, A. (2014). Indigenous Peoples and the Jurisgenerative Moment of Human Rights. *California Law Review*, 102.

Chauvel, R. and Bhakti, I. N. (2004) *The Papua Conflict: Jakarta's Perceptions and Policies*. Washington: East West Centre.

Committee on Economic, Social and Cultural Rights, General Comment 12, Right to adequate food (Twentieth session, 1999), UN Doc. E/C.12/1999/5 (1999). Adopted by Human Rights Treaty Bodies, UN Doc. HRI/GEN/1/Rev.6 at 62 (2003).

De Gaay Fortman, B. (2010). *Political Economy of Human Rights: Rights, Realities and Realisation*. New York: Routledge.

de Schutter, O. (2009). Large-scale Land Acquisitions and Leases: A Set of Minimum Principles and Measures to Address the Human Rights Challenge. In: *Report of the Special Rapporteur on the Right to Food*, Olivier de Schutter. New York: Human Rights Council, United Nations.

de Schutter, O. (2014). Final Report: The Transformative Potential of the Right to Food. In: *Report of the Special Rapporteur on the Right to Food*, Olivier de Schutter. New York: Human Rights Council, United Nations.

Deiniger, K and Byerlee, D. (2011). *Rising Global Interest in Farmland: Can It Yield Sustainable and Equitable Benefits?* Washington, DC: World Bank.

Government of Indonesia. (2010). Grand design Pengembangan pangan dan energi skala luas. Jakarta: Ministry of Agriculture.

GRAIN (2012). GRAIN Releases Data Set with over 400 Global Land Grabs (23 February 2012). Available at: www.grain.org/article/entries/4479-grain-releases-data-set-with-over-400-global-land-grabs

Hadiprayitno, I. (2010). Food Security and Human Rights in Indonesia. *Development in Practices*, 20(1).

Hadiz, V. (2004). Decentralization and Democracy in Indonesia: A Critique of Neo-Institutionalist Perspectives. *Development and Change*, 35(4).

Hale, C. R. (2002). Does Multiculturalism Menace? Governance, Cultural Rights and the Politics of Identity in Guatemala. *Journal of Latin American Studies*, 34.

Hathaway, O. A. (2002) Do Human Rights Treaties Make a Difference? *Yale Law Journal*, 111.

Human Rights Council (Twenty-fifth session 2014). Report submitted by the Special Rapporteur on the right to food, Olivier de Schutter, UN Doc. A/HRC/25/57, 24 January 2014.

Koh, H. H. (1996). Transnational Legal Processes. *Nebraska Law Review*, 75.

Levitt, P. and Merry, S.E. (2009). Vernacularization on the Ground: Local Uses of Global Women's Rights in Peru, China, India and the United States. *Global Networks*, 9(4).

Mechlem, K. (2004). Food Security and the Right to Food in the Discourse of the United Nations. *European Law Journal*, 10(5).

Merry, S. E. (2006). Transnational Human Rights and Local Activism: Mapping the Middle. *American Anthropologist*, 108.

Moubray, J. (2007). The Right to Food and the International Economic System: An Assessment of the Rights-Based Approach to the Problem of World Hunger. *Leiden International Law Journal*, 20.

Obidzinski, K., Takahashi, I., Dermawan, A., Komarudin, H. and Andrianto, A. (2013). Can Large Scale Land Acquisition for Agro-Development in Indonesia Be Managed Sustainably? *Land Use Policy*, 30.

Sumardjono, M. (2012). Pragmatism UU Pengadaan Tanah. *Kompas*, 7 June 2012.

Topidi, K. and Fielder, L. (2013). *Transnational Legal Processes and Human Rights*. Surrey: Ashgate.

Widjojo. M. S. (ed.) (2010). *Papua Road Map: Negotiating the Past, Improving the Present, Securing the Future*. Jakarta: LIPI.

Zakaria, R. Y., Kleden, E. O. and Franky, Y. L. (2011). *MIFEE Tak Terjangkau Angan Malind*. Jakarta: Pusaka.

Zoomers, A. (2010) Globalisation and the Foreignisation of Space: Seven Processes Driving the Current Global Land Grab. *Journal of Peasant Studies*, 37(2).

6 Foucault's evaluation of the UN call for human rights in global food governance

Jonathan Liljeblad

In May 2008, the United Nations High Commissioner for Human Rights (UNHCHR) Louise Arbour issued a call to include human rights in food governance. Arbour stated that while food crises can be addressed through humanitarian operations, such aid is only a short-term solution and that a longer-term response requires an emphasis on human rights (United Nations, 2008). Arbour's reasoning is that food crises are largely driven by deeper issues of distribution, with food being denied as a part of a wider pattern of ongoing exclusionary practices against marginalized groups. This means that the denial of food, while a violation of the human right to food, is likely only a component of a broader violation of human rights in general. According to Arbour, humanitarian food aid, in focusing on the alleviation of immediate hunger problems, tends to ignore these greater issues and so constrains itself from resolving the underlying larger-scale factors of exclusion driving food crises. As a result, a more complete resolution of food issues requires a more comprehensive effort that encompasses patterns of marginalization, something that Arbour sees as a primary concern for the international human rights system (United Nations, 2008).

While the UNHCHR's statements were ostensibly directed at the issue of food aid during the 2008 global hunger crisis, it is possible to take her comments as a reflection of the distribution component of global food governance in that they share a common theme of "a lack of access to adequate food" (United Nations, 2008). For the UNHCHR, hunger is a significant function of inequalities in food distribution and such inequalities, because they are driven by exclusionary practices against marginalized peoples, have human causes. This means that resolution of hunger can be mitigated by changes in human behavior, and thus led to the UNHCHR's call for human rights to change the human behavior responsible for inequality.

This chapter is a critique of the UNHCHR's call for human rights and uses the theories of Michel Foucault to assert that the international human rights system of the United Nations is insufficient to address the issues used by Louise Arbour to justify the inclusion of human rights in global food governance. Following Foucault, the analysis argues that the various trends in global food governance foster a power structure that subordinates individuals and groups in global food governance and that the status of individuals and groups can be improved by empowering them to advance their own interests against the states, institutions, corporations, and non-governmental organizations (NGOs) that dominate food governance. The analysis then seeks to evaluate the capacity of the international human rights system of the United Nations to fulfil Foucault's expectations.

This chapter begins by identifying the dominant trends in global food governance, with the major paradigms comprising approaches that focus on state-centric international institutions, privatized free-market approaches, or public–private "stakeholder" arrangements. The chapter then notes that these paradigms of governance involve actors consisting of states, international institutions, NGOs, or corporations. Absent within such governance structures are individuals and groups. As a result, the chapter observes that the international human rights system, because of its concern for the welfare of individuals and groups, appears to fill a neglected area in global food governance and thus justifies the UNHCHR's call for human rights in food governance.

This chapter proceeds to evaluate the potential for human rights to address the interests of individuals and groups within global food governance, applying the theories of Michel Foucault to determine to what extent the international human rights system empowers individuals and groups to assert their interests against the hegemony of states, international institutions, corporations, and NGOs that dominate global food governance. The discussion shows how Foucault is relevant in describing the nature of power relations in global food governance, and then uses Foucault to prescribe how such power relations can be changed to improve the subordinate status of individuals and groups. The analysis finishes by taking such a prescription to highlight the ways in which international human rights can satisfy or dissatisfy Foucault's requirements.

The UNHCHR's call in relation to the general trends in food governance

The UNHCHR's call to integrate human rights with global food issues stands in stark contrast to the current era of global food governance. The difference between human rights and the structure of global food governance becomes clear when compared against each other. Global food governance following World War II falls into several major identifiable trends: state-centric transnational approaches to facilitate the flow of food products and food science (Barrett and Maxwell, 2005; Gupta, 2004; Lin, 2012; Phillips, 2006), privatized free-market approaches to foster international food business (Barrett and Maxwell, 2005; Gupta, 2004; Lang, 2009; Lang and Barling, 2012; Phillips, 2006), or public–private partnership arrangements that revolve around "stakeholders" comprising states, corporations, and NGOs (Busch, 2011; Kaan and Liese, 2011; Lang and Barling, 2012; Osterveer and Sonnenfeld, 2012; Phillips, 2006). Despite their differences, these trends have arisen in an era largely marked by an increased industrialization of agriculture, with food industries transitioning away from individual farmers and local markets toward multinational corporations servicing transnational markets whose consumption is fueled by a growth in transnational agricultural financial instruments, proprietary agricultural knowledge, and specialized agricultural science (Gupta, 2004). The benefits of such changes in countering global hunger is subject to debate, with critics like Joyeeta Gupta (2004) charging that the various forms of global food governance produce a regime in which hunger is a systemic problem, with poorer populations consistently suffering from inadequate food and excess malnutrition. Defenders like Robert Paarlberg (2002) counter that the issues of hunger are not systemic within the global food system but rather a result of distribution and production problems within individual nation-states, and that the international system's efforts to address hunger are stymied by internal issues inside countries.

It should be noted that the actors at the center of the debate tend to be those involved in the various global food governance trends: transnational state-based institutions, multilateral state-led arrangements, multinational corporations, or NGOs. Absent from the array of actors are the entities directly receiving food: the individuals and groups whose consumption and need for food is the underlying driver of efforts to improve food production and distribution. The absence of individuals and groups from global food governance is not insignificant, since it places individual and groups in a subordinate status within global food governance and locates them at the margins of decisions over food production and distribution. This poses issues of sovereignty and justice, since it means that the concerns of individuals and groups over the violation of land rights, access to food, continuation of local culture, and individual livelihoods are suppressed beneath the interests of states, international institutions, corporations, and NGOs (Allen, 2008; Barrett and Maxwell, 2005; Huish, 2008; McMichael, 2003; Rosset, 2008). As a result, the interests of those in need of food are disconnected from the activities of the actors involved in controlling food.

In a sense, such conditions underlie the UNHCHR's desire to associate human rights with global food governance. Human rights ostensibly apply to individuals and groups of human beings (Freeman, 2002: 73; Lillich et al., 2006: 2). As a result, human rights directly address the actors at the margins of global food governance and thereby address an area of global food issues not covered by the predominant models of governance. In recognizing that food distribution is a reflection of exclusionary practices that create a hierarchy of those who receive food versus those who do not, the UNHCHR brings the topic of food governance under the purview of human rights and its concerns for the welfare of marginalized human beings.

It may appear possible to oppose the exercise of human rights in global food governance by arguing that the concerns of individuals and groups are already represented in food decisions via proxy, in that all human beings are represented by their respective national governments, the international institutions those governments join, corporations whose products are sold to consumers, and the myriad NGOs, both domestic and international, who assume consumer interests. This is the model in the current global food regime, with the welfare of vulnerable populations subject to the actions of states, international institutions, corporations, and NGOs to grant and administer entitlements of food aid, aid networks, and aid distribution points (Sen, 1999; Watts, 2000; Watts and Bohle, 1993). Such actions are justifiable to a degree, since it is possible that under conditions of hunger "societies become breeding grounds for instability, civil unrest, terrorism and demagogues" (Sheeran, 2008) that can disrupt regional and international order (Essex, 2011).

Such an argument, however, suffers in several respects. For example, the role of NGOs as representatives for individuals and groups is often challenged by the power of states, international institutions, and corporations, who tend to favor each other in setting food policies and thus exclude non-state and non-corporate actors from food governance (Clapp and Murphy, 2013; Kaan and Liese, 2011). For their part, national governments and international institutions generate their own issues in asserting the needs of the hungry. The United States, for example, denied food aid to Ethiopia in the mid-1980s as a geopolitical action to punish Ethiopia's alliance with the Soviet Union and discourage its potential purchase of Soviet military equipment (Barrett and Maxwell, 2005; Shepherd, 1985). International institutions, because of their dependence on the contributions of member states, are susceptible to domination by the behavior of dominant members, with an example being the World Food Programme and the critics who charge that its behavior is subject to the vicissitudes of the internal politics of its largest donor, the United States (Barrett and Maxwell, 2005; Clapp, 2012). Even in cases where food is provided on humanitarian grounds, rather than on the basis of geopolitics, states and international institutions encounter challenges in recipient areas in terms of gaining cooperation from affected governments and securing the absence of endemic violence opposing food distribution efforts (Blouin and Pallage, 2008; Paarlberg, 2002: 23). Notable examples of cases where food distribution was thwarted include Sudan in 1988, where food delivery was blocked or seized by opposing forces within a chaotic conflict zone; Somalia in 1994, where food was regularly seized by militias struggling for political control; North Korea in 1995, where the government denied international access to assist famine-stricken areas; or Afghanistan in 2001, where food shipments were stymied by ongoing violence (Deng and Minear, 1992; Natsios, 1996). More recently, there were accusations that Robert Mugabe used food as a coercive tool in the 2013 Zimbabwe election (Laing, 2013) and charges that the opposing forces in the Syrian conflict denied food distribution to selected populations as a combat tactic (Sengupta, 2014). In cases like these, the states, international institutions, corporations, and NGOs that comprise the dominant actors in the global food regime are either incapable or unwilling to advance the needs of starving people and so are not always capable proxies for the interests of individuals and groups. Such deficiencies point to a need for options that promote the welfare of individuals and groups. Given the concern of the international human rights system to do exactly this, it becomes easier to recognize the value of human rights in global food governance and hence identify the basis for the UNHCHR's call.

The connection of human rights to global food governance, however, requires some evaluation as the relevancy of the former with the latter. Justification of human rights in global food governance requires a demonstration of relevancy in terms of human rights sharing common issues with global food governance and human rights resolving those issues in ways global food governance does not. The above discussion demonstrates a compatibility between the two in terms of human rights addressing an area neglected by trends in global food governance, but it does not show whether human rights is capable of sufficiently resolving the area of neglect. This chapter seeks to provide such an evaluation, using a postmodern analysis with the theories of Michel Foucault.

From a theoretical perspective, the omission of individuals and groups from the debates over global food governance is understandable, since much of the academic field of international relations uses theories that see the world otherwise. The focus on nation-states and international institutions, for example, is consistent with the precepts of realist/neo-realist and liberal/neo-liberal philosophies, which as paradigms in international studies espouse the primacy of nation-states (in the case of realism/neo-realism) or international institutions and commercial entities (in the case of liberalism/neo-liberalism) in global affairs and belittle the significance of individuals or groups as relevant subjects of study (Nau, 2008; Snyder, 2004). For its part, constructivism looks to alternative actors beyond nation-states and international institutions and so can address the questions of NGOs, corporations, and other non-state entities (Nau 2008; Snyder 2004). But constructivism invariably focuses on actors associated with transnational societal transformations and so tends to bypass the behavior of individuals and local groups in transnational issues (Nau, 2008; Roskin and Berry, 2009). One exception in constructivism, however, is the area of postmodernism, whose concern for the inequalities in power relations make it more sensitive to the welfare of "the marginal, the peripheral, the excluded" and hence more receptive to making the status of individuals and groups in governance something worthy of study (Rosenau 1992: 8). Postmodernists, in particular, would recognize that the current structure of global food governance tends to favor control by nation-states, international institutions, NGOs, and corporations, and so creates a hierarchy of power that places them in a position of dominant hegemony that excludes individuals and groups from governance. This marginalizes individuals and groups to a subordinate status with an inferior ability to control the outcomes of a global food regime. With little power, individuals and groups are left with little capacity to advance their concerns and hence little possibility of addressing their needs.

Of particular relevance among postmodern perspectives are the theories of Michel Foucault, whose work focuses specifically on the dynamics of power and the inequalities in power relations between marginal and dominant actors. Foucault provides insights that identify not only why the status of individual human beings in the power inequalities in global food governance is problematic, but also highlight how such inequalities can be rectified so as to improve their status – and hence better advance their interests. Hence, Foucault has the potential to generate (1) a descriptive framework that is consistent with human rights concerns for the marginal status of individuals and groups within global food governance and (2) prescriptive guidance to address such problems.

It should be noted that the question of power relations is also a concern of other theorists besides Foucault. In particular, issues of structure arising from power inequalities is a central concern for neo-Marxist perspectives, who follow Karl Marx's focus on the struggles between classes to control the forces of production. In a sense, the global food regime conveniently fits with such conceptions, with the states, corporations, and NGOs involved in global food governance constituting dominant classes holding control over the forces of production in terms of the cultivation and distribution of food, and individual human beings constituting subordinate classes with little control over food outside their own hunger for it.

The nature of neo-Marxist theories, however, poses issues relative to Foucault and the integration of human rights in global food governance. First, while Marx provides useful descriptions of the nature of power relations in the global food regime, his theories generate prescriptions of a different character, with the conceptualization of production driving inequalities leading to a "revolutionary moment" wherein the dominant are overthrown by the lower classes. This is problematic for those who seek to avoid radical overthrow of the existing international system – such as the UNHCHR, who presumably avers revolution of the international system in favor of working through it, due in no small measure to its place within the institution of the United Nations that is constructed around nation-states and its call for human rights which are themselves dependent upon enforcement by nation-states. Foucault, in contrast to Marx, does not necessarily foresee revolution but instead conceives of a more dialectical scenario wherein power relations are in a state of constant flux, with the interactions between technologies of power and technologies of the self ensuring that someone is in a position of domination and someone is in a position of subordination. Second, Marx's theories, in looking to the nature of power demarcating the hierarchy of different classes, essentially searches for a structuralist account involving large-scale social forces, and so overlooks the question of human beings at the scale of individuals or groups behaving as actors within global food governance. Foucault, in contrast, centers his theories around the place of the marginalized in discourse, and so more directly conforms to the individual and group focus of human rights.

Placing human rights and global food governance under Foucault

Application of Foucault's theories to the power inequalities in global food governance commences with recognition of food governance as a "discourse." Foucault conceived of "discourse" as "practices that systematically form the objects of which they speak" (1972 [2010]: 49). He interpreted this expansively, taking the concept of discourse to include speech, writing, actions, or symbols that generate frameworks that structure the development and movement of information, ideas, and meanings between people (Hunt and Wickham, 1994). For Foucault, delineation of a discourse is important because its structure is a mechanism of inclusion and exclusion toward actors and their viewpoints and thereby is determinative in the distribution of power (Hunt and Wickham, 1994: 8–9). In addition, by controlling who and what is involved in the exchange of information, ideas, and meanings, a discourse directs the potential outcomes it may take. In this way, "power and knowledge directly imply one another" (Foucault, 1977: 27–28; Hunt and Wickham, 1994: 12), with both constituting and being constituted by the social networks hosting the interactions of discourse. This means that for Foucault, power is not something held by actors but rather is something that moves fluidly in the relations between them (Foucault, 1978 [1990]: 93–102).

Foucault's notion of discourse is broad enough to encompass the range of actors present within the various post-World War II trends in global food governance: under Foucault, states, international institutions, business entities, NGOs, and the individuals and groups subordinate to them can all be interpreted as actors engaged in verbal, written, or physical interactions over ideas about food production, food distribution, and food consumption. Thus, the states and state-based international institutions associated with state-centric approaches, the private entities involved in free-market approaches, and the "stakeholders" comprising public–private partnerships are all engaged in a discourse to assert their own ideas regarding food. Similarly, the relief forces, governments, opposing sides in conflict zones, militias, and other parties struggling over food can be seen as actors engaged in a discourse on food governance. In addition, the populations who receive or are denied food are also actors in a global discourse of food.

The differences between these actors are their relative differences in capacity to exert their worldviews about how food is to be treated. Within Foucault's framework, this means that actors differ in their ability to control the discourse, whether in terms of the communication of information and meanings about food or the outcomes that arise in the treatment of food. Foucault attributed the capacity to control discourse to what he labelled as "technologies of power," which he defined as the various means employed by dominant actors to include or exclude knowledge and ideas to influence the identity of other actors in a discourse (Foucault, 1988). For Foucault, the inclusion or exclusion of knowledge and ideas meant the inclusion or exclusion of not just actors but also the outcomes advocated by those actors – including outcomes that allowed those in positions of hegemonic power to manipulate the subordinate status of those existing at the margins of discourse. This means that the ability to include or exclude knowledge and ideas in the discourse over food constitutes power, and hence that the disparities among actors in their ability to include or exclude knowledge and ideas demarcates the inequalities of power between them. Such processes are manifested in the various models of post-World War II global food governance, wherein control over decision-making, and hence the inclusion and exclusion of knowledge and ideas used in decision-making, is vested in states, international institutions, corporations, or NGOs. By excluding individuals and groups, these post-World War II trends in global food governance exclude their knowledge and ideas from the governance discourse, and thus reduce their power to influence decisions over food. In this way, the models of global food governance function as technologies of power that empower states, international institutions, corporations, and NGOs to be hegemons and disempower individuals and groups. Such power inequalities between actors in the global food discourse form a structure that sustains the dominant and marginalizes the subordinate. Phrased in Foucauldian terms, the structure of global food governance is one of power inequalities that include states, corporations, and NGOs exercising power in decisions over food and exclude individual human beings, with the technologies of power sustaining the dominance of the former and the subordination of the latter.

A Foucauldian description of the power relations in global food governance is useful not just because it explains the marginal status of individual human beings beneath nation-states, institutions, corporations, and NGOs, but also because it leads to a prescriptive insight regarding how such power inequalities can be mitigated. In opposition to the "technologies of power" that differentiate the dominant from the subordinate, Foucault introduced the term "technologies of the self," which he used to refer to the mechanisms that allow subordinate actors to control their own identities and so empower them to influence their own status relative to those holding hegemonic control (Foucault, 1988). For Foucault, such mechanisms operate by allowing marginalized actors greater ability to control the inclusion or exclusion of their knowledge and ideas in a discourse. In effect, technologies of the self provide the marginalized with greater agency in the structure of power inequalities in a discourse. Foucault's thoughts suggest that it is possible to improve the marginal status of individual human beings in global food governance by working to enable technologies of the self that allow them greater agency to engage the hegemony of nation-states, international institutions, and NGOs in a discourse of food. The substance of such technologies of the self would be those mechanisms that allow individual human beings to include or exclude the knowledge and ideas affecting their interests within the global food discourse.

In a way, the UNHCHR's call for greater emphasis on human rights in global food governance is consistent with Foucault's prescription for technologies of the self. Human rights apply equally to all human beings and are granted to individuals and groups (Freeman, 2002: 73; Lillich et al., 2006: 2), which means that human rights encompass the marginal actors excluded from the discourse of global food governance: individuals and groups. In addition, human rights are not legal rights dependent upon the consent of states or other political authorities but instead are moral rights that are inherent to human beings (Freeman, 2002; Langlois, 2009; Lillich et al., 2006: 2), and so provide individuals and groups with autonomy against the elements holding hegemonic status in the power structure of global food governance. Moreover, human rights are entitlements that allow holders of rights to seek claims against others who obstruct their enjoyment of those rights (Freeman, 2002: 61), and so human rights empower individuals and groups with a measure of agency to work against the power structure of the global food regime. Phrased in Foucauldian terms, by empowering individuals and groups to pursue claims against others, human rights allow those who have been excluded from a discourse to assert knowledge and ideas related to their interests into such a discourse, and thus enable them to mitigate their marginal status by facilitating their capacities to engage the discourses of hegemonic power. In this way, human rights could be construed as technologies of the self that allow the individuals to work against the power inequalities between themselves and the states, international institutions, corporations, and NGOs that dominate global food governance. Thus, the OHCHR, in calling for a greater emphasis on human rights in global food governance, may appear to be promoting a technology of the self in the discourse of food.

Foucault's evaluation of human rights in global food governance

A correlation between human rights and Foucault, however, should be viewed with caution, since the potential of human rights to be a technology of the self is delimited by how much they fulfill Foucault's vision of empowering those at the margins to work against power inequalities. To be consistent with a Foucauldian vision, technologies of the self must exist that allow the marginalized to engage with those holding hegemonic positions over unequal power relations. This means that if human rights are to be technologies of the self they must allow individuals and groups to work against the dominant actors in the discourse of global food governance. In addition, if they are to be technologies of the self, human rights must exist in a way that they can be claimed by rights-holders, in the sense that they are not just *de jure* expressions of moral claims via legal rights but also *de facto* instruments that offer rights-holders access and utility in advancing their status against the forces of domination. This section asserts that it is not clear that the international human rights system meets these conditions for technologies of the self.

With respect to the first requirement, Foucault's criteria for technologies of the self asks that human rights allow those in subordinate positions of power to engage those holding hegemonic positions over unequal power relations. This means that human rights must enable individuals and groups to work against the dominant positions held by states, international institutions, corporations, and NGOs in the discourse of global food governance. Unfortunately, it is not clear that the international human rights system meets this requirement, since the treaties that comprise the system limit themselves to cases of human rights violations by states and thus omit international institutions, corporations, and NGOs from the jurisdiction of their treaty bodies. There are efforts to pursue greater accountability of non-state actors toward human rights in the form of a

United Nations agenda on business and human rights centered around corporate social responsibility (UNHCHR 2014) and calls to promote the extraterritorial jurisdiction of states as a way of ensuring non-state actors follow the human rights obligations of states (de Schutter, 2006; King, 2009). Such efforts, however, are in a somewhat nascent stage, with the United Nations agenda focusing on the promotion of voluntary principles and standards and the calls for extraterritorial human rights obligations encountering resistance from powerful states (King, 2009; UNHCHR, 2014), leaving individuals and groups in an uncertain position against non-state actors. As a result, with respect to both state and non-state actors, there is a glaring shortfall in individuals and groups seeking to use their human rights as a means of engagement with the hegemonic powers in global food governance. While the international human rights system may provide a measure of options for individuals or groups against the dominant position of states, international institutions, corporations, and NGOs, such options do not act to alter the power inequalities with respect to these hegemonic actors in the global food discourse. As a result, human rights do not adequately empower the marginalized to engage those holding dominant positions in global food governance, and do not meet Foucault's requirement for a technology of the self.

With respect to the second requirement, Foucault's notion of technologies of the self indicates that human rights must offer access and utility to rights-holders in terms of providing ways for rights-holders to successfully pursue remedies for human rights violations. To a degree, access and utility exists in the form of *de jure* mechanisms for individual or group complaints for violations of human rights that allow petitioners to pursue claims for violations of human rights at various levels: domestic courts, regional courts, and the international system of human rights (OHCHR 2014a; Smith 2007: 141). In the international system of human rights, individuals and groups can pursue claims for violations of their human rights via bodies created by either the United Nations Charter ("UN Charter") or the United Nations human rights treaties (Butler, 2004; Dantas, 2012; OHCHR, 2014a). Under the UN Charter, communications may be filed through the Human Rights Council (UNHRC, which replaced the previous Commission on Human Rights) (UNHRC, 2014a) under its Complaint Procedure (UNHRC, 2014b) or its Special Procedures (UNHRC, 2014c) (which replace the Section 1503 and 1235 procedures of the previous Commission on Human Rights). Under the United Nations human rights treaties, victims of human rights violations can exercise individual complaint mechanisms that involve the committees established under their respective treaties ("UN treaty bodies" or "treaty bodies"): the International Convention on Civil and Political Rights (ICCPR) under its First Optional Protocol creates the Committee on Human Rights (CHR); the Convention on the Elimination of Racial Discrimination's Article 14 offers the Committee on the Elimination of Racial Discrimination (CERD); the Convention Against Torture's Article 22 forms the Committee Against Torture (CAT); the Optional Protocol of the Convention on the Elimination of Discrimination Against Women establishes the Committee on the Elimination of Discrimination Against Women (CEDAW); the Optional Protocol of the Convention on the Rights of Persons with Disabilities promulgates the Committee on the Rights of Persons with Disabilities (CRPD); the Optional Protocol of the International Covenant on Social, Economic, and Cultural Rights creates the Committee on Economic, Social, and Cultural Rights (CESCR); and the Convention on Enforced Disappearances' Article 31 establishes the Committee on Enforced Disappearances (CED) (OHCHR, 2014c).

The UNHRC and the various UN treaty bodies provide different ways for individuals and groups to take action against human rights violations by states. For the UNHRC, both the Complaint Procedure and the Special Procedures allow individuals and groups to submit information about human rights violations to the OHCHR. Under the Complaint Procedure, communications received by the OHCHR Human Rights Council Branch are screened by a Working Group on Communications (WGC), who forwards the ones that show "consistent patterns" and "reliably attested" human rights violations to a Working Group on Situations (WGS), who then generates a confidential report that documents the pattern of human rights violations and issues recommendations for the UNHRC (2014b). Under the Special Procedures, communications received by the OHCHR are directed to country-specific or theme-specific investigations of human rights abuses, each of which is responsible for screening and evaluating the claims of human rights violations and publishing the results of the investigations in public reports that are submitted at each regular session of the UNHRC (2014c). For both the Complaint Procedure and Special Procedures, individuals and groups are not treated as parties seeking remedies against a state for specific human rights violations, but instead are treated as sources of evidence regarding a state's "pattern" of human rights violations (UNHRC, 2014b). In contrast to the UNHRC, the UN treaty bodies offer greater flexibility to address specific claims of individuals or groups, in that treaty bodies do not necessarily have to look for "systematic" violations but can act upon particular incidents of "serious" or "grave" violations of human rights (Butler, 2004: 19, 43–44; OHCHR, 2014c). For the UN treaty bodies, the complaint process begins with a petition to the OHCHR Petitions and Inquiries Section, who conducts an initial screening of the petition and forwards it to the appropriate treaty body for examination on admissibility and merit (Dantas, 2012; OHCHR, 2014c). While proceedings of a treaty body in regard to a complaint are kept confidential, information involved in meetings to monitor state behavior following the conclusion of a treaty body investigation are public (OHCHR, 2014b, 2014c).

Based on the procedures provided by the UNHRC and the treaty bodies of the various UN human rights treaties, there appear to be complaint mechanisms available for individuals and groups against the actions of states under the international human rights system. By serving to advance the concerns of individuals and groups against states, the international human rights system exhibits a potential to satisfy Foucault's criteria for technologies of the self in that the UNHRC and the UN treaty bodies constitute what Foucault might see as the empowerment of individuals and groups who are the marginalized actors against states who are the hegemons in global food governance. Moreover, in accepting communications from individuals and groups, the treaty bodies seem to make themselves accessible to those holding subordinate positions in the discourse of global food governance. In essence, the treaties that form the basis of the international human rights system present a *de jure* expression of mechanisms that appear to satisfy Foucault's requirements of technologies of the self.

Such an appearance, however, is illusory, since the complaints system fostered by the UNHRC and UN treaty bodies suffers from a number of issues which frustrate the *de facto* ability of individuals to seek remedies, and so impede the aspirations of those seeking technologies of the self that work against the hegemons of the discourse over global food governance. First, the outcomes of UNHRC and UN treaty body proceedings have a debatable status: the UNHRC is limited to performing a review, delivering requests to change, or issuing recommendations on proper behavior to an offending state (UNHRC, 2014d); similarly, the UN treaty bodies, while they claim that their decisions are legally binding (CHR, 2008; Dantas, 2012: 203; *Sooklal* v. *Trinidad and Tobago* (2000)), are limited to issuing recommendations and invitations to offending states to adjust their behavior (Butler, 2004: 44–46). As a result, compliance is also limited, with the UNHRC or treaty bodies having little ability to compel violating states to respond to their findings (the CHR, for example, reports that only about 30 percent of state replies indicated satisfactory compliance to its recommendations) (Butler, 2004: 47). In addition, the jurisdiction of the UNHRC and treaty bodies are not universal but instead are limited to state parties: while the UNHRC, as a United Nations Charter body, is empowered to review all members of the United Nations (OHCHR, 2014d), the treaty bodies are subjected to greater restrictions – as of 2014 the ICCPR's First Optional Protocol creating the CHR has only 115 parties (UN Treaty Collection, 2014a), the CERD has 177 parties (UN Treaty Collection, 2014b); the CAT has 115 parties (UN Treaty Collection, 2014 c); the Optional Protocol for CEDAW has 104 parties (UN Treaty Collection, 2014d); the Optional Protocol for the CRPD has 80 parties (UN Treaty Collection 2014e); the Optional Protocol for CESCR has 13 parties (UN Treaty Collection, 2014f); and the CED has 42 parties (UN Treaty Collection, 2014g). Further, even before arriving at the questions of enforcement, compliance, and jurisdiction, there is the presence of admissibility rules in the UNHRC and the UN treaty bodies that threaten to obstruct the filing of petitions by denying individual claimants any standing to seek relief: (1) a "local remedies" rule that requires claimants to exhaust all remedies within their country even if they believe them ineffective before pursuing relief through the UNHRC or a treaty body; (2) a "non-duplication" rule that, apart from the CERD, prohibits a treaty body from responding to an individual claim if it is already being heard by another UNHRC Complaint Procedure, UNHRC Special Procedure, or UN treaty body (Dantas, 2012; de Schutter, 2010: 805–831; Udombana, 2003; UNHRC, 2014b); and (3) a *ratione temporis* rule that limits complaints to a treaty body to violations that occurred after a treaty entered into force In addition, the First Optional Protocol to the ICCPR holds a "causality" requirement that asks petitioners to demonstrate a causal link between an alleged violation of human rights and an accused offending state (Dantas, 2012).

Such a body of issues is problematic, since it suggests that human rights do not exist in a way that offers access or utility to rights-holders seeking to advance their status against the forces of domination. The inability of the UNHRC or UN treaty bodies to issue legally binding remedies or compel compliance means that individual petitioners are not likely to challenge the powers of states – they may be able to secure international decisions from the UNHRC or UN treaty bodies in their favor, but those decisions will not necessarily translate into changes in state behavior and hence entail no substantive change in the power relations between the individual petitioner and the accused state. Moreover, the limited number of state parties to the various international human rights treaties means a restriction in the jurisdiction of treaty bodies, with individual petitions limited to those people from countries which are state parties and claims through the treaty bodies limited to those countries which are state parties. Further, the presence of admissibility rules pose a major obstruction for individuals seeking relief: the "local remedies" rule places the burden of proof on petitioners, imposing real financial and physical burdens on those in indigent or exigent circumstances (e.g., cases of severe poverty, conflict, anarchy, non-functional or dysfunctional courts, corrupt or hostile governments, wherein petitioners place themselves at risk to seek domestic remedies); the "non-duplication" rule can potentially extend the time needed to pursue a claim in the event that it is denied by one human rights body and subsequently filed with another, and thereby impedes the opportunity for relief for claimants unable to dedicate the time necessary to accommodate a potential succession of petitions; the *ratione temporis* rule effectively excludes an entire body of marginalized actors by denying petitions for violations that occurred before a treaty entered into force; and the "causality" requirement can render petitions inadmissible for lack of evidence, creating a burden for petitioners who lack the capacity to accumulate or preserve evidence due to a lack of capacity (e.g., indigence) or a condition of vulnerability (e.g., living under a hostile state unwilling to admit to its human rights violations). Phrased in Foucauldian terms, such a body of issues results in a system that maintains the primacy of states and restricts the number of petitioners able to use it. This effectively acts as a means of exclusion against individuals and groups from the protection of human rights treaties, and thereby sustains their subordination beneath the power of states. This is ironic, because it means that an international human rights system that claims to assist the empowerment and inclusion of marginalized peoples in discourses of power inequalities engages in its own practices of subordination and exclusion against the marginal actors it is supposedly meant to serve. The findings of this evaluation of the international human rights system as a Foucauldian technology of the self is presented in Table 6.1.

In sum, from a Foucauldian perspective human rights are insufficient to accomplish what they are meant to achieve: the mitigation of power inequalities and improvement in the status of individuals and groups within global food governance. If international human rights are to be a technology of the self – that is, if the UNHCHR's call for human rights in global food governance is to satisfy Foucault's concerns for the status of the marginalized in a discourse, there must be changes in the international human rights system that make it more capable of empowering individuals and groups to work against the hegemonic actors in the global food regime. As indicated by the findings of the above evaluation, one area for change would be in an expansion of the types of actors subject to human rights obligations, such that the UNHRC and international human rights treaties encompass not just violations committed by states but also those committed by international institutions, corporations, and NGOs. This would allow fuller engagement by individuals and groups against the full range of dominant actors in current global food governance. Another area for change would be to increase the access and utility provided by individual complaint mechanisms to potential petitioners to the UNHRC and UN treaty bodies: issues of enforcement and compliance can be addressed by allowing treaty bodies to do more than issue recommendations or invitations to offenders to change their behavior but instead issue legally binding decisions; and issues of compliance can be mitigated by encouraging states to become parties to the various international human rights treaties. Similarly, issues of

Table 6.1 Evaluation of the international human rights system under Foucault's technology of the self

Requirements constituting Foucauldian technologies of the self	*Status of international human rights system with respect to each requirement*
Allow those in subordinate positions of power to engage those holding hegemonic positions	International human rights system provides complaint mechanisms for rights-holders under UN Human Rights Council and various UN human rights treaty bodies, but there is an issue in that they only apply against states
Offer access and utility to those in subordinate positions in terms of providing ways for rights-holders to pursue remedies for human rights violations	Technologies of the self exist for rights-holders in the form of the complaint mechanisms of the UNHRC and UN treaty bodies, but there are issues of access and utility in terms of: • Enforcement • Compliance • Jurisdiction • Admissibility

admissibility can be eased by eliminating the "local remedies" rule so petitioners do not have to demonstrate that they have exhausted all potential remedies in their countries, eliminating the "non-duplication" rule so that a petitioner can file complaints with multiple treaty bodies at the same time, and eliminating the *ratione temporis* rule to allow complaints for violations that occurred before a treaty came into force. Moreover, the demands of the "causality" requirement can be eased by reducing or eliminating the burden of proof upon petitioners to demonstrate a causal link between an alleged violation of human rights and an accused offending state (Dantas, 2012).

Unfortunately, the prospects for such types of changes are dubious, since individual complaint mechanisms of the UNHRC and UN treaty bodies are associated with the United Nations and its human rights treaties, all of which are dependent upon the approval of state parties for change, meaning that the empowerment of those at the margins through changes in the UNHRC or UN treaty bodies is at the mercy of actors currently within the dominant hegemony in global food governance. Such hegemony is not incentivized to cede its power, since it is contrary to the self-interest of states to facilitate an expansion, whether in terms of their enforceability, compliance rate, jurisdiction, or admissibility, in the individual complaint mechanisms of the international human rights system if it entails a loss in state sovereignty. Similar issues also exist with respect to the non-state actors that hold hegemonic positions alongside states in global food governance. For example, United Nations efforts to foster corporate social responsibility involve voluntary principles and standards that are dependent upon corporations integrating international human rights within their business practices (UNHCHR, 2014), but doing so is contrary to the self-interest of corporations if it means a loss in corporate profits. Another iteration of this theme follows the calls for states to exercise extraterritorial jurisdiction as a way of promoting human rights: extraterritorial jurisdiction allows a state to exert control over its subjects outside its own borders, and thereby allows the imposition of that state's obligations to human rights upon non-state actors anywhere in the world (de Schutter 2006; King, 2009), but such a scenario is resisted by powerful states who see it as contrary to their self-interest to encourage a world where all states claim the ability to interfere with each other's sovereignty. As a result, the prospects for changes to the international human rights system that might empower individuals and groups in global food governance are frustrated by the system's reliance upon action by dominant actors who are predisposed against such action.

Hints at a more promising area for those at the margins of global food governance may be found by noting that the UNHCHR's call for human rights is essentially a legal approach tying moral claims to legal mechanisms that are meant to address inequalities in power relations. Power, however, is also the subject of politics, particularly in regard to issues of "who gets what, when, how" (Lasswell, [1936] 1990) endemic to discussions of food production and distribution. As a result, an alternative approach – or at least a supplemental one

– to the UNHCHR's turn to law may be a look to politics directed at resolving the exclusionary nature of global food governance through a greater inclusion of individuals and groups in decision-making. An example of this is the effort of the International Institute for Environment and Development (IIED) to "democratise" governance of food systems by supporting citizen participation in the policy-making (IIED, 2014). A similar approach is advocated by the United Nations Special Rapporteur on the Right to Food Olivier de Schutter in his final report to the HRC, dated January 24, 2014, wherein he criticizes the current global food system for its environmentally unsustainable practices and its failures to address widespread hunger (de Schutter, 2014a). De Schutter, in his presentation of the report to the HRC, states that "at the local, national, and international levels, the policy environment must urgently accommodate alternative, democratically-mandated visions" and that "food democracy must start from the bottom-up, at the level of villages, regions, cities, and municipalities" (de Schutter, 2014b).

The idea of "democratizing" global governance is one associated with a transnational movement to tie local politics to global policy, largely by promoting the influence of individuals and groups upon global governance processes (Dahlberg, 2001; Hoogesteger, 2012; Patomaki, 2003). Adopting a democracy-oriented political approach to global food governance does have the potential to avoid the issues associated with a human-rights-centric legal one in that (1) a democratic process, if it is inclusive, allows for greater bargaining and consensus-building relative to the adversarial nature of a legal-style hearing and so suggests a greater likelihood of a greater number of actors complying with its decisions; (2) a democratic political process can be structured that allows individuals and groups to interact with states, international institutions, corporations, and NGOs in policy-making decisions, and thus allows individuals and groups to engage with the full range of hegemonic actors involved in global food governance; and (3) a democratic political process is not bound by legal rules of admissibility and hence allows more consideration of a greater array of information between actors. As a result, politics, especially democratic politics, exhibits a potential to empower the marginalized actors in global food governance in ways that human rights does not. This provides promise that justifies further exploration of political approaches that satisfy Foucault's requirements for a technology of the self that is accessible and effective for marginalized individuals and groups to work against the dominant hegemony of states, international institutions, corporations, and NGOs in the global food discourse.

Conclusion

This chapter critiqued the UNHCHR's call for human rights using the theories of Michel Foucault to assert that human rights are insufficient to address the issues used to justify their inclusion in global food governance. The chapter began by noting how the UNHCHR's call to integrate human rights with food issues seeks to aid the welfare of individuals and groups that are marginalized from a global food system dominated by governance models involving states, international institutions, corporations, and NGOs. This chapter then evaluated the potential for human rights to assist the status of individuals and groups within global food governance, applying the theories of Michel Foucault to determine to what extent the international human rights system empowers individuals and groups to assert their interests against the hegemonic actors in global food governance. The chapter showed how Foucault is relevant in describing the nature of power relations in global food governance, and used Foucault to prescribe how such power relations need to be changed to improve the subordinate status of individuals and groups. The analysis takes such a prescription to highlight the ways in which international human rights can satisfy or dissatisfy Foucault's requirements.

The UNHCHR shares a common concern with Foucault for the status of subordinate actors marginalized by unequal power relations with dominant hegemons. The UNHCHR, through an international human rights system meant to protect individuals and groups against the actions of states, asserts rights protecting the former against the latter. Foucault, in describing power relations as an interaction of technologies of the self held by the subordinate against the technologies of power held by the dominant, indicates that individuals and groups can work against hegemonic power to the extent that there are accessible and effective technologies of the self. This chapter, however, found that under Foucault human rights fall short of a goal to protect the marginalized actors in the global food discourse, with the international human rights system exhibiting issues in accessibility and effectiveness that render its use problematic – in short, under Foucault, the international human rights system is questionable as a technology of the self empowering individuals and groups to assert their interests against the states, international institutions, corporations, and NGOs that dominate global food governance. As a result, it fails to address the UNHCHR's underlying concern regarding the subordinate status of individuals and groups in the global food system. The chapter consequently found that if the UNHCHR is to better address its concerns, then there must be changes allowing individuals and groups to more easily pursue more claims within the international human rights system against a greater range of actors involved in global food governance, or the international human rights system must be supplemented by work through political mechanisms involving democratized global governance that allows individuals and groups to participate in decision-making over food.

References

Allen, Patricia (2008) "Mining for Justice in the Food System: Perceptions, Practices, and Possibilities." *Agriculture and Human Values* 25(2): 157–161.

Barrett, Christopher and Daniel Maxwell (2005) *Food Aid After Fifty Years: Recasting Its Role*. New York: Routledge.

Blouin, Max and Stephanie Pallage (2008) "Humanitarian Relief and Civil Conflict." *Journal of Conflict Resolution* 52(4): 548–565.

Busch, Lawrence (2011) "The Private Governance of Food: Equitable Exchange or Bizarre Bazaar?" *Agriculture and Human Values* 28: 345–352.

Butler, Israel (2004) "A Comparative Analysis of Individual Petition in Regional and Human Rights Protection Mechanisms." *University of Queensland Law Journal* 23(1): 22–53.

Clapp, Jennifer (2012) *Hunger in the Balance: The New Politics of International Food Aid.* Ithaca, NY: Cornell University Press.

Clapp, Jennifer and Sophia Murphy (2013) "The G20 and Food Security: A Mismatch in Global Governance?" *Global Policy* 4(2): 129–138.

Committee on Human Rights (CHR) (2008) *General Comment 33, CCPR/C/GC/33,* November 5, 2008. Available at: www2.ohchr.org/english/bodies/hrc/docs/CCPR.C.GC.33.pdf

Dahlberg, Kenneth (2001) "Democratizing Society and Food Systems: Or How Do We Transform Modern Structures of Power?" *Agriculture and Human Values* 18(2): 135.

Dantas, Carla (2012) "Right of Petition by Individuals within the Global Human Rights Protection System." *SUR-International Journal on Human Rights* 17: 187–208.

Deng, Francis and Larry Minear (1992) *The Challenges of Famine Relief.* Washington, DC: Brookings Institution.

de Schutter, Olivier (2006) "Extraterritorial Jurisdiction as a Tool for Improving the Human Rights Accountability of Transnational Corporations." Presentation to Seminar of the Office of the High Commissioner of Human Rights, Brussels, Belgium, November 3–4, 2006. Available at: www.reports-and-materials.org/Olivier-de-Schutter-report-for-SRSG-re-extraterritorial-jurisdiction-Dec-2006.pdf

de Schutter, Olivier (2010) *International Human Rights Law.* Cambridge: Cambridge University Press.

de Schutter, Olivier (2014a) *Final Report: The Transformative Potential of the Right to Food.* United Nations Human Rights Council, A/HRC/25/27. Available at: www.srfood.org/images/stories/pdf/officialreports/20140310_finalreport_en.pdf

de Schutter, Olivier (2014b) "Democracy and Diversity Can Mend Broken Food Systems – Final Diagnosis from UN Right to Food Expert." Available at: www.srfood.org/en/democracy-and-diversity-can-mend-broken-food-systems-final-diagnosis-from-un-right-to-food-expert

Essex, Jamey (2011) "Idle Hands Are the Devil's Tools: The Geopolitics and Geoeconomics of Hunger." *Annals of the Association of American Geographers* 102(1): 191–207.

Foucault, Michel ([1972] 2010) *The Archaeology of Knowledge and Discourse on Language.* New York: Pantheon.

Foucault, Michel (1977) *Discipline and Punish: The Birth of the Prison.* New York: Vintage.

Foucault, Michel ([1978] 1990) *The History of Sexuality.* New York: Vintage.

Foucault, Michel (1988) "Technologies of the Self," in Luther Martin, Huck Gutman, and Patrick Hutton (eds.), *Technologies of the Self.* New York: Routledge.

Freeman, Michael (2002) *Human Rights.* Malden: Polity.

Gupta, Joyetta (2004) "Global Sustainable Food Governance and Hunger: Traps and Tragedies." *British Food Journal* 106(5): 406–416.

Hoogesteger, Jaime (2012) "Democratizing Water Governance from the Grassroots: The Development of Interjuntas-Chimborazo in the Ecuadorian Andes." *Human Organization* 71(1): 76–86.

Huish, Robert (2008) "Human Security and Food Security in Geographical Study: Pragmatic Concepts or Elusive Theory?" *Geography Compass* 2(5): 1386–1403.

Hunt, Alan and Gary Wickham (1994) *Foucault and Law.* Boulder, CO: Pluto.

International Institute for Environment and Development (IIED) (2014) Available at: www.iied.org/strengthening-local-voices-governance-food-systems-environment

Kaan, Christopher and Andrea Liese (2011) "Public Private Partnerships in Global Food Governance: Business Engagement and Legitimacy in the Global Fight against Hunger and Malnutrition." *Agriculture and Human Values* 28: 385–399.

King, Hugh (2009) "The Extraterritorial Human Rights Obligations of States." *Human Rights Law Review* 9(4): 521–556.

Laing, Aislinn (2013) "Zanu PF: Using Food Aid to Build Support Ahead of Elections." *Telegraph*, May 5, 2013. Available at: www.telegraph.co.uk/news/worldnews/africaandindianocean/zimbabwe/10038751/Zanu-PF-using-food-aid-to-build-support-ahead-of-Zimbabwe-elections.html

Lang, Tim (2009) *Food Security and Sustainability: The Perfect Fit.* London: Sustainable Development Commission.

Lang, Tim and David Barling (2012) "Food Security and Food Sustainability: Reformulating the Debate." *Geographical Journal* 178(4): 313–326.

Langlois, Anthony (2009) "Normative and Theoretical Foundations of Human Rights," in Michael Goodhart (ed.), *Human Rights.* New York: Oxford University Press.

Lasswell, Harold ([1936] 1990]) *Politics: Who Gets What, When, How.* London: Peter Smith.

Lillich, Richard, Hannum Hurst, S. James Anaya, and Dinah Shelton (2006) *International Human Rights* (4th edn). New York: Aspen.

Lin, Ching-Fu (2012) "SPS-Plus and Bilateral Treaty Network: A 'Global' Solution to the Global Food-Safety Problem?" *Wisconsin International Law Journal* 29: 694–734.

Locke, John (2003) *Two Treatises on Government.* New Haven, CT: Yale University Press.

McMichael, Philip (2003) "Food Security and Social Reproduction: Issues and Contradictions," in I. Bakker and S. Gill (eds.), *Power, Production, and Social Reproduction.* New York: Palgrave Macmillan.

Natsios, Andrew (1996) "Humanitarian Relief Interventions in Somalia: The Economics of Chaos." *International Peacekeeping* 3(1): 68–91.

Nau, Henry (2008) *Perspectives on International Relations.* Washington, DC: CQ Press.

Office of the High Commissioner for Human Rights (OHCHR) (2014a) *Human Rights Bodies.* Available at: www.ohchr.org/en/hrbodies/Pages/HumanRightsBodies.aspx

Office of the High Commissioner for Human Rights (OHCHR) (2014b) *Human Rights Bodies – Complaints Procedures.* Available at: www.ohchr.org/EN/HRBodies/TBPetitions/Pages/HRTBPetitions.aspx

Office of the High Commissioner for Human Rights (OHCHR) (2014c) *Human Rights Treaty Bodies – Individual Communications.* Available at: www.ohchr.org/EN/HRBodies/TBPetitions/Pages/IndividualCommunications.aspx

Office of the High Commissioner for Human Rights (OHCHR) (2014d) *United Nations Human Rights Council.* Available at: www.ohchr.org/EN/HRBodies/HRC/Pages/HRCIndex.aspx

Osterveer, Peter and David Sonnenfeld (2012) *Food, Globalization and Sustainability.* New York: Routledge.

Paarlberg, Robert (2002) *Governance and Food Security in an Age of Globalization.* Washington, DC, USA: Food Policy Research Institute.

Patomaki, Heikki (2003) "Problems of Democratizing Global Governance: Time, Space, and the Emancipatory Process." *European Journal of International Relations* 9(3): 347.

Phillips, Lynne (2006) "Food and Globalization." *Annual Review of Anthropology* 35: 37–57.

Rosenau, Pauline (1992) *Post-Modernism and the Social Sciences.* Princeton, NJ: Princeton University Press.

Roskin, Michael and Nicholas Berry (2009) *IR: The New World of International Relations.* London: Longman.

Rosset, Peter (2008) "Food Sovereignty and the Contemporary Food Crisis." *Development* 51(4): 460–463.

Sen, Amartya (1999) *Development as Freedom.* New York: Knopf.

Sengupta, Somini (2014) "UN Orders Both Sides in Syria to Allow Humanitarian Aid." *New York Times,* February 22, 2014. Available at: www.nytimes.com/2014/02/23/world/middleeast/un-orders-both-sides-in-syria-to-allow-humanitarian-aid.html?_r=0

Sheeran, Josette (2008) *Hunger as a National Security and Global Stability Issue.* Keynote Address, Women's Foreign Policy Group, September 29, 2008. Washington, DC. Available at: http://home.wfp.org/stellent/groups/public/documents/newsroom/wfp189715.pdf

Shepherd, Jack (1985) "Ethiopia: The Use of Food as an Instrument of US Foreign Policy." *Issue: A Journal of Opinion* 14: 4–9.

Smith, Rhona (2007) *International Human Rights* (3rd edn). New York: Oxford University Press.

Snyder, Jack (2004) "One World, Rival Theories." *Foreign Policy* 145: 52–62.

Sooklal v. *Trinidad and Tobago* (2000) Comm. No. 928/2000, UN Doc CCPR/C/73/D/928/2000 para. 7.

Udombana, Nsongurua (2003) "So Far, So Fair: The Local Remedies Rule in the Jurisprudence of the African Commission on Human and Peoples' Rights." *American Journal of International Law* 97(1): 1–37.

United Nations (2008) "Solution to Food Crisis Must Address Inequalities – UN Human Rights Chief." Press release, May 22, 2008. Available at: www.un.org/apps/news/story.asp?NewsID=26762&Cr=food&Cr1=crisis#.Uzd1GRAyBNU

United Nations High Commissioner of Human Rights (UNHCHR) (2014) *Business and Human Rights.* Available at: www.ohchr.org/EN/Issues/Business/Pages/BusinessIndex.aspx

United Nations Human Rights Council (UNHRC) (2014a) *United Nations Human Rights Council.* Available at: www.ohchr.org/EN/HRBODIES/HRC/Pages/HRCIndex.aspx

United Nations Human Rights Council (UNHRC) (2014b) *Human Rights Council Complaint Procedure.* Available at: www.ohchr.org/EN/HRBodies/TBPetitions/Pages/HRTBPetitions.aspx

United Nations Human Rights Council (UNHRC) (2014c) *Special Procedures of the Human Rights Council.* Available at: www.ohchr.org/EN/HRBodies/SP/Pages/Welcomepage.aspx

United Nations Human Rights Council (UNHRC) (2014d) *Complaint Procedure of the Human Rights Council Frequently Asked Questions.* Available at: www.ohchr.org/Documents/HRBodies/ComplaintProcedure/FAQs_HRC.doc

United Nations Treaty Collection (UN Treaty Collection) (2014a) https://treaties.un.org/Pages/ViewDetails.aspx?src=TREATY&mtdsg_no=IV-5&chapter=4&lang=en

United Nations Treaty Collection (UN Treaty Collection) (2014b) https://treaties.un.org/Pages/ViewDetails.aspx?src=TREATY&mtdsg_no=IV-2&chapter=4&lang=en

United Nations Treaty Collection (UN Treaty Collection) (2014c) https://treaties.un.org/pages/ViewDetails.aspx?src=TREATY&mtdsg_no=IV-9&chapter=4&lang=en

United Nations Treaty Collection (UN Treaty Collection) (2014d) https://treaties.un.org/Pages/ViewDetails.aspx?src=TREATY&mtdsg_no=IV-8-b&chapter=4&lang=en

United Nations Treaty Collection (UN Treaty Collection) (2014e) https://treaties.un.org/Pages/ViewDetails.aspx?src=TREATY&mtdsg_no=IV-15-a&chapter=4&lang=en

United Nations Treaty Collection (UN Treaty Collection) (2014f) https://treaties.un.org/Pages/ViewDetails.aspx?src=TREATY&mtdsg_no=IV-3-a&chapter=4&lang=en

United Nations Treaty Collection (UN Treaty Collection) (2014g) https://treaties.un.org/Pages/ViewDetails.aspx?src=TREATY&mtdsg_no=IV-16&chapter=4&lang=en

Watts, Michael (2000) "The Great Tablecloth: Bread and Butter Politics, and the Political Economy of Food and Poverty", in G. L. Clark, M. P. Feldman, and M. S. Gertler (eds.), *The Oxford Handbook of Economic Geography.* Oxford: Oxford University Press.

Watts, Michael and Hans Bohle (1993) "The Space of Vulnerability: The Causal Structure of Hunger and Famine." *Progress in Human Geography* 17(1): 43–67.

7 Sustaining food production in the Anthropocene

Influences by regulation of crop biotechnology

Mark Perry[1]

Introduction

It is appropriate that the current era has been given the moniker the Anthropocene,[2] where human interference in every aspect of life is creating changes at ever-greater rates. From genes to the global ecosphere, human activity is the cause of change. The production of food is no exception. In the current global economy, where the movement of food products are seen as a part of world trade, trying to establish harmonisation on the regulation of biotechnological innovation and its application to crop production, as well as systemising the regulatory steps that can be taken to help to achieve this, can be seen as a desirable outcome of international negotiations.

Putting aside the question of the technologies involved, the common aim, and one that echoes the desires of farmers, breeders and consumers over millennia, is for high productivity and greater output solutions that do not rely on raised levels of inputs, such as fuel, fertilisers, water, pest controls and so forth. Typically these inputs depend on depleting the reserves of natural resources. Although this is a global issue, developed nations struggle to implement harmonised policies that support food security. Often the issues have not been addressed at all on a cooperative basis, while many developing and least developed nations, which are in a worse state for food supply, have barely addressed the problem even from an internal perspective. There are even less comprehensive regulatory approaches to address the challenges brought by agriculture. In terms of focus on agricultural biotechnology the picture is even bleaker. However, there is general agreement among most nations that there is a need to take into account the contributions of science to improve access to food (see UN, 2015; ICESR, art. 11). There is an overall consensus among nations that methods of food production need to be improved, including through the application of science. Article 11(2) of the International Covenant on Economic, Social and Cultural Rights holds:

> The States Parties to the present Covenant, recognising the fundamental right of everyone to be free from hunger, shall take, individually and

through international co-operation, the measure, including specific programmes, which are needed:

a) To improve methods of production, conservation and distribution of food by making full use of technical and scientific knowledge, by dissemination knowledge of the principles of nutrition and by developing or reforming agrarian systems in such a way as to achieve the most efficient development and utilisation of natural resources;
b) Taking into account the problems of both food-importing and food-exporting countries, to ensure an equitable distribution of world food supplies in relation to need.

The recorded challenges that face the global food supply this decade are multitudinous: some are novel, such as increases in extreme climatic variation and growing vigilance over the use of pesticides, others are exacerbations or continuations of problems from the last century, such as increasing population pressure, and regions that can be regarded as lacking the rule of law and security for citizens. It has been said that the benefits of the Green Revolution (GR) dating from the 1960s have reached maximum potential, and further gains are limited as the crops from those developments make demands for greater levels of fertilisers and irrigation, that are arguably not sustainable. Some solutions to the demands for greater supply of foodstuffs may be seen to lie in the use of biotechnology to develop *improved* food crops that require fewer inputs during cultivation and harvest for the same or better outputs. However, the claims to benefits and improvements are highly contentious, with some arguing that such products are not enhanced, or indeed that they are harmful. There have been diverse approaches taken around the world to the regulation of biotechnology's application to crop development that need to be examined in the light of issues surrounding food security.

Food security

The right to 'adequate food' is a basic human requirement, and seen globally as a human right (ICESR, art. 11). We all consume foodstuffs, with consumption globally ranging from excessive to insufficient. Having regular access to a range of good primary food products is clearly an essential requirement for all persons, following air and water.[3] For much of the planet there have been concerns with food security for centuries, and this is becoming an imperative issue again, even in developed nations, with threats to productivity discussed below.[4] Historically, particularly in regional agricultural localities, the cycle of feast or famine has followed the climatic and pest variations from year to year.[5] The 1960s saw the introduction of new seed stock, such as the dwarf, hardy and productive IR8 rice variety. The drive for higher productivity was at least somewhat in response to the threat of massive famine in India in the late 1950s, which in turn was stimulated in part by the flowering of bamboo.[6] The introduction of these new varieties of short, strong and high yield varieties saw the birth of the 'Green Revolution'.[7] There were two international agricultural research centre programmes, one for rice in the Philippines and one for maize and wheat in Mexico, that led the development of the high yield wheat and rice crops. This application of technology, which was developed through what today we call conventional seed stock production, or traditional breeding (primarily to distinguish plants produced from those forms of plant breeding that involve recombinant DNA techniques), provided the world with huge increases in global yields for cereal crops. For example, since 1970 production has improved significantly in the targeted crops, with global cereal production more than doubling in the period 1970 to 2012 (FAO, 2013).[8]

The benefits flowing from the GR have not been criticism free. One aspect that is generally accepted is that it has led to a reduction in biodiversity in agricultural products. However, the same can be said of any successful product that is adopted by industrial multinational producers. Other critics point out that the gains made using these high yield crops depend on increased inputs of fertiliser and water, and that these yield increases have come at an environmental cost that is not sustainable (see e.g. Jones et al., 2013).[9] Other arguments focus on the misapplication of required inputs, as well as bad management practices, the use of financial incentives and economic structuring, rather than inherent problems with the high yield varieties.

The environmental consequences were not caused by GR technology per se, but rather, the policy environment that promoted injudicious and overuse of inputs and expansion of cultivation into areas that could not sustain high levels of intensification, such as the sloping lands. Output price protection and input subsides – especially fertiliser, pesticide and irrigation water – distorted incentives at the farm level for adopting practices that would enhance efficiency in input use and thereby, contribute to sustaining the agricultural resource base. Where the policy incentives were corrected, farmers quickly changed behaviour and adopted more sustainable practices. For example, the removal of pesticide subsides in Indonesia in the early 1990s led to a dramatic drop in insecticide use (Pingali, 2012, p. 12304).

Whatever view is held of the application of traditional breeding techniques, the rate of increased productivity gains from the early decades of the GR has declined. However, the need for greater productivity has not abated. Without being unduly negative, the outlook for food security for much of the world's population by 2050, on the face of it, is desolate. The undeniable population increases, spreading desertification, extremes in climatic variation, pollution, greed and the multitudinous other afflictions facing the human race will be a major factor in the availability of food, and shall likely reach critical levels in the course of the next few decades. The United Nations Department of Economic and Social Affairs, Population Division, is now predicting a global population of 8.1 billion by 2025 and 9.6 billion within 35 years, with most increases happening in developing nations. This will naturally increase the demand for a sustainable food supply, especially in those regions that are already food poor (UN, 2012).[10] Land degradation and desertification is occurring at an alarming rate, with 12 million hectares per annum being lost to drought and desertification (UNCCD, n.d.).[11] Climatic variations have also been the subject of much debate over the last two decades, but there are few sceptics left who deny that there is currently a change in climatic factors that are not beneficial to humanity.[12] The United Nations predicts that by 2050, unless there are changes in agricultural production, there will be dramatic drops in food production due to climate change (UNCCD, n.d.). In 2007 to 2008 another problem came to the fore highlighting structural problems in the global food security. The cost of rice nearly doubled in a period of three months with many other staples not far behind, with the rapid price rises in basic foodstuffs leading to food riots in countries dispersed as 'Guinea, Mauritania, Mexico, Morocco, Senegal, Uzbekistan and Yemen' (Bradsher, 2008).

A plethora of solutions have been proffered for improving access to food, and addressing the issue of food security, ranging from food-focused approaches such as improved and fairer product distribution systems, better preservation of foods that are produced, and avoidance of waste from farm to fork,[13] through to perspectives at a larger level of granularity such as political stability, and justice. However, few would challenge the need to at least examine the possibilities to get more crop output for less input – that is, to reduce the environmental burdens associated with growing crops but produce more food. There is dire need for international cooperation on the production of foodstuffs, as well as their acceptance in the marketplace, that will cope with the changing conditions in a manner that does not rely on depleting the natural reserves, whether through irrigation and input nutrient requirements or negatively impacting the environment, such as air, and land.

There is no 'magic bullet', no one single solution to provide food security. In terms of crop production, the Food and Agriculture Organization comments (FAO, 2002, p. 3):

> There are three main sources of growth in crop production: expanding the land area, increasing the frequency with which it is cropped (often through irrigation), and boosting yields. It has been suggested that we may be approaching the ceiling of what is possible for all three sources.

Numerous challenges face the global food supply in the twenty-first century: some are novel, such as increases in extreme climatic variation; others are exacerbations of problems from the last century, such as increasing population pressure. The benefits provided by the GR from the 1960s are reaching maximum potential, and their deployment continues to make demands for a greater supply of fertilisers and irrigation that may not be sustainable. Arguably, there are solutions that lie in the application of newer biotechnology methods to develop advanced food crops, ones that require fewer inputs on cultivation for the same or better outputs. It is clear that in looking for solutions to the challenges to food security there is an urgent need to at least consider increased productivity.[14] There have been diverse approaches taken around the world to the regulation of biotechnology's application to crop development, but the issue of whether these crops are better, in terms of inputs and outputs rather than good or evil, or can offer sustainable solutions is first addressed below.

Crop production – the promise of biotechnology

The advances in biology since the 1960s have provided the basis for a broad range of biotechnologies that offer benefits in enhanced crop production, including improved breeding, gene mapping, trait mapping, traditional gene targeting and recombinant DNA techniques. There are undoubtedly potential dangers too, ranging from mono-cropping,[15] to seed monopolies,[16] to unintended biological outcomes.[17] The triggering of regulation of new crops varies significantly from state to state. Most nations look to regulate based on the type of technology involved in the creation of the plant with desired traits. A notable exception to this is Canada, as discussed below, which looks to regulate plants with 'novel traits' independent of the means by which they were developed. There are many applications of biotechnology that can be used and are used to provide advantageous outcomes from crop production with a given input (see e.g. Abdel-Aziz et al., 2015). However, given the focus from the media and other vocal parties on plants created through recombinant DNA techniques, often given the name genetically modified organisms (GMOs),[18] the focus will be on crops produced by these means,[19] and using the publicly accepted understanding of GMO to include transgenic, intranenetic and cisgenic crops.[20]

During the 1950s, and following some remarkable insights into the workings of plant crown gall disease (see e.g. Braun, 1958), where tumours are formed on plants, studies began to focus on how the *Agrobacterium Tumefaciens* integrates parts of its own DNA into that of the plant. This became the basis for the use of the *agrobacterium* as a means of accomplishing gene transfer into plants.[21] It should be noted that such gene insertion occurs in nature without human intervention, and can be considered a 'natural process' in much the same way that using yeast to make bread rise is a natural process, even though bread does not exist without human intervention:

> The wide host range of *Agrobacterium* (even wider now that monocot transformation is facile) inspired the idea that DNA incorporation may be a universal phenomenon. But perhaps the most important legacy from *Agrobacterium* has been its inspiration of confidence that foreign gene integration, even though DNA is sometimes delivered artificially, *is a perfectly natural process*. My most fervent wish is that well-meaning environmental proponents will come to recognize this and embrace the technology based on it.
>
> (Chilton 2001, p. 13, emphasis added)

Other techniques have also been developed for inserting genes into plants, such as microinjection, where the DNA is injected into the host cell being transformed by transportation on a non-reactive carrier such as gold or tungsten, where a phage is used rather than the *agrobacterium*. This process is sometimes called using a 'gene gun'. However, *agrobacterium* is still the major means of inserting molecular constructs for particular traits, i.e. GMO creation for crops. Whatever the technique, the result is a plant carrying introduced sequences where they would not have had them before.

The first transgenic field trials were with tobacco in France in 1986 (James and Krattiger, 1996, p. 31). The first field trial of a transgenic food crop was planted on 1 June 1987 at the Plant Breeding Institute, Cambridge, UK, one day before Monsanto's (Jefferson, 2006, p. 17). This was the dawn of the age of application of the new biotechnology to crop production in the field. The first food crop that was genetically modified by these techniques was Calgene's FlavrSavr tomato, which came onto the market in 1994. Although the trait for FlavrSavr was slower ripening and resistance to rotting, it was not a great commercial success. The deployment and approval of several other 'version one' GMOs soon followed with glyphosate resistance,[22] and those expressing proteins from *Bacillus Thuringiensis*,[23] being among those first on the market. Bt corn was introduced in 1996, soon followed by 'Roundup Ready'[24] soybeans and many other crops.

The potential for these plant developments is huge, giving plants (as well as other organisms such as bacteria, and some animals) possible traits that include herbicide resistance (e.g. Monsanto, 2015), raised laurate levels in plant seed fats (CERA, 2015), resistance to pest attacks (ISAAA, 2015), virus resistance (Gonsalves et al., 2004), stress resistance (Zhang et al., 2000), vitamin enhancement (Dubock, 2013), vaccines (Abdullah et al., 2008; Norris, 2005), growth rate (Blakeslee, 1994; FAO, 2015), better insulin (Xavier-Filho et al., 2003; Shama and Peterson, 2004), and even apples that resist browning of their flesh when exposed to air. The arguments as to whether these developments in biological science are angelic or evil are beyond the scope of this chapter, and an area of much vitriolic debate. However, the legal systems in most nations have legislation and regulation that directly or indirectly influences the possibility of such developments reaching the field and fork.

Regulation

Many jurisdictions are currently struggling to find a balance in forming a regulatory framework for biotechnology between the extremes of unrestrained technology and exercising caution to the extent of stifling innovation. Countries are typically facilitating control of technology by the implementation of government policy through regulation, either directly by legislation or through some other designated body. The fundamental purpose underlying the policy directing such regulation, is to control the use of biotechnology to an extent that minimises risk while maximising production potential. In the production of crops, the focus is on output traits and whether there is harm in the use of the 'crop as product'. Although this can be seen in various approaches to regulation, the trigger for regulation varies from dependence on the process by which the crop is produced (such as the European Union, Japan, Australia), where it is the molecular transformation processes that trigger regulation, or on the novelty of product itself, such as in the USA and Canada. Furthermore, the triggering of legal processes varies considerably from country to country. A few examples are given to illustrate the divergence of approaches at the regulatory level.

The European Union looks to regulate deliberate release into the environment of GMOs (see Commission Directive 2001/18/EC on the deliberate release into the environment of genetically modified organisms, p. 1). This is followed by a process that is summarised in Figure 7.1, but there is also an overlay of state jurisdictional mechanisms.

A small number of European states, including Spain, Portugal and Germany, allow some cultivation of GMOs. But only two GM plants are under cultivation, the Monsanto Bt corn, MON810 which is used for animal feed and starch production, mainly in Spain, and BASF's Amflora potato, used to produce pure starch for paper and textile production. Although the European Commission approved the potato in 2010, BASF withdrew it from the EU market in 2012, despite the approval process taking 14 years.

Figure 7.1 GM plant regulation in the European Union

The European Commission has recently released its Proposal for a Regulation of the European Parliament and of the Council and allows the Member States the option of restricting or prohibiting the use of GM food and feed on their territory (COM(2015) 177, final). It follows the review of the decision processes on GMOs in the EU (European Commission, 2015). It should be noted that individual states in Europe have had *de facto* bans on GMOs by invoking the 'Safeguard Clause' in article 16 of Commission Directive 2001/18/EC on the deliberate release into the environment of GMOs to provide reasons for them not to allow the production of such products in their country.

In Australia, regulation aims to address the use of specific means of creation of the crop, in this case recombinant DNA technologies under the Gene Technology Act 2000 (Cth) and the Gene Technology Regulations 2001 (Cth). These regulations aim 'to protect the health and safety of people, and the environment, by identifying risks posed by or as a result of gene technology, and by managing those risks through regulating certain dealings with genetically modified organisms' (Gene Technology Act, 2000 (Cth), s. 3).

In addition to the federal legislation, Australian states have adopted their own schemes of management. For example, the long title of the Genetically Modified Crops Management Act 2004 of South Australian states it is:

> An Act to provide for the designation of areas of the State for the purposes of preserving for marketing purposes the identity of certain food crops according to whether they are genetically modified crops or non-genetically modified crops; to provide for the segregation of genetically modified food crops and their products in appropriate cases; to provide for associated regulatory powers; to provide certain protections with respect to the spread of genetically modified plant material; and for other purposes.

It defines 'genetically modified organism' or 'GMO' as a genetically modified organism within the meaning of the Gene Technology Act 2001 (SA) (Genetically Modified Crops Management Act 2004 (SA), s. 3).

Canadian legislation takes a product approach and looks to regulate the use of plants with 'novel traits', regardless of the techniques used for their creation.[25] The determination of whether the novel trait is permissible varies with the intended use of the plant. However, many would not consider the Canadian approval process to be particularly rigorous, as can be seen as the approval of GMOs with stacked traits, where previous individual traits such as pest resistance and herbicide resistance are 'stacked' into one plant to give multiple traits. Such plants have been rapidly approved in Canada, largely on the basis of an individual trait being approved in a prior application.

There are conflicts in perceptions of the need for, and risk of, using modern biotechnology to address food production issues, but, given the pressure to develop crops that are more resistant (typically, to environmental stresses), it is likely that the use of second-generation GMOs, those with stacked traits or other targeted areas of improved productivity such as drought resistance, is going to be even more widespread in the future.

Many developing and least developed nations are in a worse state than developed nations – they lack comprehensive regulatory systems to address the challenges brought by agricultural biotechnology (though some nations are in the process of developing such systems) (Karky and Perry, 2013; Nicita and Gourdon, 2013). Even in jurisdictions such as Australia, which have regulations in place, these regulations fail to specifically address such issues as inadvertent transference of GMOs to areas where they may, sometimes due to the perception of stakeholders, cause economic loss. This is illustrated in the recent decision in *Marsh* v. *Baxter* [2014] WASC 187, where the competing interests of an organic farmer and a grower of genetically modified canola were heard. In this case, the plaintiff lost organic certification for his crops (not canola) due to the unintended transfer of genetically modified canola seeds from his neighbour's property. He failed in his attempt to recover his losses from his neighbour under the tort of nuisance. One of the issues was that the certification should not have been removed from the plaintiff's land. An appeal has been heard in the Western Australia Court of Appeal, and a decision awaited.

There are other legal restraints that vary from jurisdiction to jurisdiction, ranging from liability for adventitious presence,[26] and the control of the ability to use seed due to patents or end-user agreements.[27] These may be seen as secondary regulatory issues that influence the adoption of newly developed crops.

In developing nations there are many fundamental issues for crop production, primarily the protection of the natural resources, the ability for crop survival, and even subsistence farmers to have access to improved seed for sowing. These concerns are often reflected in legislation that tries to address the issues such as a biopiracy of local resources, and the ability for farmers to save seed. In Bhutan, for example, the Biodiversity Act of Bhutan 2003 aims to combat attempts of illegal access to traditional biotechnology resources, such as native vegetation, and also protects the rights of farmers and breeders, including informal selection, to the plant varieties. It also aims to aid Bhutanese access to foreign plant varieties, which could be used by Bhutan farmers (see Biodiversity Act of Bhutan 2003, art. 2).

The international approach to regulation of GMOs has been largely reactive rather than proactive, responding to the pressures that such product use has put on trade or local policy. The main international action to date has occurred under the auspices of the Codex Alimentarius Commission (CAM), which is a joint commission of the World Health Organization and the Food and Agricultural Organization (FAO), both of which are United Nations Specialized Agencies.[28] CAM has been tasked with establishing health and safety standards and regulating international food trade, and can be seen as a powerful influence on international food regulation developments (see Perry and Karky, 2013). The Sixth Session of the Codex Alimentarius Ad Hoc Intergovernmental Task Force on Foods Derived from Biotechnology, for example, set up a working group on the low-level presence (adventitious presence) of GMOs, chaired by the USA and co-chaired by Germany and Thailand, in 2006. The Task Force put a proposed draft forward, and had it considered at the Seventh Session at the Task Force's September 2007 meeting in Chiba, Japan (Codex Alimentarius Commission, 2007).[29] The main advances on the international front have been under the auspices of CAM and the FAO in terms of assembling a database of GMO products, where each 'transformation event' that has been produced from using recombinant DNA techniques is identified, coded and added to the resource (FAO, n.d.), and the adoption of the Guideline for the conduct of food safety assessment of foods derived from recombinant-DNA plants (see Codex Alimentarius Commission, 2009).

There are many tensions that arise with the application of new technologies. Some can be easily resolved with legislation and regulation – think of car traffic rules replacing those governing horses. However in recent years the effectiveness of regulation that doesn't meet the needs of consumers of the technology are legion (think of the laws relating to the governance of the internet). Biotechnology is complex, and difficult to understand. It relates to life, something dear to everyone's heart. Regulation needs to be such to protect life, but not stifle the ability to improve the lives of many.

Conclusion

The instances of regulation illustrated herein are a small sample of the overall fragmented regulatory picture, but they aim to show that even in such a globalised market as crop production there are regulatory influences on the adoption of technologies that vary from widespread adoption to outright or *de facto* bans on GMO production. It is likely that the GMOs in the food chain are safe, despite press to the contrary, particularly in the European Union, and not one person has been shown to have died from eating a GM product. However, there is unfortunately much irrefutable evidence over the last four decades to show that many millions have died of starvation, as well as several more millions of people who continue to suffer from malnutrition. Looking back to the 1960s, commentary is pertinent to the developments of today:

> This new revolution can be as significant and as beneficial to mankind as the industrial revolution of a century and a half ago. To accelerate it, to spread it, and to make it permanent, we need to understand how it started and what forces are driving it forward. Good luck – good monsoons – helped bring in the recent record harvests. But hard work, good management, and sound agricultural policies in the developing countries and foreign aid were also very much involved.
>
> (Gaud, 1968)

The revolution since that time is the application of recent biotechnology advancements, such as recombinant DNA techniques, to crop production. Food security in the coming decades must improve to avoid some of the scourges that afflict humankind. The requirements for good understanding and widespread education regarding the new technologies that have been deployed widely over the last two decades is not being met by proponents of the technologies nor aided by anti-GMO polemics based on pseudoscience and fear mongering. Civil society requires our governance structures to ensure that such technologies can be managed through regulatory processes to give us global food security, control of risk and fair deployment, and, it is hoped, to avoid greed and monopolisation of basic resources such as seed. It is possible for a sustainable future for food security to take advantage of biotechnology with greater levels of penetrance if international cooperation is able to become more homogenised and effective, in the hope that this will lead to improved crop production without the current degradation of arable lands and excessive depletion of natural resources.

Notes

1 The author thanks Kylie Lingard, Ph.D. candidate, for her great research assistance in the preparation of this chapter.
2 'I began using the term "Anthropocene" in the 1980s, but never formalised it until Paul contacted me." (Steffen et al., 2011, citing biologist Eugene Stoermer).
3 The question of the quality of foodstuffs available, particularly the trend in developed countries to consume processed mass-produced packaged products, is outside the scope of this chapter which looks at the production of primary products.
4 The World Food Summit of 1996 defined food security as existing 'when all people at all times have access to sufficient, safe, nutritious food to maintain a healthy and active life' (WHO, 2015).
5 There is also the issue of human disruption of access to food through conflict, which has been a common cause of displacement and famine, and a tragedy that is likely to continue into the future.
6 While some bamboos only flower every 40 years or so, when they do come into flower they produce prodigious amounts of seed which in turn leads to a large spike in the rat population. This has long been seen as a predictor of local famine in the vicinity of such mass flowering varieties of bamboo (see Nag, 1999).
7 The first published use of the term is attributed to William Gaud who worked for the United States Agency for International Development before joining the International Finance Corporation in the late 1960s (see Gaud, 1968). Gaud's 1968 address to the Society for International Development is of particular significance in that it noted several of the issues that are apparent today, including the raised requirements for irrigation and fertiliser for the high yielding seeds, the political issues related to providing aid to developing nations, and the policies required to support better farming outcomes.
8 The gains in 'total factor productivity' (as well as direct gains in yield) can be seen across a wide range of crops between 1960 and 2000, as well as considerations of regional variations (see Evenson and Gollin, 2003). Later FAO analysis show similar results. For example, global cereal production increased over 2.1 times in the period from 1970 to 2012 (FAO 2013). Khush (1999, p. 646) notes: 'The 1960s was a decade of despair with regard to the world's ability to cope with the food-population balance, particularly in the tropics ... Thanks to the widespread adoption of "Green Revolution" technology, large-scale famines and social and economic upheavals were averted. Between 1966 and 1990, the population of the densely populated low-income countries grew by 80%, but food production more than doubled.'

9 Jones et al. (2013) look at the stripping of macro- and micro-nutrients from soils, and notes that India has had decades of such soil impoverishment. Jones et al. (2013, p. 860) conclude: 'Although technology brought about one successful Green Revolution in agriculture from 1950–70, the systems agriculture created were inherently leaky and unsustainable from a nutrient perspective.'

10 The current world population is around 7.2 billion. The predictions for future world populations are naturally uncertain, with the projection given being the 'medium variant' and high and low variants one billion more or less.

11 Due to metrics and methodologies used in the five major global assessments between 1977 and 2003 resulting 'in a plethora of degradation estimates ranging 15% to 63% of global degradation and 4% to 74% of dryland degradation' (Safriel, 2007, p. 1). However, whatever the 'true' value of degradation, any increase is going to result in lower ability to produce foods.

12 Although the latest report on the future from the Australian government recognises climate change as an issue for the future, it bizarrely states the obvious (Commonwealth of Australia, 2015): 'Governments must continue to plan for the potential economic and environmental effects of climate change. Some economic effects may be beneficial – where regions become warmer or wetter this may allow for increased agricultural output – while others may be harmful. For example, lower rainfall may reduce crop yields, or transport infrastructure (such as roads, ports and rail networks) may become more susceptible to damage from extreme weather events' (p. 42). This is rather like saying flooding may be good in some areas for frogs.

13 Some estimates put the food wastage at around 30 per cent of all produced. For example, Gustavsson et al. (2011, p. 4) found '[r]oughly one-third of the edible parts of food produced for human consumption, gets lost or wasted globally, which is about 1.3 billion ton per year'. Gustavsson et al. (2011, p. v) also identified that most wastage occurs in developed nations, 'per capita food waste by consumers in Europe and North-America is 95–115 kg/year, while this figure in sub-Saharan Africa and South/Southeast Asia is only 6–11 kg/year'.

14 There are naturally many other issues in this complex arena, such as food justice (see e.g. Kennedy and Liljeblad, 2016).

15 Although it should be noted that the dangers associated with reduced biodiversity are also applicable to any crop that is grown from a single strain, as are much of the products from industrial agriculture. However, there were many earlier instances where reliance on a single crop that failed led to severe food shortages, such as the Irish Great Famine of the 1840s. The potato of choice in Ireland at the time was the Irish Lumper, one of poor quality but high productivity, and also a variety that was highly susceptible to fungal blight (Buchanan, 2012).

16 One view of this is put by Shiva (2014, p. 11): 'However, farmer-bred and farmer-saved seeds are not seen as contributing to growth. They create and renew life but don't lead to profits. Growth begins when seeds are modified, patented and genetically locked, leading to farmers being forced to buy more every season.' Nature is impoverished, biodiversity is eroded and a free, open resource is transformed into a patented commodity. Buying seeds every year is a recipe for debt for India's poor peasants. And ever since seed monopolies have been established, farmers' debt has increased. More than 270,000 farmers caught in a debt trap in India have committed suicide since 1995.

17 For example, the StarLink Corn Affair, a variety of corn that was prohibited for human consumption due to its containing attributes that were similar to known human allergens contaminated some corn supply in many US states, which led to depressed prices, and risk to human health (see Beebe 2004; see generally Perry and Karky, 2013).

18 These transgenic plants/animals are typically called genetically modified organisms (GMOs) – which although a misnomer, as nearly all crop plants and domesticated

animals have been genetically modified through human intervention, whether by traditional breeding or by other more drastic mutagenesis approaches, is one that has gained popular usage and acceptance. A subset of organisms created in this way are known as transgenics, where the genes introduced are taken from a different organism, and hence the disparaging 'frankenfoods' and other monikers. For a description of the techniques involved with transgenic animals, such as the 'onco-mouse' (Harvard mouse) (see Perry and Krishna, 2001).

19 The global area of crops that were GMO in 2014 was put at 181 million hectares, with a value of US$15.7 billion: '[This represents] 22% of the US$72.3 billion global crop protection market in 2013, and 35% of the US$45 billion global commercial seed market. Of the US$15.7 billion biotech crop market, US$11.3 billion (72%) was in the industrial countries and US$4.4 billion (28%) was in the developing countries' (James, 2014).

20 There is some divergence of the meanings of these terms, but generally cisgenesis is using genes, promoters and terminators that originate from the recipient plant; intragenesis is genes, promotors, terminators from sexually compatible gene pool of recipient plant (for detailed discussion on variations in the definitions, see Holme et al., 2013).

21 The fascinating story of this development is recounted in Chilton (2001).

22 The crop plant is transformed to resist the herbicide glyphosate so that the crop can be sprayed with the herbicide without its being killed, and thus weed pressure is reduced and yield improved. It is not generally recognised that prior to the recombinant DNA techniques used to create glyphosate resistant plants, some herbicide resistance had been bred into varieties by hybridisation techniques of earlier years (see Harrison, 1992).

23 The crop plant is transformed to include genes that express proteins from the soil bacterium *Bacillus Thuringiensis* to kill certain insects, such as corn borer without the need for pesticide sprays. It should be noted that pesticide sprays made with *Bacillus Thuringiensis* are still used, and considered by some to be 'natural'.

24 Roundup Ready is the moniker for the Monsanto glyphosate resistant crops, the herbicide carrying the trademark 'Roundup'.

25 This is the responsibility of the Canadian Food Inspection Agency (CFIA) under the Plant Protection Act 1990 (SC) c. 22 and the Seeds Act 1985 (RSC) c. S-8. The CFIA was established by the Canadian Food Inspection Agency Act 1997 (SC) c. 6.

26 The German Genetic Engineering Act, for example, imposes strict liability on damages from GMOs up to €85 million.

27 Some countries do not allow patenting of seeds, for example, only the constructs in the seeds, whereas in others the whole plant and seed may be patented. The European Patent Convention prohibits the patenting of plant varieties, as does the common law in Canada, but other jurisdictions allow for the patenting of plants, which in turn leads to issues with seed saving by farmers.

28 The Commission has a long history of over a century. It was formally established as part of the joint World Health Organization and Food and Agricultural Organization in 1963 (see Shubber, 1972).

29 The United States had made a similar proposal to form an ad hoc taskforce on LLP at the 5th Session in 2005, but it was not accepted at that time.

References

Abdel-Aziz, N. A., Salem, A. Z. M, El-Adawy, M. M, Camacho, L. M, Kholif, A. E., Elghandour, M. M. Y. and Borhami, E. (2015). Biological treatments as a mean to improve feed utilization in agriculture animals: An overview. *Journal of Integrative Agriculture*, *14*(3), 534–543.

Abdullah, M. A., ur Rahmah, A., Sinskey, A. J. and Rha, C. K. (2008). Cell engineering and molecular pharming for biopharmaceuticals. *Open Medicinal Chemistry Journal, 2*, 49–61.

Beebe, L. (2004). In re StarLink Corn: The link between genetically damaged crops and an inadequate regulatory framework for biotechnology. *William and Mary Environmental Law and Policy Review, 28*(2), 511–537.

Biodiversity Act of Bhutan (Water Sheep Year) 2003.

Blakeslee, S. (1994). Gene transplant speeds salmon growth rate. *New York Times*. Retrieved from www.nytimes.com/1994/09/20/science/gene-transplant-speeds-salmon-growth-rate.html

Bradsher, K. (2008). High rice cost creating fears of Asia unrest. *New York Times*. Retrieved from www.nytimes.com/2008/03/29/business/worldbusiness/29rice.html?fta=y&_r=0

Braun, A. (1958). A physiological basis for autonomous growth of the crown-gall tumor cell. *Proceedings National Academy of Science, 44*(4), 344–349.

Buchanan, D. (2012). *Taste, Memory: Forgotten Foods, Lost Flavors and Why They Matter.* Vermont: Chelsea Green Publishing.

CERA (2015). *GM crop database: CGN-89465–2 (23–18–17, 23–198)*. Retrieved from http://cera-gmc.org/GmCropDatabaseEvent/23–18–17,%2023–198

Chilton, M.-D. (2001). Agrobacterium: a memoir. *Plant Physiology, 125*(1), 9–14.

Codex Alimentarius Commission (2007). *Codex Ad Hoc Intergovernmental Task Force on Foods Derived from Biotechnology: provisional agenda (7th session)*. Rome: FAO/WHO, CX/FBT 07/7/1.

Codex Alimentarius Commission (2009). Guideline for the conduct of food safety assessment of foods derived from recombinant DNA plants (CAC/GL 45–2003). In: WHO/FAO eds. *Foods Derived from Modern Biotechnology*. Rome: WHO/FAO.

Commission Directive 2001/18/EC of 12 March 2001 on the deliberate release into the environment of genetically modified organisms and repealing Council Directive 90/220/EC.

Commonwealth of Australia (2015). *2015 Intergenerational Report: Australia in 2055.* Canberra: Commonwealth of Australia.

Dubock, A. (2013). Golden Rice: A long-running story at the watershed of the GM debate. *Bioscences for Farming in Africa*. Retrieved from: www.goldenrice.org/PDFs/GR_A_long-running_story.pdf

European Commission (2015). *Communication from the Commission to the European Parliament, the Council, the European Economic and Social Committee and the Committee of the Regions: reviewing the decision-making process on genetically modified organisms (GMOs)*. Brussels: EC.

Evenson, R. E. and Gollin, D. (2003). Assessing the impact of the Green Revolution, 1960 to 2000. *Science, 300*(5620), 758–762.

FAO (2002). *Towards 2015/2030 World Agriculture: Summary Report*. Rome: FAO, 2002, p. 3. Available from: ftp.fao.org/docrep/fao/004/y3557e/y3557e.pdf

FAO (2013). *Statistical Yearbook: World Food and Agriculture*. Rome: FAO.

FAO (2015). *Genetic biotechnologies* [online]. Available from: www.fao.org/fishery/topic/14796/en [accessed 4 May 2015].

FAO (n.d.). *FAO GM foods platform*. Retrieved from www.fao.org/food/food-safety-quality/gm-foods-platform/browse-information-by/oecd-unique-identifier/en

Gaud, W. S. (1968). The Green Revolution: Accomplishments and apprehensions. Society for International Development. Retrieved from www.agbioworld.org/biotech-info/topics/borlaug/borlaug-green.html

Gene Technology Act 2000 (Cth).

Gene Technology Act 2001 (SA).

Gene Technology Regulations 2001 (Cth).

Genetically Modified Crops Management Act 2004 (SA).

Gonsalves, D., Gonsalves, C., Ferreira, S., Pitz, K., Fitch, M., Manshardt, R. and Slightom, J. (2004). Transgenic virus resistant Papaya: From hope to reality for controlling Papaya ringspot virus in Hawaii. *APSnet*.

Gustavsson, J., Cederberg, C. and Sonesson, U. (2011). *Global Food Losses and Food Waste: Extent, Causes and Prevention*. Rome: FAO.

Harrison, H. (1992). Developing herbicide-tolerant crop cultivars: Introduction. *Weed Technology*, *6*(3), 613–614.

Holme, I. B., Wendt, T. and Holm, P. B. (2013). Intragenesis and cisgenesis as alternatives to transgenic crop development. *Plant Biotechnology Journal*, *11*, 395–407.

International Covenant on Economic, Social and Cultural Rights 1966 (opened for signature 16 December 1966, entered into force 3 January 1976) 993 UNTS 3 (ICESR).

ISAAA. (2015). *Bt Insect Resistant Technology*. Retrieved from https://isaaa.org/resources/publications/pocketk/6/default.as

James, C. (2014). *Global Status of Commercialized Biotech/GM Crops in 2014*. Ithaca, NY: ISAAA.

James, C. and Krattiger, A. F. (1996). *Global Review of the Field Testing and Commercialization of Transgenic Plants: The First Decade Of Crop Biotechnology*. Ithaca, NY: ISAAA.

Jefferson, R. (2006). Science as social enterprise: The CAMBIA BiOS initiative. *Innovations: Technology, Governance, Globalization*, *1*(4), 13–14.

Jones, D., Cross, P., Withers, P. J. A., DeLuca, T. H., Robinson, D. A., Quilliam, R. S., Harris, J. M., Chadwick, D. R. and Edwards-Jones, G. (2013). Nutrient stripping: The global disparity between food security and soil nutrient stocks. *Journal of Applied Ecology*, *50*(4), 851–862.

Karky, R. and Perry, M. (2013). World Trade Organization obligations and legislative policy: Choices in developing countries for biotechnology. *International Trade Law Journal*, *22*(1).

Kennedy, A. and Liljeblad, J. (2016). *Food Systems Governance: Challenges for Justice, Equality and Human Rights*. London: Routledge.

Monsanto (2015). *Agricultural Seeds*. Retrieved from www.monsanto.com/products/pages/monsanto-agricultural-seeds.aspx

Nag, S. (1999). Bamboo, rats and famines: Famine relief and perceptions of British paternalism in the Mizo Hills (India). *Environment and History*, *5*(2), 245–252.

Nicita, A. and Gourdon, J. (2013). *A Preliminary Analysis on Newly Collected Data on Non-Tariff Measures*. Geneva: UNCTAD.

Norris, S. (2005). *Molecular Farming*. Ottawa: Parliamentary Information and Research Service.

Perry, M. and Karky, R. (2013). Agriculture under threat – a crisis of confidence? The solution: Redefine adventitious presence maximum levels from zero to zero++. *Canadian Journal of Law and Technology*, *11*, 25–47.

Perry, M. and Krishna, P. (2001). Making sense of mouse tales: Canada lifeform patents topsy-turvy. *European Intellectual Property Review*, *23*(195).

Pingali, P. (2012). Green Revolution: Impacts, limits, and the path ahead *PNAS, 109*(31), 12302–12308.

Proposal for a Regulation of the European Parliament and of the Council, amending Regulation (EC) No 1829/2003 as regards the possibility for the Member States to restrict or prohibit the use of genetically modified food and feed on their territory, COM(2015) 177, final.

Safriel, U. N. (2007). The assessment of global trends in land degradation. In: Sivakumar, M. and Ndiang'ui, N. (eds), *Climate and Land Degradation*. Berlin: Springer, 1–38.

Shama, L. M. and Peterson, R. K. D. (2004). The benefits and risks of producing pharmaceutical proteins in plants. *Risk Management Matters*, *2*(4), 28–33.

Shiva, V., 2014. How economic growth has become anti-life. *Green Social Thought*, 11–12.

Shubber, S. (1972). The Codex Alimentarius Commission under international law. *International and Comparative Law Quarterly*, *21*(4), 631–655.

Steffen, W., Grinevald, J. Crutzen, P. and McNeill, J. (2011). The Anthropocene: conceptual and historical perspectives. *Philosophical Transactions of the Royal Society*, *369*(1938), 842–867.

UN (2012). *World Population Prospect: The 2012 Revision (Data Sources and Meta Information)*. Retrieved from http://esa.un.org/wpp

UN (2015). International Covenant on Economic, Social and Cultural Rights. Retrieved from: https://treaties.un.org/doc/Publication/MTDSG/Volume%20I/Chapter%20IV/iv-3.en.pdf

UNCCD (n.d.). *Desertification Land Degradation and Drought: Some Global Facts and Figures*. Retrieved from www.unccd.int/Lists/SiteDocumentLibrary/WDCD/DLDD%20Facts.pdf

WHO (2015). *Food Security*. Retrieved from www.who.int/trade/glossary/story028/en

Xavier-Filho, J., Oliveira, A. E. A., da Silva, L. B. Azevedo, C. R., Venâncio, T. M., Machado, O. L. T., Oliva, M. L., Fernandes, K. V. S. and Xavier-Neto, J. (2003). Plant insulin or glucokinin: A conflicting issue. *Brazilian Journal of Plant Physiology*, *15*(2), 67–78.

Zhang, J., Klueva, N. Y., Wang, Z., Wu, R., Ho, T. H. D. and Nguyen, H. T. (2000). Genetic engineering for abiotic stress resistance in crop plants. *In Vitro Cellular and Developmental Biology*, *36*(2), 108–114.

8 Plant genetic resources interdependence

Reintegrating farmers into the global food system

Chidi Oguamanam

Introduction

The Food and Agriculture Organization (FAO) of the United Nations defines food security as a "situation in which all people at all times have physical and economic access to sufficient, safe and nutritious food to meet their dietary needs and food preferences for an active and healthy life" (FAO, 2006, p. 1).[1] As an interdisciplinary concept in continuous evolution, other definitions of food security abound (Lang and Barling, 2012). The same is true in regard to variations in interpreting details of the key elements of the food security concept embedded in the FAO and other definitions (FAO, 2003, 2006). Aside from the productionist or supply – physical and economic access – aspects of food security include issues of 'dietary needs,' 'food preferences,' and 'healthy life' and involve increasingly open considerations in the pattern of food production that shifts the food security discourse to a broader food system theory (Lang and Barling, 2012).

For many cultural communities in the developing world, important aspects of such considerations include agro-biodiversity, dietary diversity, the production and access to culturally appropriate foods in the context of human dignity as an addition to a rights-based approach to food. For the most part, food security has evolved to embrace a combination of production and sufficiency of food for hunger relief on the one hand, and, on the other, interrelated social, ecological, justice, equity, health and complex arrays of issues in the dynamics of global food production and supply.

FAO statistics on the trends and figures related to agro-biodiversity and agricultural change over the last century show that smallholder farmers or traditional agriculturalists are deserting "their multiple local varieties and land races for genetically uniform, high-yielding varieties" (FAO, 2004, p. 3). As a consequence, the world has lost 75 percent of plant genetic diversity since the 1900s. Worldwide, 30 percent of livestock breeds are under the risk of extinction. Out of the estimated 250,000 to 300,000 edible plant species, humans have been able to use only 150 to 200, which roughly translates to 4 percent. Out of that number, three crops (maize, wheat, and rice) are the main food sources, contributing almost 60 percent of plant-derived calories and proteins consumed by humans (FAO, 2004, p. 3).

This chapter outlines the historical interdependence over the sourcing of plant genetic resources for food and agriculture (PGRFA) and, indeed, of worldwide agricultural production and associated inequity in the global food system. It explores the factors that contribute to the above outlined dismal global profile of monoculture and agro-biodiversity, as well as its complicity in escalating the food insecurity situation in developing countries and traditional centers of crop genetic diversity. The chapter argues that one of the important governance challenges of food security, nay food system, in the twenty-first century is the need for a proactive de-escalation of the contemporary monocultural trend. It underscores the promotion of agro-biodiversity through the reinvigoration of farmer-centered agricultural practices of the indigenous and local communities (ILC) in developing countries.

Global interdependence of plant crop genetic resources

According to Jack Kloppenburg Jr. (1988, p. 46), "plant genetic resources (PGRs) encompass the total range of plant germplasm [i.e. hereditary material contained in every cell] available in the global gene pool." The reference to PGRFA is an emphasis on the use and relevance of strategic plants for propagation, food, and related agricultural productions "through farmer selection, conventional breeding and modern biotechnological techniques" (Ramarez et al., 2013, p. 39). Russian botanist Nikolai Vavilov's groundbreaking work demonstrates an uneven distribution of PGRs across the world. The Vavilov Centers of genetic diversity serve as a starting point for grasping the extent of the geographical and corresponding geopolitical disparity associated with the prevalence of world PGRs. Vavilov's outline of the geographical origins of various cultigens identifies 640 most significant human-tendered crops. Alfred W. Crosby notes, "five hundred crops in Vavilov's list belonged to the Old World [virtually the rest of the world excluding the Americas], and one hundred to the New" (2003, p. 170). On the basis of Vavilov's list, much fuss has been made about the genetic barrenness and richness of the so-called global north and south respectively. However, a critical study of the historic traffic, interactions and undergirding ecological dynamics of global genetic resources at the scale of both flora and fauna (Crosby, 2004; Kloppenburg, 1988) unveils the interdependence imperative, perhaps more than the geographic disequilibrium.

In what he calls a rough picture of the "overarching web of interdependence," Kloppenburg (1988, p. 180) provides an insightful analysis of Vavilov's Centers of genetic diversity. Out of the 10 centers, at 30.8 percent, West Central Asia has the lowest dependence indices (i.e. percentage of the region's food production derived from non-indigenous crop variety) in relation to the remaining nine regions. It is closely followed by Indo-Chinese at 33.2 percent, Hindustanean/West Central Asia at 48.6 percent, and Latin America at 55.6

percent. Of the rest, Chino-Japanese are credited with 62.8 percent; Africa 87.7 percent; Euro-Siberian 90.8 percent; and Australian and North America, both with 100 percent dependence indices. In quasi-cumulative terms, the Central Asiatic and Latin American regions are the originating sources of crops that account for 65.5 percent of the world's food crops. A combination of key food crops from Latin America (maize, potato, cassava, sweet potato) and two key crop varieties from West Central Asia (wheat and barley) results in the two regions alone being the source of six out of the seven most significant global food crops.

Holistically, six regions, corresponding to virtually all of the world's developing countries are the sources of plant genetic richness "that has provided the base for fully 95.7 percent of global food production" (Kloppenburg, 1988, p. 181). North America, Australia, Mediterranean, and Euro-Siberia – regions of concentration of world's industrialized countries (excluding Japan) – have virtually 100 percent dependence indices on non-indigenous crop diversity. Collectively, their indigenous crop base contributes only 4.5 percent of world crop variety. Yet, with a robust agro-economic base, these regions are today's global breadbaskets.

But the gene-rich and gene-poor geopolitical binary is far from being as simple as it sounds. Genetic dependence is an obligate universal phenomenon and not an exclusive albatross of a specific region (Halewood et al., 2013). For example, not many champions of Africa's genetic diversity appreciate the marginal 4 percent contribution officially ascribed to the region in the genetic base of global food crop production, not to mention the continent's 87.7 percent dependence index.

Perhaps the most striking aspect of the overarching web of interdependence is the pivotal position of Latin America. Latin America is the originating region of diversity of key agricultural and industrial crops, including maize, cassava (manioc), potato, sweet potato, cocoa, cotton, rubber, and tobacco. Add those crops to the two major ones of West Central Asiatic origin of diversity, namely wheat and barley, and the two regions are the source of 76.4 percent, 87.2 percent and 85.4 percent of food crop production from North America, Euro-Siberia and the Mediterranean respectively (Kloppenburg, 1998, p. 182). However, despite the unparalleled contribution of Latin America to global crop genetic diversity, Kloppenburg notes that the region "looks to Chino-Japanese crops (especially soybeans) for 15.8 percent of its food crop production" (1998, p. 182). He also adds that "[e]ven Africa makes significant contribution to regions as diverse as Hindustan (12.8 percent), Latin America (7.8 percent), and North America (3.6 percent) with millets and sorghums" (1988, p. 182).

The processes of global transmissions and dispersals of crop genetic diversities that account for the present web of interdependence have been variously documented from diverse disciplinary perspectives, including those that focus on ecology, biology, natural history, geography, colonialism, imperialism, global geo-economic politics, and various combinations of insights from these and other disciplines. Most of the accounts suggest that crop dispersals or plant genetic transmissions are both inevitable phenomena and incidences within the coterminous trail of human and other biotic experiences. Indeed biology remained a complementary aspect of the various scientific and political renditions of the accounts of the trans-Atlantic and trans-Pacific encounter, or the historic narratives of the multiple hemispheric contacts, including those between the so-called Old and New Worlds. Europe's foray into Africa, Asia, Latin America, North America, and the rest of the New World had complexly interlinked political, ecological, economic, colonial, religious, and, perhaps most importantly, biological undertones. For Alfred Crosby (2004), Jared Diamond (1997) and Richard Manning, there is a consensus that "at its root conquest was biological" before it was anything else (2004, p. 57).

Historically, human interventions through artificial selections and cultural mediations complemented the natural selection process and thus account for development of land races. The latter are traditionally or locally adapted and "genetically variable populations that exhibit different responses to pests, diseases and fluctuations in environmental conditions" (Kloppenburg, 1988, p. 46). Well before the colonial and industrial interventions that shaped the destiny of modern agriculture, domestication of plants and organized crop production occurred first among indigenous and local community peasantries of the third world (Hawkes, 1983). Their cultural practices and insights have remained critical for "the development within any one species of thousands of land races" (Kloppenburg, 1988, p. 46) and, subsequently, for agro-biodiversity, sustainable agriculture, and, ultimately, food security.

Agro-industry: monoculture and wealth creation without diversity

Dependence worldwide on only three major crops, maize, wheat and rice, is a symbolic indicator of the anemic state of global agro-biodiversity. As a notion, agro-biodiversity or biodiversity in agriculture attracts diverse conceptual emphasis. The exploration of those will not detain us here. In its elementary rendition, agro-biodiversity refers to the robustness in the dynamic or healthy state of "interactions between the environment, genetic resources and management systems and [epistemological] practices used by culturally diverse peoples … [in agricultural production]" (FAO, 2004, p. 1). It "encompasses the variability of animals, plants and micro-organisms that are necessary for sustaining key functions of the agro-ecosystem, including its structure and processes for, and in support of, food production and food security" (FAO, 2004, p. 1; FAO, 1999). Agro-biodiversity and agro-ecosystem are mutually reinforcing concepts. Agro-biodiversity comprises all components of biodiversity at all biotic levels, including genetic, species, and notably diversity of ecosystems conducive for agricultural production, which are designated agro-ecosystems.

Notwithstanding the complex abundance of human, ecological, and various other undercurrents conducive for agro-biodiversity, humankind exploits only an estimated mere 4 percent of higher plant species for food. Significantly, only a few industrialized countries of Euro-American heritage produce conservatively an estimated 67 and more than 70 percent of global wheat and maize exports, respectively. These two crops are the "most important of the big three grain crops that account for two-thirds of the world's nutrition" (Manning, 2004, p. 52). Therefore, although the so-called third world or underdeveloped parts of the world are the sources of global crop diversity, in practical terms, they are not recognized as major food producers. Rather, countries such as Canada, United States, Australia, and European Union states where the historic PGRs dependence indices are virtually 100 percent, constitute the world's breadbaskets of sorts.

The present anemic state of our agro-biodiversity and agro-ecological base reflects a continuation of structural, ideological and epistemic fault lines in agricultural production. The fifteenth-century foundational genetic revolution sparked mainly via the Columbian Exchange (Crosby, 2003) took on a more organized, intense and opportunistic tenor in the twentieth-century courtesy of the Green Revolution (GR) (Conway, 1999). Well before the global GR, the US was far ahead of many industrialized countries in aggressive and systematic collection of germplasm from centers of crop diversity. The US patent office's involvement in this practice dates far back to 1839 and it is characterized as the origin of public agricultural science (Kloppenburg, 1988, p. 15).

Under the urgency to remedy the post-World War II global hunger crisis, the US, mainly through its private sector, led by the Ford and Rockefeller Foundations embarked on intensive scientific research and development (R&D). The focus of the R&D was the introduction of diverse techniques, inputs such as synthetic fertilizers and pesticides to boost the development of high-yielding varieties of major crops and cereals. The GR supervised new agro-management processes including the use of irrigation and generous distribution of seeds of monocultures notably hybridized grains, especially maize.

Between the eighteenth and nineteenth centuries, the US and most of Europe had established robust public sector-driven R&D in agricultural science through universities and various research centers (Dutfield, 2008). However, the turn of the twentieth century marked the "developments in science [notably relating to the discovery of rDNA] that would catalyze the transformation of plant breeding and establish the hegemony of the scientist rather than the farmer as the principal producers of new crops varieties" (Kloppenburg, 1988, p. 66). At the time of the GR (1940s–1960s), the private sector had assumed substantial control of agricultural R&D in the United States, Europe and other industrialized countries.

The GR marked the twentieth-century creation of international agricultural research centers (IARCs),[2] as premier *ex situ* international seed banks under a global commons model. Now named the CGIAR-Consortium, the Centers started with only two, sponsored by the Ford and Rockefeller Foundations.[3] They have since increased to 15 under the auspices of the former Consultative Group on International Agricultural Research.[4] As part of the FAO agenda, they operate at the intersection of public and private sector R&D partnership for "reducing rural poverty, increasing food security, improving human health and nutrition, and ensuring sustainable management of natural resources" (CGIAR, n.d. p. 1).

In terms of significance, Kloppenburg (1988, p. 15) notes that the creation of the IARCs courtesy of the GR "was the product not only of an effort to introduce capitalism into the countryside but also of the need to collect systematically the exotic germplasm required by the breeding programs of the developed nations." Through the GR:

> Western science not only made the seed the catalyst for the dissolution and transformation of pre-capitalist agrarian social formations, it also staffed an institutional network that has served as a conduit for the extraction of plant germplasm from the Third World.
>
> (Kloppenburg, 1988, p. 15)

GR typifies the American vision of agriculture as an industrial, scientific, and capitalist endeavor. Agriculture evolved as an incidence of necessity for immigrant survival, and was further consolidated in the context of colonial exploitation of natural resources, slave labor and incidental trade and commerce (Schlebecker, 1976). In essence, agricultural industrialization was a capitalist endeavor. Just before the GR, America had a breakthrough in hybridization science and technology they applied to corn, arguably the world's most important food crop. That development which "shook the foundation of American agriculture" (Manning, 2004, p. 90) gave scientists and breeders an upper hand in the quest not only to control the obligate regenerative capacity of seeds but also to control farmers' practice of use and exchange of farm-saved seeds.

Further and later scientific and technological developments in agriculture that explore and exploit the role of genes or applications of recombinant rDNA insights (also known as agro-biotechnology) have reduced agricultural production to the control of seeds and their genes, a process in which genetic information or data are now highly prized proprietary assets. Naturally, genes of a few elite germplasm or monocultures (corn, wheat, rice, canola, potatoes, etc.), with global economic and market significance, as opposed to those of diverse land races, are the central focus of agricultural innovation and production. In the present and last centuries, the concentration on elite germplasm involves fast-paced and essentially corporate-driven R&D that pursues transformation of agriculture from its natural mission of food production to wealth creation (Manning, 2004).

Consequently, industrial agricultural production is now a complex chain of activities that deliberately creates and exploits sequences of opportunities in the preservation, marketing, branding, packaging, transportation, customization of food and allied products. Furthermore, it comprises and emboldens multifaceted actors in a value chain that relegates or marginalizes farmers and several considerations critical to agro-biodiversity. In its focus on wealth and capital creation – which are not automatically coterminous with food security and agro-biodiversity – industrial agriculture leverages on commercial opportunities associated with agro-chemical or multifarious agro-external inputs. Additionally, it exploits commercial opportunities at the sub-industrial borderline between food and medicine, especially pursuant to emergent but uncertain applications of agricultural biotechnology in the making or 'pharming' of so-called functional or medicinal foods (e.g. bio-fortification) (Oguamanam, 2011; Ryan-Harshman, 1997).

In a counterintuitive way, Manning (2004, p. 188) taps at the dissonance of industrial agriculture from food production when he provocatively suggests that "[w]hat agriculture grows is not food but commodities, grain not to eat but to store, trade, and process." He reflects further: "[c]onsider the range of plants humans consume, the hundreds of species. That is food. Consider that two-thirds of our calories come from wheat, rice and maize. Add sugar and you have nearly a complete picture of commodities." He contends that industrial agricultural commodities can be distinguished from real food that comes from *farming*.[5]

Equity gaps, law, and governance challenges over PGRs

Since the founding of the IARCs and their transformations, access to the benefits of R&D that use global PGRFA between developing and industrial countries has remained contentious. Implicated in the conflict are the roles of capital, law, and power to exclude non-industrial or informal actors in agricultural production. It is undisputed that "[n]o region can afford to isolate itself – or be isolated – from access to plant germplasm in other regions of diversity" (Kloppenburg, 1988, p. 184). That fact is at the heart of the interdependence of the global food system. For this simple reason, historically, PGRs are considered common heritage of humankind. As such, ideally, all dealings with them should take the nature of open and sustainable stewardship for inclusive innovation.

The point of departure, however, is that Western capitalist industrial and scientific approach to agriculture as symbolized in the agricultural model (supervised by the GR and its continuing transformation to the extant agricultural biotechnology) conceives common heritage to mean free access to genetic resources in ILC and centers of crop diversity. Owing to epistemic hubris, that model is aloof or insensitive to the contributions of alternative knowledge associated with *subcultural*[6] categories in their dealings with PGRs. Only the interventions of various forms of plant scientists and breeders within the Western scientific module are perceived as capable of adding value to naturally occurring germplasm.

Yet, undeniably, ILCs or traditional agriculturists in the regions of crop diversity were the first to domesticate crop species.[7] There is a world of difference between specific domestic/ated species and their wild relatives. The motivations of traditional farmers and agriculturists are not exclusively capitalist or wealth creation. Given the correlation between biological or genetic diversity and cultural diversity, agro-ecological necessity and cultural considerations are at the heart of the breeding activities of ILCs or traditional farmers.

The intersections of food, culture and identity, which are mostly evident in ILCs, implicate the often-underemphasized aspects of food security. As well, the intersections engage the role of traditional knowledge in agricultural innovation. In relation to formal plant scientists or breeders, no less demanding or exacting is the time and efforts which traditional farmers or agriculturalists expend in the domestication or progressive adaptations of raw germplasm into anthropomorphic beneficial varieties. Kloppenburg (1988, p. 46) observes that the objective of the early informal breeders and, of course, their progenies, was "not high yield but consistency of production. And the result of their efforts was development of greater inter- and intra-specific generic variability in particular and relatively confined geographic regions."

The failure to recognize values added to genetic resources by both immemorial and contemporary traditional agriculturalists, and descendants of ancient civilizations who pioneered crop domestication, has critical ramifications for food security and sustainable agro-biodiversity. Law, specifically intellectual property law, is a vital superstructure for this state of artificial disequilibrium that is at the heart of the governance challenge of global food security. Historical attempts through multiple regime platforms to recognize and reward the contributions of traditional agriculturists both in regard to their knowledge, innovation and practices associated with their land races, and their ability to partake in the benefits from outside innovation paradigms continues to be resisted.

Through the invocation of intellectual property rules and its limited application to only formal scientists' industrial crop improvement techniques, industrialized countries exploit the common heritage approach to PGRs. Using various historic channels, they indulge in unfettered acquisitions of exotic germplasm. Yet they insist on imposing various hurdles, including trade barriers and intellectual property tolls, i.e. patents, plant breeders' rights, licenses, etc. on stakeholders in the regions of crop genetic diversity. It does not matter that those stakeholders were the first to transform the freely obtained germplasm and that all others build upon their immemorial and dynamic stewardships.

The first putative arrangement toward equitable application of the common heritage approach was through the IARCs system of the 1960s. It was designed to enable American and, later, industrialized countries' researchers to acquire PGRs from centers of crop diversity and to freely make accessible to source countries any benefits arising from R&D on such materials under a trust arrangement. The system was rocked by crisis of confidence, especially in regard to the ambiguous role of private sector partners and their doubtful commitment to public interest management approach to the global pool of genetic resources under a common heritage principle (Oguamanam, 2012;

Mgbeoji, 2006). Arguably, lack of a clear legal framework, especially in regard to access to PGRs innovations under the IARCs to regions of crop diversity, and continued erosion of confidence in the system warranted the need for a legal framework.

That quest resulted in the 1983 International Undertaking on Plant Genetic Resources for Food and Agriculture. The Undertaking's objective was to "ensure that plant genetic resources of economic and/or social interest, particularly for agriculture, will be explored, preserved, evaluated and made available for plant breeding and scientific purposes" under the auspices of the FAO Commission on Genetic Resources for Food and Agriculture (CGRFA). It reiterated the notion of common heritage and free and unrestricted access to PGRs. Also, it recognized rights premised on the contributions of farmers at the centers of crop genetic origin in improving PGRs, i.e. 'farmers' rights.'

Yet the crisis of confidence over the equitable rendition of the common heritage principle over the utilization of global pool of PGRs continued, when major industrialized countries snubbed the Undertaking and refused to provide support for it. Between 1983 and 2001, concerted efforts at multiple regimes crystallized in some compromise between the needs of developing and industrialized countries resulting in important impacts on the global governance of PGRs. The hallmark of those efforts was a shift in the orientation or interpretational modification of the notion of free access to genetic resources and the consequential recalibration of the common heritage approach.

Between 1983 and 2001, changes in international environmental law, especially courtesy of the 1992 Rio Convention on Environment and Sustainable Development (Rio '92) were to alter conventional thinking on the notion of genetic resources as common heritage of humankind. Specifically, the Convention on Biological Diversity (CBD) recognized unequivocally "the sovereign rights of states over their natural resources, [and that] the authority to determine access to genetic resources rests with the national governments and is subject to national legislation" (Article 15). The CBD as well as other instruments from Rio '92, notably Agenda 21[8] also bolstered the pivotal nature of the knowledge, innovations and practices in ILCs in the improvement of PGRs. Article 8(j) of the CBD underscores the essence of those practices in conservation of biological resources and the need to involve their stakeholders in equitable access and benefit sharing over the utilizations of genetic resources. Through its elaborate provisions on indigenous knowledge, the 2007 United Nations Declaration on the Rights of Indigenous Peoples provided further momentum on the subject.

The CBD's endorsement of PGRs as sovereign property creates a conflict with the Undertaking's continued propagation of the common heritage approach. Not only was the Undertaking not supported by industrialized countries, whatever relevance it had was eroded by the CBD-led transformations in international environmental law in relation to the governance of PGRs. In the meantime, the CBD's major work programs on access and benefit sharing (ABS) over utilizations of genetic resources, and on knowledge innovations and practices of indigenous and local communities provided a conducive opportunity and impetus for developing countries to pressure the FAO for the transformation of the Undertaking onto a binding treaty instrument. The resulting document was the 2001 International Treaty on Plant Genetic Resources for Food and Agriculture (Plant Treaty). The treaty represents a global legal framework on the governance of PGRFA on the basis of sovereign rights of nations over their genetic resources within an equitable ABS scheme. The Plant Treaty reflects the inevitable nature of regime overlap and interface as part of the governance challenges of PGRFA and, by extension, food security (Oguamanam, 2015a).

To underscore the regime interface between the FAO and the CBD, Article 1 of Plant Treaty outlines its objectives as follows: "[C]onservation of and sustainable use of plant genetic resources for food and agriculture and fair and equitable sharing of benefits arising from their use, in harmony with the Convention on Biological Diversity for sustainable agriculture and food security." It establishes a multilateral system (MLS) for a global commons pool of PGRs under an ABS framework. The MLS scheme supervises the utilization of 64 annexed PGRs, including those under the control of CGIAR Consortium's IARCs. It also supports continuing addition of more PGRs into the common pool by way of new accessions. So far, the Governing Body of the treaty has consolidated its operational workings with the CGIAR Consortium. It has signed agreements with the IARCs that require the latter to comply with prototype standard material transfer agreements (SMTAs) and other equitable ABS requirements in their dealing with PGRs resources acquired from contracting parties. The SMTA is a contractual document that "articulates the fine details and terms of exchange of genetic resources in the MLS as prescribed under Article 12.4" of the Plant Treaty (Oguamanam, 2015a).

Central to the SMTAs is the requirement that products of R&D improvements arising from genetic resources acquired from the MLS's common pool would be made freely available. Hence the SMTA places an embargo on parties from claiming intellectual property rights (IPRs) over such products. Where parties insist upon making such claims, or otherwise commercializing their products, they are required to pay prescribed royalty fees into a trust account, the Benefit Sharing Fund (BSF). The BSF is dedicated to funding and supporting R&D needs, including agro-biodiversity and PGRs conservation practices, especially of stakeholders, in developing countries, least developed countries and countries with economies in transitions. These categories in some ways correlate with the historic centers of crop genetic diversity.

Not only has the regime overlap between the CBD and the FAO's Plant Treaty reimagined the common heritage principle over PGRs, it has also re-envisioned and consolidated the operative framework of a common's approach to PGRs from its historic origins in the 1960s under a novel ABS framework. The Plant Treaty is the first practical instrument for the implementation of ABS albeit with a limited focus on PGRFAs. Ten years after the Plant Treaty came into effect, the CBD consolidated the notion of equitable

ABS, extending it to all forms of genetic resources and associated local knowledge under the auspices of the 2010 Nagoya Protocol on Access to Genetic Resources and the Fair and Equitable Sharing of Benefits Arising from their Utilization to the Convention on Biological Diversity, which came into effect in 2014.

Intellectual property and escalation of inequity

Despite the strides in the CBD and FAO's Plant Treaty, significant constraints on agro-biodiversity and global food security can be located at the intersection of the two regimes with the Union for the Protection of New Varieties of Plants (UPOV) and the World Trade Organization's (WTO) Agreement on Trade Related Aspects of Intellectual Property Rights (TRIPS). These two instruments are pivotal sites for strengthening proprietary control of PGRs innovation under the industrial agricultural model. They do not accommodate alternative agricultural innovation and knowledge framework of traditional agriculturalists, notably ILC smallholder farmers in regions of crop diversity. Both the UPOV and the TRIPS agreement promote strong IPRs protection over R&D in PGRs. While the UPOV is exclusively dedicated to promoting the interests of plant breeders, via plant breeders' rights, TRIPS accommodates overlapping and concurrent protection for both plant breeders' and biotechnology patent rights even in developing countries with no pre-existing laws on intellectual property in agriculture. TRIPS represent a major international initiative for the extension of intellectual property protection over life forms – an unpopular idea in many ILCs at the centers of crop diversity.

The UPOV was established in 1961 simultaneous to the formation of the IARCs. It was the brainchild of European countries, especially those that had an early advantage in plant breeding. As an organization dedicated exclusively to safeguarding the proprietary interest of plant breeders, UPOV is premised on the epistemological license that hardly reckons with the contributions of farmers or traditional agriculturalists to improvements of PGRFAs. In the orientation of UPOV, farmers are free riders in the use of genetic resources, through their customary practice of sharing and exchanging of farm-saved seeds (Borowiak, 2004). Farmers were therefore seen as obstacles to a viable breeding industry. As such, they are targets of regulatory containment. It did not matter that in many ILCs at the centers of crop origin and diversity, farmers doubled as breeders. Under the UPOV, dichotomization of farming from breeding was critical (Dutfield, 2008) as agriculture is reduced to merely the control of the seed.

Not surprisingly, many industrialized country founders of the UPOV and the United States pushed back on two major defining features of the earlier International Undertaking, namely the accommodation of farmers' rights and the free and unrestricted access to PGRs. The result of that intervention was articulated in the 1989 FAO Conference, also known as Keystone Dialogues, which clarifies that plants that are subject of PBRs protection under the UPOV cannot be freely available as envisaged under the International Undertaking. This singular compromise marked a symbolic concession by developing countries on the validity of intellectual property in PGRs (Aoki and Luvia, 2007) well before the TRIPS agreement. Keystone also endorsed the idea that common heritage does not necessarily mean that access to PGRs would be free. Thereby, it prepared the ground for further transmutation of the concept to accommodate the right of states to determine terms of access to the genetic resources within their territories pursuant to their sovereign rights. Finally, Keystone did not overturn the International Undertaking's idea of farmers' rights. However, it preferred to leave the concept in its vague rendition in the Undertaking.

The extent to which the resulting transformation of the International Undertaking into the Plant Treaty further advanced the interests of farmers as stakeholders in food security and agro-biodiversity is debatable. However, whatever contributions the Plant Treaty may have made in regard to the farmers' rights are diminished. The Treaty preserved the pre-existing obligations of parties under the UPOV. For industrialized countries, a key obligation was the protection of breeders' interest, which is in conflict with those of farmers. In addition, under Article 12.3 (d) of the Plant Treaty, prohibition of proprietary claims over genetic resources or their genetic components obtained from the MLS applies only to those that are in the form in which they were received. This provision is among the most precarious aspects of the Plant Treaty as it lends the Treaty to multiple interpretations. This includes interpretations that allow the continued use of intellectual property as a discriminatory legal regime to support formal techno-scientific improvements on PGRs while sustaining the regime of disdain over the contributions of informal traditional agriculturalist and farmers at the centers of crop genetic diversity.

The latest revision of the UPOV, in 1991, places strict restrictions on a farmer's ability to use and exchange farm-saved seeds, even as it subjects any stakes farmers may have in PGRs to the overarching interest of breeders. Conversely, UPOV 1991 contains an elaborate range of breeders' rights, which includes their ability to exercise lien over farmers' harvests in some cases. In the unrelenting bid to privilege industrial approach to agricultural production and innovation, developed countries insist that the UPOV PBRs regime should be the default standard of protection. This is so notwithstanding that the TRIPS agreement recognizes the rights of individual states to enact own *sui generis* PBRs laws.

Similarly, the Plant Treaty vests on national governments the responsibility to implement farmers' rights. However, the expectation that developing countries can leverage on that responsibility may be naïve. Recently, aggressive proselytization of the UPOV PBRs has resulted in a significant increase in the number of developing countries that have signed onto the 1991 Act of the UPOV. Consequently, despite the Plant Treaty's elaborate, even if opaque, provisions on farmers' rights, many developing countries, even those with non-existent plant breeding industry, have ratcheted interest in protecting plant breeders' rights (Oguamanam, 2015b). This systemic marginalization of farmers has ramifications for food security and agro-biodiversity.

The food security and food system imperative

The evolution of food security as a concept between the early and the middle of the twentieth century in which the GR is also located, focused on a food "productionist policy paradigm" (Lang and Barling, 2012, p. 316). Under that paradigm, a global responsive and centralized strategy to tackle the burden of hunger through the deployment of capital and promotion of "a productionist agricultural technology solution" (Lang and Barling, 2012, p. 315) received priority. As evident in the GR, environmental sustainability issues, including agro-biodiversity, natural resource depletion, and various sociocultural considerations integral to the complexities of emergent global food needs attracted little critical attention in the strategy to mitigate food insecurity. For as long as food production was ratcheted up through industrial agriculture's high-yielding harvests that fed the world's hungry (Avery, 2001) all seemed well.

However, as a concept in continuing evolution, food security discourse has, without denying the productionist aspect, since ruptured. Tim Lang and David Barling (2012) amply synthesize the complex perspectives on food security in their appraisal of the concept. They conclude that the evolutionary trajectory of food security discourse bodes a return to first principles "in terms that were first debated in the late 18th century Enlightenment: what sort of food system is environmentally, socially and economically sustainable?" (p. 321). From a food systems approach, then, multifarious considerations emerge, especially those that are hardly addressed under capitalist and market-oriented monocultural industrial agricultural production paradigm.

Aside from its exposure of systemic issues at the intersections of modern agriculture and global food supply, a food systems approach brings into contention the roles of much more diverse actors, including women, smallholder traditional farmers, or traditional agriculturalists. Their alternative epistemic methods of dealing with diverse landraces, and their conceptions of agriculture as a cultural and social cohesion process as opposed to market and capital-driven industrial production enterprise for wealth creation are equally of interest in determining equitable governance approaches to food security. In this model, deeper regard for agro-biodiversity and agro-ecological considerations provide an important counterpoint to industrial monoculture and help to highlight the health concerns over nutritionally narrow global caloric base (Altieri, 2003). Those considerations are aspects of evolving conceptions of food security that are underexplored in productionist paradigm, which now is a subject of fading integrity.

Systemic control of global food supplies via industrial models of food production, supply and marketing chains account, in part, for the globalization of environmental and health pressures associated with food consumption. Dependence on a few industrially produced monocultures and livestock excessively supplied and consumed put pressure on the environment and agro-ecosystems through an increase in greenhouse gas emissions and the overall high costs of energy and external agro-inputs, not to mention costs of operating agro-allied industries. In addition, superfluous production and consumption of industrial monoculture foodstuff, especially meat and dairy, contribute to the epidemic of obesity; first in the developed world, and now rapidly spreading to developing countries. As many countries and regions, notably China, India, and Brazil, increase their rank of new affluent middle class, they make nutritional transitions – altering their diets toward "more complex, sweeter, fattier, processed foods, which in turn generate diet-related ill-health patterns associated with the affluent" (Lang and Barling, 2012, p. 314). The perpetuation of this pattern demonstrates the dissonance between increased food production and food security within a distressed global food system.

Ironically, the integration of agricultural production and food supplies into the globalized trade regime has limited the role of states and emboldened those of corporations in decision making over policies on food security. Under the extant globalized trade order, the ability of ILC farmers to leverage on growing varieties of nutritionally rich traditional landraces to boost dietary and health benefits runs into a brick wall vis-à-vis capital's focus on the production and marketing of lucrative monocultures. In addition, as the global intellectual property in agriculture privileges breeders and other hi-tech actors, it undergirds intense corporate concentration in agro-pharmaceutical and allied industries. There is paucity of support for local production of culturally appropriate food by peasant farmers.

Proprietary right holders in agriculture, especially plant breeders, want to respond that breeders' rights do not constrain ILC smallholder farmers' liberty to use their traditional land races any way they deem fit to advance their food security. What they ignore, is that when there is no concrete incentive for farmers' value added to PGRs, any such improvements are open to appropriation by breeders whose rights are legally secured and privileged (Oguamanam, 2015b). Moreover, smallholder farmers continue to abandon their diverse local varieties for genetically uniform and often proprietary alternatives. Apart from lack of incentives at local and international levels to support their stewardship of traditional land races, the latter are regarded as inferior by local bureaucrats and are rarely included in publicly approved seed lists (Dutfield, 2008, p. 42).

Under the present design of global agricultural economy, ILCs at the historic centers of origin of crop genetic diversity have little control over their food and dietary preferences. Their alternative epistemic approaches to agricultural production and propensity of such methods for moderating biodiversity loss and reinvigorating interests in complex structural environmental factors that are critical for the sustainability of modern agricultural production system are hardly engaged. These and various other considerations are integral aspects of food security from a food systems lens. And they are collectively linked to agro-biodiversity and agro-ecological ethics of sustainability (Altieri, 2003).

Because of the foregoing gaps, food security remains a contested proposition in regard to its conceptual foundation and with respect to the operative emphasis of any proponent of the concept across time, space, and interest. Nonetheless, more holistic approaches shift the discourse from a consumerist template into one that melds multiple considerations, including but not limited to, environmental sustainability, epistemic pluralism, economic and trade justice, health, nutrition and dietary diversity; and agro-biodiversity, etc.

Central to the progressive evolution of food security is the idea of food sovereignty. Essentially an ILC smallholder peasant farmer-led thinking, food sovereignty seeks a change in the control of food from current globalized network of transnational corporations to smallholder farmers. It allows communities, peoples, and cultures to take ownership over their food systems, as well as leverage upon improved rural infrastructures and knowledge systems, including their own, to deploy agricultural knowledge to produce food (GRAIN, 2012; Shiva, 2007, p. 50). A food sovereign model does not deny the obligate interdependence of the global supply of PGRs; however, it rejects the strategic elimination of traditional farmers by industry and capital as stakeholders in agriculture production. Additionally, because it is a grounded, capacitation, and participatory model, food sovereignty is capable of addressing inherent genetic erosion of the present monocultural profile of global agriculture by reinvigorating interest in the generic richness of traditional land races.

Conclusion: reintegrating farmers into the global food system

A major feature of the dominance of an industrial agricultural model in the global food system is its relocation of power and influence from off the land and off traditional agriculturists and smallholder peasant farmers, to complex layers of actors that are empowered by capital. As a consequence, smallholder farmers and their various contextual parallels across the globe are systematically displaced in modern agriculture. For the most part, they are presently left with little option, if any, to practice agriculture both as a way of life and a form of ecological stewardship and social cohesion. Farmers have been indirectly coerced onto the global monocultural bandwagon of industrial agriculture, as evident in their progressive jettisoning of the traditional landraces, because of radically shrinking space for their (farmers') relevance and operation in the global food system (Oguamanam, 2007). Industrialized countries have made the shift from traditional to industrial farming or agriculture. However, that transition came at expensive costs to agro-biodiversity and agro-ecological sustainability. Consequently, it has perpetuated legal and cultural hierarchies of power and dependence of the global south – the traditional centers of crop genetic diversity – on the global north with a negative outcome for food security.

The evolutionary trajectory of agriculture in Europe and especially in US and the other parts of the New World demonstrates that agriculture is first a necessary tool for immigrant survival. It later transformed into an opportunistic instrument for servicing industry, trade, and colonialism whereof the deployment of capital enhanced agriculture's potential as a pivotal enterprise in wealth creation. Historically, in Europe, the US and virtually all industrialized countries, agriculture transitioned from land-based labor-intensive experience to a mechanized practice that enhanced rapid de-ruralization of those societies. Unlike in most ILCs in the global south, in Europe and its colonial outposts in the New World, there are no robust affinities that link people, land, culture, and agriculture. The transition to agro-industrialization fitted with the pragmatic logic of capital. Moreover, the relocation of labor from land was readily cushioned through complex capital-driven stakeholders, including transporters, marketers, packagers, producers, processors, wholesalers, warehousemen, retailers, and open-ended actors within the agricultural supply and value chain. Since the 1900s there has been a progressive decline in the farming populations in many of those societies from 60 percent to, presently, under 1 percent (Jöhr, 2012; Bello, 2004) without any correlating impact on their ability to boost food production.

The replication of monocultural capital-driven agricultural models in ILCs or among peasant farming communities in the south, for example, the Philippines, Mexico, parts of China and Africa, has not produced the same results as it did in the West (Bello, 2009). In those countries and regions the displacement of peasant agricultural populations, who have cultural affinities with land, has resulted in social stress and chronic poverty and, often, political rupture (Bello, 2009). As well, such attempt reflects the globalization of monoculture and a linear epistemic and ideological model of agricultural production that has yet to address agro-biodiversity and agro-ecological gaps, which are vital to sustainability and food security.

Today, despite the strides of industrial agriculture, 80 percent of the world's estimated 1 billion hungry (located mainly in Asia and sub-Sahara Africa) still depend on smallholder farmers for their food needs (FAO, 2012). The GR's focus on the formalization of agricultural production in traditional communities, as well as its support for those with credit, the politically well connected and those with formal title to land, historically, pressured and exposed ILC farmers to negative conditions and consequences. Several decades later, the globalization of trade has stamped huge footprints of transnational corporate convergence in agro-biotechnology in a manner that escalates the stress on traditional farmers. Under extant IPRs, smallholder farmers are targeted as objects of regulatory containment and suppression. But history bears out their resilience. Rather than fade, hope is on a resurgent plane over the role of smallholder farmers in attaining a food secure world. Lang and Barling (2012) capture the sentiment when they note that "a counter-narrative has emerged ... [which] proposes that small-scale farming is important for land care; that smallholder and female-run productivity per hectare can be high; and there is more social value in raising their output further than in driving them from the land" (p. 318). For them, "[t]his revitalizes an old element in classical economics: how to define efficiency. Should it be in capital terms or ecological terms, in output per unit of labour or per hectare?" (p. 318).

An equitable integration of smallholder farmers into the global food system in a manner that empowers and not problematizes the traditional practices associated with their diverse landraces is important for food security and sustainability. Efforts to support the rights of ILC farmers and address the agricultural needs of rural communities in developing countries and regions of crop diversity under the auspices of the International Treaty are encouraging. But they remain limited in terms of real and potential impacts. They can easily be neutralized by the phenomenon of offshore agricultural land grab that is rapidly displacing smallholder farmers in Africa and elsewhere (Oguamanam, 2015b). At best, such efforts under the Plant Treaty are symbols of compromise within the global political economics of agriculture that have historically accentuated the marginalization of smallholder farmers.

Aside from minimal international effort, developing countries and regions of crop diversity have to be proactive to strategically enhance the integration of the diverse land races of ILCs into the official seed system. Through strong national and regional collaborative approaches in the global areas of crop genetic diversity and homes of ILC smallholder farmers, it is possible to stem the tide of genetic erosion. Similarly, it is feasible to reverse ongoing progressive jettisoning of the traditional landraces and farmers' fascination with industrial agriculture's high-yielding monocultures. There is still wiggle room within the global legal architecture for the governance food system to advance a bottom-up approach to food security via the food sovereignty model and related frameworks. Under such models, it is conceivable to reposition smallholder farmers, enabling them to capitalize on their model of agricultural production; one that represents an agro-epistemic and agro-ecological niche not filled by industrial agriculture (Manning, 2004, p. 191). The reinvigoration of smallholder farmers as stakeholders in agricultural production and food security within the global food system alongside progress in industrial agriculture would provide the basis for reconsideration of efficiency at a meeting point between capital and ecological imperative. Agriculture can still be a capital and wealth creation endeavor. But it can be moderated by cultural and ecological imperatives under an equitable global food system. The farmer must not be inhibited from what farmers do: grow food. And other stakeholders in agricultural production do not necessarily have to operate at the expense of farmers and food security of the world's most vulnerable.

Notes

1 The definition is credited to the World Food Summit in Rome, 1996.
2 Specifically, the International Rice Research Institute and the International Centre for the Improvement of Maize and Wheat.
3 Ibid.
4 In 2008, the organization officially changed its name to just "CGIAR", which it claims reflects some transformations in its modus operandi.

5 Manning (2004) makes a bold and admittedly inchoate distinction between farming and agriculture; and between food and commodities. According to him, while farming is the business of growing food, healthy food, that is, agriculture produces commodities on industrial scale for purpose of wealth creation in which food (not necessarily healthy food) is an incidental but not the most important part (pp. 188–190).

6 That is within an analytical framework in which the Euro-American is the dominant culture and the rest are ascribed the status of alternatives or simply 'othered' or called subcultures

7 Manning (2004), however, contends that agriculture (which would include domestication of plants and animals) evolved "independently in at least five different places on the planet." He avers that humans did not create agriculture "in a very real sense, it created us. Plants domesticated us" (p. 186).

8 Agenda 21 is a statement of general governance principles for global environmental protection from sustainable development prism for the 21 century arising from the United Nations Conference on Environment and Development, Rio de Janeiro, Brazil, June 3–14, 1992.

References

Agenda 21 (1992). Retrieved from https://sustainabledevelopment.un.org/content/documents/Agenda21.pdf

Agreement on Trade Related Aspects of Intellectual Property Rights. (1994). Annex IC of the Marrakesh Agreement Establishing the World Trade Organization, 1896 UNTS 299; 33 ILM 1197. Retrieved from www.wto.org/english/tratop_e/trips_e/t_agm0_e.htm

Altieri, M. A. (2003). The Case against Agricultural Biotechnology. Briefing Paper, Croptwatch. Retrieved from www.corpwatch.org/article.php?id=7030

Aoki, K. and Luvai, K. (2007). Reclaiming Common Heritage Treatment in the International Plant Genetic Resources Regime Complex. *Michigan State Law Review*, 35.

Avery, D. (2001) Genetically Modified Organisms Can Help Save the Planet, in Gerald Nelson (ed.), *Genetically Modified Organisms in Agriculture*. San Francisco: Academic Press.

Bello, W. (2009). *The Food Wars*. London: Verso.

Borowiak, C. (2004). Farmers' Rights: Intellectual Property Regimes and the Struggle over Seeds. *Politics and Society*, 32(4), 511–543.

CGIAR (n.d.). About Us. Retrieved from www.cgiar.org/who-we-are

Convention on Biological Diversity (1992). Text of the CBD. Retrieved from www.cbd.int/convention/text/default.shtml

Conway, G. (1999). *The Doubly Green Revolution: Food for all in the Twenty-First Century*. Auburn: Comstock.

Crosby, A. W. (2004). *Ecological Imperialism: The Biological Expansion of Europe, 900–1900*. New York: Cambridge University Press.

Diamond, J. (1997). *Guns, Germs, and Steel: The Fates of Human* Societies. New York: Norton.

Dutfield, G. (2008). Turning Plant Varieties into Intellectual Property: The UPOV Convention. In G. Tansey and T. Rajotte (eds.), *The Future Control of Food: A Guide to International Negotiations and Rules on Intellectual Property, Biodiversity and Food Security*. London: Earthscan.

FAO (1999). Agricultural Biodiversity. Paper presented at Conference on Multifunctional Character of Agriculture and Land, Background Paper no. 1, Maastricht, the Netherlands. www.fao.org/mfcal/pdf/bp_int.pdf

FAO (2003). Trade Reforms and Food Security: Conceptualizing the Linkages. Retrieved from ftp.fao.org/docrep/fao/005/y4671e/y4671e00.pdf

FAO (2004). What Is Agrobiodiversity? Retrieved from ftp.fao.org/docrep/fao/007/y5609e/y5609e00.pdf

FAO (2006). Food Security (Policy Brief no. 1) Retrieved from ftp.fao.org/es/ESA/policybriefs/pb_02.pdf

FAO (2012). Smallholders and Family Farmers. *Sustainable Pathways*. Retrieved from www.fao.org/fileadmin/templates/nr/sustainability_pathways/docs/Factsheet_SMALLHOLDERS.pdf

GRAIN (2012). The Great Food Robbery: How Corporations Control Food, Grab Land and Destroy the Planet. Retrieved from www.grain.org/article/entries/4501-the-great-food-robbery-a-new-book- from-grain

Halewood, M., I. Noriega and S. Louafi (eds.), *Crop Genetic Resources as a Global Commons: Challenges in International Law and Governance*. London: Earthscan.

Hawkes, J. G. (1983). *The Diversity of Crop Plants*. Cambridge, MA: Harvard University Press.

International Treaty on Plant Genetic Resources for Food and Agriculture (2001). [Plant Treaty]. Retrieved from www.planttreaty.org/content/texts-treaty-official-versions

International Union for the Protection of New Varieties of Plants (2011). UPOV Lex. Retrieved from www.upov.int/upovlex/en/acts.html

Kloppenburg Jr, J. R. (1988). *First the Seed: The Political Economy of Plant Biotechnology 1492–2000*. New York: Cambridge University Press.

Lang, T and Barling, D. (2012). Food Security and Sustainability: Reformulating the Debate. *Geographical Journal*, 178(4), 313–326.

Manning, R. (2004). *Against the Grain: How Agriculture has Hijacked Civilization*. New York: North Point Press.

Nagoya Protocol. (2010). Access to Genetic Resources and Fair and Equitable Sharing of Benefits Arising from their Utilization to the Convention on Biological Diversity. Retrieved from www.cbd.int/abs/text/default.shtml

Oguamanam, C. (2007). Tension on the Farm Fields: The Death of Traditional Agriculture? *Bulletin of Science, Technology and Society*, 7(4), 260–273.

Oguamanam, C. (2011). Toward a Constructive Engagement: Agricultural Biotechnology as a Public Health Incentive in Less Developed Countries. *Journal of Food Law and Policy*, 7(2), 257–296.

Oguamanam, C. (2012). *Intellectual Property in Global Governance: A Development Question*. London: Routledge.

Oguamanam, C. (2015a). Implementing the International Treaty on Plant Genetic Resources for Food and Agriculture – A Regulatory and Intellectual Property Outlook. In E. Marden and N. Godfrey (eds.), *Innovation in Agricultural Genomics: Overcoming Complexities in the Intellectual Property Regulatory Complex*. Vancouver: UBC Press.

Oguamanam, C. (2015b). Breeding Apples for Oranges: Africa's Misplaced Priority over Plant Breeders' Rights. *Journal of World Intellectual Property, Journal of World Intellectual Property 8 AUG 2015 DOI: 10.1111/jwip.12039*. Retrieved from http://papers.ssrn.com/sol3/papers.cfm?abstract_id=2553363

Oguamanam, C. (2015 forthcoming). Sustainable Development in the Era of Bioenergy and Agricultural Land-Grab. In S. Alam, S. Atapattu, C. G. Gonzalez and J. Razzaque (eds.), *International Environmental Law and the Global South*. Cambridge: Cambridge University Press.

Ramirez, M, Ortiz, R., Taba, S., Sebastián, L., Peralta, E., Williams, D. E., Ebert, A. W. and Vézina, A. (2013). Demonstrating Interdependence in Plant Genetic Resources for Food and Agriculture. In M. Halewood, I. Noriega and S. Louafi (eds.), *Crop Genetic Resources as a Global Commons: Challenges in International Law and Governance*. London: Earthscan.

Ryan-Harshman, M. (1997). Food Biotechnology: Food Industry, Nutrition and Public Health. *Proceedings of the Nutrition Society*, 56, 845–854.

Schlebecker, J. T. (1976). *Whereby We Thrive: A History of American Farming, 1606–1972*. Iowa: Iowa State University Press.

Shiva, V. (ed.) (2007). *Manifestos on the Future of Food*. Cambridge, MA: South End Press.

United Nations Declaration on the Rights of Indigenous Peoples. (2007). UN General Assembly Resolution, adopted October 2, 2007, A/RES/61/925. Retrieved from www.refworld.org/docid/471355a82.html

9 Contaminated land law of China

A possible way to achieve food safety?

Xiaobo Zhao[1]

Introduction

Food safety has become a deep-set concern in China. Frequently reported cases of food poisoning have deepened the spreading fears among the Chinese people. It has been reported that Cadmium-contaminated rice, for example, which was first identified in South China's Guangdong province in 2013, has found its way onto people's dining tables (Wong, 2013). As estimated by the Ministry of Environmental Protection (MEP) of China, one-sixth of arable land (about 50 million acres) in China has suffered soil pollution (Ministry of Environmental Protection, 2013). More than 8 million acres of China's farmlands are so polluted that they are now not suitable for planting crops (Wong, 2013). At the same time, more than 13 million tons of crops harvested each year were contaminated with heavy metals and 22 million acres affected by pesticides (Wong, 2013). This is a clear reminder that soil pollution, which has been continuously accumulating over the past decades, is eroding the foundation of the country's food safety and becoming a real threat to the public health. This is important, as China has 22 percent of the global population, but only 13 percent of the world's arable land (FAOSTAT Database, 2014). Land contamination and food safety therefore have the potential to substantially threaten the food security of the nation. The increasing amount of contaminated land has been identified as the main contributor to the ongoing food safety crisis in China.

This chapter looks at the intrinsic connections between two most significant issues—the land contamination and food safety crisis faced by China. Based on a consensus that land contamination is one of the major contributors to food contamination, this chapter will argue that proper systems to improve the quality of arable lands and food in China should be incorporated into the contaminated land legislation at a national level. The structure of this chapter is as follow: first, it briefly reviews the current scale, causes, and impacts of soil contamination in China; second, there is a discussion as to how contamination laws can be used to improve the food safety situation in China; and, third, the recommendation of several regimes that should be considered by Chinese environmental legislatures and policymakers, based on a comparative study to world approaches with regard to contaminated land management is made.

Land contamination and its impacts on food safety in China

Status quo of land contamination in China

For a long time, land contamination in China was perceived as relatively rare. But today, a growing number of people have started to realize that land contamination is a widespread problem as inherent consequences of historical industrial and waste disposal practices. From 2005 to 2013, the MEP and the Ministry of Land Resources jointly conducted the first National Soil Pollution Survey, which covered 2.4 million square miles of land across mainland China (Wong, 2013). In April 2014, the MEP released the results of the survey. The report showed that approximately 16.1 percent of the country's total lands, including 19.4 percent of farmland, had been polluted. Human industrial and agricultural activities are considered to be the main sources of land pollution. More specifically, factory waste products, irrigation of land by polluted water, the improper use of fertilizers and pesticides, and the breeding of livestock have all contributed to the farmland pollution (Wong, 2013). The survey also found that 82.8 percent of the polluted land was contaminated by inorganic materials such as cadmium, nickel, and arsenic. The levels of these materials in the soil have risen sharply since the 1990s. The level of cadmium had risen by 50 percent in the southwest, 10 percent in coastal areas, and 40 percent in other regions. While the geographical factors have been considered, the overall soil contamination situation in southern China is much worse than in northern China (Ministry of Environmental Protection of PRC, 2014).

Causes of land contamination in China

Generally speaking, land contamination could be caused by municipal and industrial pollution activities and farming practices. In the context of a sharp rise in economic and social development over the past decade, the cumulative effect of industrial and agricultural pollution is thought to be the main reason for nationwide land contamination (Ministry of Environmental Protection of PRC, 2014). Pollution from mining industries, the overuse of fertilizers and pesticides, and the polluted water irrigation on arable lands, are the main contributors of land contamination.

In China, farming practices have been identified as one of the main causes of land contamination and the rise of adverse effects is being noticed by increasing numbers of people (Grazer, 2009; Weili et al., 2004). Common practices include the over application of pesticides, chemical fertilizers, animal and poultry excrement and sludge, sewage irrigation, discarded residues of agricultural plastic membranes and mulching. Most of these practices can be classified as nonpoint source pollution (NSP) (Ritter and Shirmohammadi, 2001, p. 1; Zhao, 2013).[2] In China, nearly one-third to half of all NSP arises from farming practices. It was suggested by an incomplete investigation in 2009, that about 100,000 km^2 of agricultural land has been polluted by pesticides, chemical fertilizer, wastewater irrigation, heavy metal pollution, and plastic film (Environmental Issues and Countermeasures Facing New Rural Development in China Special Policy Group, 2006). Among others, researchers have pointed out that the over application of chemical pesticides and wastewater irrigation is two of the most important causes of agricultural land contamination in China (Wendong, 2007; Department of Research Center of the State Council, 2006).

China is the world's main chemical pesticide producer and the world's largest consumer of chemical pesticides and it is unsurprising that the over-application of chemical pesticides has become one of the main sources of land contamination in China. In 2007, for the first time China exceeded the US and became the world's largest chemical pesticide producer, with production totaling 173,000 tons (Zhao, 2013, p. 14). As the National Statistics Bureau of China (NSBC) revealed, there was a notable increase in the yield of chemical pesticides from 2001 to 2010. According to the MEP, the total application of chemical pesticides in China in 1983 was 862,000 tons and this rose to over 1.31 million tons in 2006. With an average of 13.97kg/ha applied to agricultural land this is higher than the rate applied to land in developed countries (Conradie and Field, 2000). By 2008, the amount of chemical pesticides used in China had risen to approximately 1.672 million tons (National Bureau of Statistics of China and Ministry of Environmental Protection of China, 2009).

The low efficiency of chemical pesticides is another problem. Although the total amount of chemical pesticides applied in China is extremely high, the effectiveness is as low as 30 percent, which means approximately 70 percent of the pesticides applied is directly diffused into the environment and accumulated in soils (Gould and Lewis, 2009). In some high-yielding districts, the frequency of spraying pesticides may be as high as 30 times per year, with the average amount exceeding 300 kg/ha, and this is reportedly increasing at a rate of 10 percent per year (Environmental Issues and Countermeasures Facing New Rural Development in China Special Policy Group, 2006). Meanwhile, a notable feature of chemical application in China is that high toxicity chemicals account for a prodigious proportion of the products applied. Research has shown that more than 30 types of organophosphorus pesticides with a total weight of 200,000 tons is applied in China, with more than 80 percent severely toxic (Environmental Issues and Countermeasures Facing New Rural Development in China Special Policy Group, 2006). In addition, persistent organic pollutants (POPs), such as the Polychlorinated Biphenyls (PCBs) and polynuclear aromatic hydrocarbons (PAHs), compound pollution and worsen the land contamination situation in the main corn producing areas (Project Group of National Program on the Development of Basic Research, 2007). POPs were widely detected in the topsoil of the Yangtze River Delta with an average radium concentration higher than the traditional organo-chlorine pesticides (such as DDT) and were considered to be a serious new territorial soil contamination problem (Project Group of National Program on the Development of Basic Research, 2007). Researchers then recommended special attention be paid to farmlands within the Yangtze River Delta, which are thought to be the most important crop lands in China (Project Group of National Program on the Development of Basic Research, 2007).

Large-scale wastewater irrigation had been encouraged in China for years, especially in the northern areas, which suffer from water shortages (Lei Luo et al., 2009). Every year, China generates a huge amount of contaminated wastewater. Until 1998, over 36,200 km^2 of land was irrigated with farmland wastewater and this accounted for 7.33 percent of the overall irrigation area and 10 percent of the surface water irrigation area. These amounts are 1.6 times larger than that used at the beginning of the 1980s (1977–1982) (Wendong, 2007). By 2009, the amount of contaminated wastewater generated in China was 5.89 billion tons, of which industrial wastewater and municipal sewage sludge accounted for 2.43 billion tons and 3.55 billion tons respectively (MEP, 2010).

Land contamination and food safety crisis of China

In China, food safety is a concept of multiple dimensions. Typically, it contains two important aspects; 'safety of food quality' and 'food security.' Safety of food quality generally refers to 'quality and safety' of agriculture products, which Art. 2 of the Agricultural Product Quality and Safety Law (2006) of China defines as 'the quality of an agricultural product meets the requirements for guaranteeing human health and safety.' The United Nations' Food and Agricultural Organization (FAO) defines 'food security' as:

> All people, at all times, have physical and economic access to sufficient, safe and nutritious food to meet their dietary needs and food preferences for an active and healthy life.
>
> (FAO, 1996)

It is well known that agricultural production highly depends on the quality of the soil. Without soil, land plants could not grow, and animals could not survive. But without healthy soil, pollutants may enter the food chain and cause harm to human beings and livestock. Land contamination, particularly farming land contamination, is now threatening the quality of agriculture products, as well as the food security of the nation.

Land contamination has greatly damaged the taste and quality of agricultural products and, in some cases, made them unsuitable for consumption because of the presence of chemical residues. Hunan Province, a large rice-growing area in the middle of China, has some of the worst polluted soils because it is one of China's top producers of nonferrous metals. Hunan produced 16 percent of the country's rice in 2012. However, in 2003, officials in Guangdong Province found that some rice had excessive levels of cadmium and most of that rice was from Hunan Province (Wongapril, 2014).

Land contamination does not only raise concerns for domestic food quality, but also for the countries that import Chinese food, including the USA.

According to a testimony given before a subcommittee of the House Foreign Affairs Committee in May 2013, food products of Chinese origin have dominated certain areas of the USA food market (Ching-Fu, 2013).[3] The level of Chinese food imports into the USA is also expected to increase by about 10 percent per annum until 2020. As a result of the huge volumes of foods imported into the USA each year, in 2011 the USA's Food and Drug Administration was only able to inspect around 2.3 percent of the total imports from China (Ching-Fu, 2013).

Tobacco is the most important economic crop in China and has also been polluted by land contamination. As some recent studies have revealed, the quality of tobacco grown has degraded. In 2010, cigarettes produced in China compared to other countries revealed that heavy metals in 13 Chinese cigarette brands have exceeded the relevant standards. For some Chinese brands, the level of lead, cadmium, and arsenic detected was nearly three times that of Canadian cigarette brands (*People's Daily Online*, 2010).[4] This means that approximately 350 million smokers in China have been potentially exposed to health risks arising from land contamination (*People's Daily Online*, 2010).

Land contamination, together with salinization, desertification, erosion, and radioactive pollution (Li, 2006), has increased the shortage of arable lands and accordingly endangered the food security of China. Food security has been a principal mission and a primary state objective for the early twenty-first century in China. Environmental pollution, population growth, and climate change are all factors that have worsened the food security of China. Scientists indicate that around 36 million ha of agricultural land have been contaminated by organics as petrochemicals, pesticides, and polycyclic aromatic hydrocarbons (Chen, 2002). Over recent decades, a number of traditional residential areas, like the Taihu Lake area, Yangtze Delta the Pearl Delta have been suffering serious pollution and eutrophication problems (Enfeng et al., 2005), due to the increasing discharge of heavy metal pollutants like Pb, Cu, and Zn into the basin (Jin et al., 2010).

The relationship between land contamination and food safety is obvious. Using wastewater irrigation as an example, heavy metals, such as mercury, cadmium, lead, chromium and arsenic, nitrogen, organochlorine, and phenols enter the soil when farmlands are irrigated by wastewater. Although it only affects a small percentage of the total arable area, those districts under wastewater irrigation are the main areas producing corn, vegetables, and fruits in China (Wendong, 2007). In addition, the over application of nitrogenous fertilizer has resulted in the nitrate content exceeding the allowable limit in agricultural products, while some phosphate fertilizers have increased the concentration of heavy metals in vegetables. One survey revealed that in China, daily arsenic intake rate was 120 percent above the acceptable limit declared by the World Health Organization (WHO) (Environmental Issues and Countermeasures Facing New Rural Development in China Special Policy Group, 2006).

It should be noted that the growing population, accelerated urbanization, existing water scarcity, and ongoing climate change are all factors that have worsened the food security situation of China. At current rates of growth, China's population will increase by 125 million by 2025. In this scenario, China will have to expand its agricultural output by 25 percent to match this population growth, yet this will have to occur in the face of increased urban and suburban development, which is encroaching on arable land (Wong, 2010).

Regulatory frameworks addressing the contaminated land issue

The Chinese government has established a comprehensive environmental law system to address environmental protection issues. The regulatory framework comprises: (1) the Constitution of China; (2) Environmental Protection Law (amended 2014); (3) other national-wide laws and regulations; (4) decrees issued by MEP (former SEPA); (5) local legislation; and (6) environmental protection standards.

Under this framework, the Constitution and environmental laws have addressed air, water, solid waste, and noise pollution. Some of these documents have been amended several times to take into account the dynamic social and economic circumstances. Land contamination, however, didn't draw much attention from the public before the 1980s (Xiaomiao, 2009). Although there are no specific laws to deal with soil contamination in China,[5] existing laws and regulations can be applied to soil contamination issues.

The Constitution of the People's Republic of China

The Constitution of the People's Republic of China is the overarching law of China.[6] Provision for environmental protection was first inserted into the Constitution in 1978. The Constitution states in Article 9 that:

> The State ensures the rational use of natural resources and protects rare animals and plants. The appropriation or damage of natural resources by any organisation or individual by whatever means is prohibited.

In addition, Art. 26 provides that: 'the State protects and improves the living environment and the ecological environment, and prevents and remedies pollution and other public hazards,' and Art. 10 thus 'organizations and individuals using land must ensure its rational use.'

The Constitution promotes protecting natural resources and controlling environmental pollution, and more importantly, it emphasizes that the protection of the soil environment is the duty of the state.

Environmental Protection Law of the People's Republic of China (as amended in 2014)

The Environmental Protection Law of the People's Republic of China[7] (EPL) is the principal law for environmental protection in China. In April 2014, the

EPL was amended and the new law came into force on January 1, 2015. Article 2 of the EPL defines 'land' as one element of the ecosystem. Article 4 demonstrates the principle of coordinated development between economic construction, social progress, and environmental protection, and defines the rights and duties for both governments and individuals with regard to environmental protection. Article 33 emphasizes that China should enhance the management of air, water, and soil, and establish relevant mechanisms to allow for investigation, monitoring and access and remediation. In addition, it also provides that the people's governments at all levels shall provide for the protection of the agricultural environment by preventing and controlling soil pollution, desertification and other negative impacts to land. One way to do this, as suggested by Art. 33 is by preventing and controlling plant disease and insect pests through the rational application of chemical fertilizers, pesticides, and plant growth hormones. Article 50 states that the central government should provide financial support by making available a special budget for the prevention and control of 'soil pollution.' The EPL also provides instructions for pollution prevention and abatement.

Other national-wide laws and regulations

Apart from the Constitution and the EPL, numerous provisions, which are embodied in laws, administrative regulations, bylaws, and governmental documents, can also be applied to deal with land contamination problems. Areas covered by those provisions include pollution prevention, natural resource protection, city planning, agricultural environment, and ecosystem protection. For example, according to Art. 35 of the Law of the People's Republic of China on the Prevention and Control of Environmental Pollution by Solid Wastes,[8] local governments should bear the costs of dealing with discarded installations or sites which have been historically used for the purpose of storage or treatment of industrial solid wastes. This law can be applied when the liable party cannot be found, or the liable parties exist, but they have insufficient capacity to discharge their liabilities.

In addition, land contamination has been addressed by laws related to land resource and agriculture management. Article 35 of the Land Administration Law of the People's Republic of China (2004)[9] provides that the People's governments at all levels shall take measures to maintain and protect irrigation and drainage facilities, ameliorate the soil to raise fertility and prevent desertification, salinization, water loss and soil erosion and pollution. The Agriculture Law of the People's Republic of China (2002)[10] has developed regimes on regulating soil contamination by encouraging the rational use of chemical fertilizer and pesticides and improving the quality of arable land. Article 58 of the law has introduced a registration system as a way of ensuring integrated agricultural environment management. Registration and/or licenses are required under Art. 21 to produce pesticides, veterinary medicines, fodder and feed additives, fertilizers, seeds, and farm machinery, which may endanger the safety of human beings and/or livestock. Similar provisions on agricultural product safety can be found in Art. 9(1) of the Regulation on Pollution-free Agricultural Product Management (2002),[11] which requires that the environmental conditions of the Pollution-free Agricultural Products producing areas should meet the specific environmental quality standards. Moreover, the Rules on Land Reclamation[12] introduces the principle of 'those who destroyed the land should be responsible for reclamation works' to rehabilitate lands damaged by digging or sinking during the construction process.

Finally, laws on water protection and general ecosystem protection can also be applied for regulating land contamination. For example, Art. 34 of the Rules for Implementation of the Law on the Prevention and Control of Water Pollution[13] provides that in cases where industrial waste water or municipal sewage are used for irrigation, agricultural administration authorities of the people's governments at the county level and above, should organize periodic monitoring of the quality of irrigation water, soil, and agricultural products, and carry out appropriate action to prevent the contamination of soil, groundwater, and agricultural products. Moreover, Art. 32(1) of the Regulation of the Nature Reserves of the PRC[14] prescribes that productive installations shall not be built in the core area or buffer zone of nature reserves.

MEP decrees and environmental standards

As the most important environmental protection authority of China, the MEP (the former State Environmental Protection Agency (SEPA)), has promulgated numerous decrees with respect to land contamination problems. For example, the secretarial office of the former SEPA promulgated the Notice on Readying for Preventing Environmental Pollution when Enterprises Make Move (2004) (RPEP Notice), which deals with contaminated land remediation issues when a company changes its location.[15] The RPEP Notice requires that all the industries, laboratories generating hazardous wastes and all entities yielding or trading hazardous wastes, should provide a soil function restoration plan based on a schedule of monitoring and testing. The monitoring report together with the restoration plan should be submitted to the relevant environmental administrative departments before they terminate their businesses or change the original land-use purpose. Environmental protection departments at various levels should consider the importance of land contamination during the process of land redevelopment.

A draft MEP decree for contaminated site management, the Interim Measures for the Soil Environment Management of Contaminated Sites (Draft) (MSEMC),[16] was issued by the MEP on December 15, 2009. This decree is (so far) the only non-technical environmental decree for the management of contaminated sites. It consists of six chapters with 29 articles. Article 2 defines 'contaminated site' as lands with soil that has been contaminated for the reason of (1) toxic and harmful materials; (2) abandoned materials; (3) mining. Article 27(3) imposes liabilities on those who fail to report on soil environmental conditions when contaminated site remediation has been completed. In addition, the polluter and/or owner of the land-use right may be liable for the land contamination. Under Art. 8 the assignees of the land-use right may be liable for investigation and remediation expenses if they fail to carry out environmental assessment before they accept the problematic land. Moreover, local governments shall bear the site remediation costs if no liable parties can be reached. As the most important decree for defining a contaminated site and associated liability issues, the deliberative draft of the measures were approved at the commission conference of the MEP in April 2011 (Wenyin, 2011).

At this time, there are no comprehensive technical guidelines or standards on soil pollution monitoring, contaminated land assessment, and soil remediation techniques at a national level. The environmental standards, Measures on the Management of Environmental Standards (1999) (MMES) are promulgated by the MEP and/or other administrative agencies to regulate specific, technical, or compliance issues. Under Art. 3 of the MMES, those standards may fall into five categories, which include: environmental quality standards, pollutant discharge or emission standards, basic environmental criteria, criteria for samples, and criteria for methodology.[17] According to Art. 5 of the MMES, the environmental quality standards and pollutant discharge standards are compulsory[18] and under Art. 3 of the MSEMC both can be divided into state standards and local standards. Land environment protection is highly dependent on two essential standards: the Environmental Quality Standard for Soils 1995[19] and the Environmental Quality Risk Assessment Criteria for Soil at Manufacturing Facilities 1999.[20] The first standard is mandatory, but it regulates agricultural land based on crop safety only. The second is not mandatory and fails to address contamination issues for future land use. The typical environmental standards about site management criteria and technical guidelines that are currently being drafted and trialed are: (1) soil environment quality standards which include, for example, the Soil Environmental Quality Assessment and Remediation Standards for Exhibition Site (Provisional for Shanghai Expo) (HJ 350-2007); (2) testing standards, which include the Soil Environmental Monitoring Technical Specifications (HJ/T166-2004), Groundwater Monitoring Technical Specifications (HJ/T164-2004) and Water Environment Monitoring Specifications (SL219-98) issued by the Ministry of Water Resources; and (3) monitoring standards, which include the Groundwater Quality Standards (GB/T14848-93), Soil Environmental Quality Standards (GB15618-1995), and Soil Environmental Quality of Industrial Enterprises (HJ/T25-1999).

Local regulations

For most local governments, there is no specific local regulation or statute relative to land contamination. However, there are a few exceptions. Generally, cities that have historically suffered from severe industry pollution have established rules to regulate contaminated site monitoring or remediation. For example, Zhejiang Province issued the Zhejiang Province Solid Waste Pollution Prevention Regulation in March 2006;[21] the Beijing Environmental Protection Bureau (EPB) delivered the Site Environmental Assessment Guidelines in January 2007;[22] Shenyang Environmental Protection Bureau, Shenyang Municipal Planning Land Resources Bureau jointly published the Management Measures of Contaminated Sites Remediation and Control of the Shenyang City (trial implementation) in 2007.[23] In addition, the Chongqing Municipal Government issued the Notice on Strengthening Industrial Contaminated Sites Treatment and Remediation in 2008, which details requirements for meticulous conduct on contaminated site risk assessments.[24]

In summary, the following issues are subject to these local regulations. First, provisions on farmland pollution control, for example, control of farmland non-point pollution,[25] ecological agriculture enhancement, farmland preservation and reclamation,[26] water sources preservation, wastewater irrigation.[27] Second, provisions on soil environmental protection in mining areas also provide for broader issues. For example, the Environmental Impact Assessment (EIA), allows the control of the pollution source within water areas and for clean production methodology. Third, solid waste pollution control, landfill gas monitoring, medical waste control, and nuclear power station radioactive control have also been prescribed for by these local regulations and rules.

A lack of statutory standards obstructs the effective management of contaminated sites, particularly in some urban areas. As a result, most recently, a series of standards and technical guidance for contaminated sites management are being drafted at a national level by research institutes commissioned by the EMP. For example, the Guidelines for Contaminated Site Risk Assessment (2009),[28] Guidelines for Soil Remediation of Contaminated Sites (2009)[29] and Technical Guidelines for Environmental Monitoring of Sites (2010)[30] are all published for comment at the time this chapter was submitted.

Problems of the current contaminated land legal frameworks

As noted earlier, in present-day China, land contamination has become one of the most serious problems that have profoundly impacted the population's health and living conditions, and arguably the sustainable development of the Chinese society. It is likely that along with rapid industrial development, agricultural modernization, and urban construction, a growing number of contaminated sites will be discovered in the near future. Although China's central government together with its affiliated ministries has made responses to this emergent crisis, it should be noted that the existing legal system is far from sufficient or effective. This is in part due to its fragmented governance, existing legislative and policy framework, weak administrative organization and capacity, and limited technical knowledge. At present, apart from several local regulations, there is no comprehensive national land contamination law in China.

The first major challenge is the lack of integrated legislation as a response to contaminated land problems. A comprehensive national legal framework with clear policy objectives and principles is a prerequisite at the central government level to deal with land contamination problems. The existing legal system for contaminated land in China lacks cohesion due to poorly integrated legislation and effective technical approaches. From experience, in the context of China and the international communities, an effective regulatory system for contaminated land requires, *inter alia*, systematic integration of all aspects, including assessment, remediation, spatial planning, aftercare, and monitoring.

Another challenge is the extremely limited supply of experienced administrators and dedicated organizations responsible for contaminated land at both the central and local levels. Insufficient technical support on the management and treatment of contaminated land commonly exists under the current legal and policy context. Land contamination prevention and control is a relatively new concern in China, and the necessary expertise and experience is still underdeveloped. In addition, it is clear that the existing legal system for regulating contaminated land is not operating optimally. For example, the Soil Quality Environmental Standard of China was developed about 20 years ago and has been heavily criticized as being unable to tackle the current problems effectively (Shuyi, 2008). Although a new standard proposal (Announcement about Amending Soil Environmental Quality Standard) has been under public review for five years, the MEP still does not have the right of final approval for this document.[31]

Under current environmental law and policy, financial incentives for cleanup and reclamation of contaminated land have not been fully developed by policymakers. This operates as a barrier to effective and efficient dealings with contaminated lands. Funding mechanisms appear in some local regulations. However, there are no properly developed or coordinated approaches that enable legislation to be appropriately implemented.

Finally, there are no adequate solutions for resolving conflicts between central and local government interests. Provisions on soil protection and prevention and control of land contamination can easily encounter weak local protectionism in China. Local protectionism has meant that local governments let their own local interests prevail over national concerns. The implementation of central directives becomes particularly challenging considering four main local governance weaknesses: (1) modest administrative capacity of local officials; (2) low accountability, as governmental structures are often not yet developed enough to effectively monitor and evaluate policies besides top-down mechanisms; (3) weak rule of law, as local courts have a fragile institutional status; (4) limited citizen representation and participation (OECD, 2009).

Developing a contaminated land regime in China

An overview of international approaches to contaminated land management

Land contamination is a worldwide phenomenon faced by both developed and developing countries. In a handful of developed countries, national site contamination laws, which include both national and/or federal legislation, and state or provincial legislation has been developed since the early 1970s (Brandon, 2013). This trend may be attributed to several major incidents of large-scale land contamination. For example, in the USA, the Love Canal incident is widely credited as being the catalyst for federal legislation (Comprehensive Environmental Response, Compensation and Liability Act 1980) on liability for cleanup of toxic sites (Fletcher, 2003; Switzer and Bulan, 2002). In the Netherlands, the incidence of heavy soil contamination at Lekkerkerk in 1980 (Brandon, 2013; De Roo, 2003), finally led to the introduction of the Soil Clean-up (Interim) Act and non-statutory Soil Clean-up Guideline in 1983 (Brandon, 2013; De Roo, 2003).[32] Those major events or a series of smaller incidents have provided sufficient political pressure to legislate on the issue in the heavily industrialized or highly urbanized countries (e.g., the USA, Netherlands, Germany, and Australia). Some other countries enacted specific contamination laws because they are more likely to feel pressure to redevelop urban areas due to land scarcity and a high population density (e.g., the UK and Japan).

To some degree, the broad experience of developed countries in terms of site contamination management can educate developing countries, particularly for countries in which the awareness of land contamination was only raised as recently as the 1990s. In fact, several leading countries, such as the Netherlands and the USA, have influenced several others to select a particular model of site contamination legislation. For example, the liability regime under CERCLA (Comprehensive Environmental Response, Compensation, and Liability Act of 1980) in the United States has been emulated in Taiwan, Japan, and partly in the provinces of Canada (Brandon, 2013).

Comparative study shows that an integrated framework of contaminated land law may comprise following key elements (Brandon, 2013). First, it should contain detailed procedures for the management of site contamination, including site identification, investigation, assessment, remediation planning, remediation works, monitoring, and aftercare. Second, it should specify the role of public authorities, private professionals, and responsible parties at each procedural stage. Third, it should also stipulate an information management system (e.g., registration scheme or a database of contaminated sites), and secure people's right to get access to those information sources. Finally, the health and safety for site workers and neighboring residents should be adequately addressed under the framework.

China remains heavily reliant on its general environmental protection legislation to regulate land-contaminating activities, and this has to date proven insufficient in addressing the problem of land contamination and the food safety crisis. With a better understanding of the nature and extent of land contamination, and its impacts on food safety, the Chinese government has realized that it urgently needs to develop a nationwide contaminated land law based on global approaches and broader international experience (Qingxin and Sibei, 2013).[33]

Analysis of mechanisms of the contaminated land law of China

Contaminated land risk assessment schemes

In the context of land contamination, risk assessment refers to the qualitative and quantitative evaluation of the risk posed to human health and/or the environment by the actual or potential presence of soil pollutants. In most developed countries, a risk assessment would be undertaken once the relevant authority, based on the initial site investigation, has made a decision that a site is sufficiently contaminated to necessitate further assessment (McCaffrey et al., 2005). The aim of the risk assessment process is to determine whether the level of contamination present at a site poses a sufficient threat to human or environmental health, making remediation necessary or advisable (Landcare Research, 2012). Assuming remedial action is recommended, the process would then lead to an evaluation of the most appropriate remediation options for the site in question.

In the UK, the risk assessment process is called 'options appraisal' (Brandon, 2013). With the introduction of the new regulatory regime for contaminated land in section 57 of the Environment Act 1995, the UK has endorsed a risk-based framework within which contaminated land can be identified, assessed, and managed (Luo, O. et al., 2009). This framework adopts the rationale and terminology from accepted international approaches to the regulation of environmental media, and it embodies the fundamental distinctions between toxicity, hazard, and risk that exist throughout environmental science. Several terms like toxicity, hazard, and risk are introduced under a risk assessment scheme. The USA has also developed a complex contaminated site risk assessment procedure under the CERCLA.

It is now commonly accepted that a clearly defined risk assessment procedure should be an integral component of the contaminated land law of China. However, in the context of China, numerous challenges exist in developing this process. For example, the lack of technical expertise available to analyze the potentially contaminating activity or its associated risks, insufficient data about a site, and an absence of financial resources for conducting a thorough investigation (Brandon, 2013).

Contaminated land remediation schemes

The benefits of remediation are mainly reflected in improvements in human and ecosystem health, or the avoidance of future degradation in health or environmental quality. The use of treatment technologies for contaminated land remediation is encouraged by agencies in many countries because they are perceived as having added environmental value compared with other approaches to remediation, such as excavation and removal, containment, or covering/revegetation. The 'added' environmental value is associated with the destruction, removal, or transformation of contaminants into less toxic forms providing a greater flexibility for site reuse (Boyd, 1999).

In the UK, cl. 43, Part IIA of the Environmental Protection Act 1990 creates a contaminated land remediation mechanism,[34] providing a statutory framework for the identification and remediation of contaminated land. The Act provides a legal definition of contaminated land and the procedures involved in its identification and remediation or cleanup. It prescribes the respective roles of the Environment Agency and the local authorities in ensuring the remediation of contaminated land, and defines the procedure for determining and apportioning liability for the cleanup. Finally, contaminated land remediation issues have also been provided by some other environmental acts and regulations, for example, the planning regime and the provisions of the Environmental Damage (Prevention and Remediation) Regulations 2009 (UK) No. 153.

When deciding whether or not specific land should be remediated, a cost–benefit method should be considered. Generally, costs of contaminated land remediation include direct and indirect costs. Direct costs comprise mostly capital and labor expenditures, which is also referred to as the 'costs of cleanup.' In the UK, the DEFRA Circular 01/2006 (Food and Rural Affairs Department for Environment, 2006) requires that such costs be taken into account when the authority is considering the cost of the proposed remediation package which includes all the initial costs (including tax) of the remedial actions, including feasibility studies, design, specification, management, and making good; ongoing management and maintenance costs; and any 'disruption costs,' such as depreciation in the value of land, or other loss or damage likely to result from carrying out the remediation (Food and Rural Affairs Department for Environment, 2006, p. 26). In addition to direct outlays, there are also indirect costs that typically include opportunity costs and institutional costs. Under the circumstance that the benefits will surpass the potential costs, the environmental authorities should consider initiating the remediation procedure.

Contaminated land liability schemes

The question of 'who should pay' is a fundamental issue of the statutory regimes under various jurisdictions. In the UK, according to Part IIA of the Environmental Protection Act 1990, the primary liability falls upon those who have caused or knowingly permitted the polluting substances to be in, on or under the land ('Class A appropriate persons'). If no Class A persons can be found, then the present owners or occupiers, called Class B appropriate persons, will be liable in default. Both the local authority and the Environment Agency play an important role under the liability regime. The contaminated land liability regime of the UK covers a broad range of commercial entities such as companies, banks, insolvency practitioners, trustees, and parent companies.

In the USA, the CERCLA[35] defines responsibility for the costs of remediation and who should be responsible for existing contamination. It contains a stringent liability scheme and creates a new cause of action; the statute establishes the nature of the new liability, the identity of liable parties, and the triggers for, remedies, and defenses to liability. Under the CERCLA, liability may be attached to a wide array of persons, called potentially responsible parties (PRPs).[36]

It is more complicated when the liability scheme for contaminated land remediation is considered in China. On the one hand, like the USA and many European countries, China has adopted the polluter pays approach in its environmental laws and regulations. However, this approach was thought not to be an effective way to address contaminated land issues, because it is often difficult to find the original polluters of a site as they have already closed down or gone bankrupt before the contamination hazard is unearthed (Luo, O. et al., 2009). In China, a large proportion of historic land contamination cases were caused by state-owned enterprises, which means liability often falls with the government (Boyd, 1999).[37]

As a result, certain characteristics are fairly constant under the contaminated land liability scheme of China: strict liability, joint and several liability, and government liability. That is, where two or more persons are appropriate persons in relation to any particular remediation action, the authority should make a decision whether any one person should be treated as not being an appropriate person associated with the remediation issue. If sites need remediation, in whole or in part, no appropriate person can be found, the enforcing authority will take over the remediation. The UK has adopted the concept of 'orphan linkage' to describe this situation where either no owner or occupier can be found for some land, or where those who would otherwise be liable are exempted by one of the statutory provisions (Zhao, 2013, p. 150). This experience could be a possible solution for cases in China where no appropriate person can be found.

Environmental liability insurance schemes

Requiring environmental remediation insurance has become common practice in various jurisdictions.[38] Most recently, attaining environmental liability insurance has been encouraged by the newly amended Art. 5 of the EPL of China. Before that, it was simply addressed by an MEP decree, the Guiding Opinions on Environmental Pollution Liability Insurance (SEPA Document No. 189). One problem is that the current insurance law and regulations are too obscure, and issues about how the existing environmental liability laws and regulations are to be applied in a land contamination case are yet to be clarified.

A number of obstacles have been observed for developing an environmental pollution liability insurance scheme in the area of contaminated land management in China. First of all, market demand is unclear. In China, the demand for environmental insurance products will largely depend on the attitude of local governments (Re, 2011).[39] The degree to which local governments introduce and rigorously enforce environmental liability laws and regulations will substantially decide the future of this insurance. Second, historical data for contaminated sites is missing. Today, databases relating to land usage and contamination situations are extremely insufficient. This makes it quite difficult to estimate the severity and frequency of loss with conventional methods (Yingbin and Xiaohui, 2011; Ying et al., 2007).[40] Third, Chinese insurance companies are lacking in underwriting experience. Finally, there are insufficient legal remedies in Chinese courts for environmental pollution cases. In some cases, although the court decided in favour of the plaintiffs, it is still unable to stop the violation, or obtain payment of compensation.

In order to establish a sustainable proper means to prevent and remediate contaminated land, governments at all levels should encourage the development of a pollution insurance market and let the 'invisible hand' of the market work for the benefit of society. First of all, it should define clearly the financial risks associated with environmental liabilities arising from land contamination and estimate their probability. Second, data collection and filing should be initiated by environmental protection agencies. Well-constructed information systems will benefit the establishment of an environmental insurance system. Third, identifying stakeholders of interest. One essential condition for a successful insurance solution is that key groups of interest (insurers and potentially insured) are able and willing to be involved in the process. Fourth, it is necessary to introduce a compulsory insurance scheme for contaminated land issues. While considering the introduction of compulsory environmental insurance for operators, the law and policymakers should carefully examine the maturity and competitiveness of the insurance market. Fifth, improving staff training to enhance the knowledge and experience of environmental management officials and insurance enterprises over environmental insurance should be undertaken (OECD, 2009).[41] Finally, it should be noted that environmental liability insurance is not the only tool for eliminating environmental crises. Therefore, it is necessary to develop various forms of financial incentive to ensure that polluters are able to meet their obligations.

Financial assistances for contaminated land remediation and redevelopment

Economics are fundamental to the progression of contaminated sites cleanup programs. In fact, the lack of adequate and affordable financing has been reported as the most significant barrier to the reuse of a contaminated site in almost all countries facing the contaminated land problem (OECD, 2009). Substantial expenditure and excess costs in terms of contaminated land reclamation are usually referred to as the 'gap' in financing (Davis and Sherman, 2010). It necessarily involves considerable expenditure in the form of site clearance, fees for consultants and analysts, removal or treatment of contaminated soil or groundwater, and gas control or other remedial measures (Tromans and Turrall-Clarke, 2008). The high costs of cleanup or remediation will inevitably act as a considerable barrier to investment in those areas needing reclamation works (Bartsch and Wells, 2003; Tromans and Turrall-Clarke 2008; Davis and Sherman, 2010). Therefore, financial assistance schemes that can generate sufficient funds to cover the reclamation costs has been considered as a necessary mechanism for jurisdictions that have contaminated land regulations.

In the UK, under s. 37 (1)(b) of the Environment Act 1995 (EA), the Environment Agency has general statutory powers to carry out any engineering operations that are conducive to or incidental to the carrying out of its functions. In principle, according to ss. 47–49 of the EA, the funding for work such as is necessary could come from government grants, borrowings or from government loans, including financial support from the Department for Environment, Food and Rural Affairs (Defra). Under the UK system, there are two major sources of contaminated land funding. The other is from special funding mechanisms set up for the reclamation of contaminated land, set up in recognition of the possible considerable expenditure of remediation (Zhao, 2013, p. 223).

In the USA, financial assurance obligations are both voluntary and compulsory and can be negotiated between the EPA and PRPs as part of the Superfund settlement process, and be included in the terms of an enforcement order (Brandon, 2013, p. 157). Financial assurance mechanisms include surety bonds, corporate guarantees, trust funds, insurance policies, corporate financial tests, and letters of credit. Occasionally, other mechanisms may be used to suit specific circumstances, such as liens over real property, deposit accounts, escrow accounts, and certificates of deposit.

Based on the above comparison, several key issues should be considered by the Chinese legislature to develop a proper funding mechanism for contaminated land remediation. Among others, fairness should be the primary concern and significant objective of the funding mechanisms. This is because, compared with other values of the regime, such as the effectiveness or long-term sustainability, fair distribution of liabilities among all potential parties seems to be the issue of greatest concern by most in Chinese society. This will consequently require fair procedures for granting applications, such as criteria for ranking and screening applications for the funding purpose, and a fair treatment to areas with different development levels. In addition, screening criteria for the application of financial instruments should also be well defined (EPA, 2010).[42]

Concluding remarks

This chapter analyzed causes and potential impacts of land contamination in China, and in particular looked at its substantial impacts on the ongoing food crisis in China. Among all possible contributors, land contamination is probably the most basic, which is continually threatening food safety in the long food supply chain. If, 10 years ago, it was a contentious issue, it now has been commonly accepted that land contamination prevention and control measures should be undertaken within a timely manner to tackle the environmental crisis in China, among which food safety is one of the most urgent.

Over the past decades, environmental laws and regulations have been developed in China to address the soil environment protection issue and a number of scattered mechanisms have therefore been established. However, what has been approved is far from adequate to address all the challenges arising from land contamination and to tackle the food quality and safety problems facing China presently. Historical legislative practices of China and the outside jurisdictions have shown that, a nationwide contaminated land law, in which a systematic contaminated land remediation mechanism, a sounder liability system, a more effective financial assistance arrangement and relevant schemes alike, should be developed to stop and control the prevailing land contamination all over the country.

The conclusion of this chapter seems to direct attention to making a new law to improve food safety by maintaining good soil quality of arable lands and safeguarding the ecological system in whole. However, this is only a theoretical assumption. After all, we should bear in mind that soil environment improvement is just one factor that may benefit food safety protection. Attention should also be given to those specific laws and regulations, as they are supposed to regulate other issues in the food chain, e.g., procedural rules for monitoring and inspecting food products.

In sum, a credible, comprehensive law on land contamination could provide relatively immediate benefits and substantial improvement for food safety, if it is widely promoted by Chinese legislatures. Moreover, if China would draw on the combined experience of developed countries over the past decades, and could adopt proper mechanisms based on its domestic conditions, the making of a nationwide contaminated land law will substantially mitigate the impacts of its food safety crisis.

Notes

1 The author would like to thank the Australian Centre for Agriculture and Law (University of New England, Australia) and the School of Law, Beijing Foreign Studies University (China), for their efforts to initiate an international discussion on this topic.
2 NSP generally refers to pollution that comes from dispersed sources such as agricultural fields, parking lots, golf courses, etc.
3 These areas include, e.g., tilapia (77.5 percent), apple juice (65.2 percent), cod (52.7 percent), processed mushrooms (34.1 percent), garlic (27.4 percent), clams (16.1 percent), frozen spinach (16.0 percent), and salmon (12.7 percent).
4 The ninth Asia Pacific Conference on Tobacco and Health was held in Sydney, Australia with the theme FCTC (Framework Convention on Tobacco Control) in Asia Pacific: Change, Challenge and Progress. More than 600 people from more than 40 countries and regions attended the conference.
5 It refers to the national level basic law. Although by the end of 2008, there were some regulations promulgated by the MEP on governing heavy metal problem, there were no laws.
6 There have been four Constitution laws since that establishment of the PRC, which were enacted in 1954, 1975, 1978, and 1982. The most recent Constitution law was promulgated by the NPC in December 1982 at the Fifth National People's Congress. It has been amended in 1988, 1993, 1999, and 2004, the latest amendment was made in 2004.
7 National People's Congress, Order No. 22, December 26, 1989, amended in April, 2014.
8 National People's Congress, Order No. 31, December 29, 2004.

9 National People's Congress, Order No. 28, August 28, 2004.
10 National People's Congress, Order No. 81, December 28, 2002.
11 Ministry of Agriculture of the PRC, General Administration of Quality Supervision, Inspection and Quarantine of the People's Republic of China, April 4, 2002.
12 People's Republic of China, State Council, January 1, 1989.
13 State Council, Order No 284, March 20, 2000.
14 Republic of China, State Council, Decree No. 167, October 9, 1994, art. 32.
15 People's Republic of China, SEPA, Decree No. 47, June 1, 2004.
16 People's Republic of China, MEP, Decree No. 1321, December 15, 2009.
17 People's Republic of China, SEPA, Decree No. 3, April 1, 1999, art. 3.
18 According to the Standardization Law, national environmental standards marked as 'GB' are mandatory standards, while those marked as 'GB/T' are voluntary standards (with the 'T' as 'recommended'). Similarly, standards issued by MEP are marked as 'HJ' are mandatory with national scope; however, those marked as 'HJ/T' are voluntary ones.
19 People's Republic of China, MEPA, GB15618-1995, March 1, 1996.
20 MEPA, HJ/T 25-1999, August 1, 1999.
21 The Regulation requires an environmental risk assessment to be carried out for contaminated soil.
22 The Guidelines mainly stipulate work procedures and technical methods for site environmental assessments within Beijing.
23 The Measures mainly stipulate the evaluation and identification of contaminated sites.
24 Chongqing City Council, Decree No. 208, June 26, 2008.
25 For example, the Regulation of Environment Protection of Shanghai City prescribes that farming producer should scientifically implicating chemicals, pesticides and agricultural film.
26 For example, the Regulation of Agricultural Ecology Protection of Anhui Province (1999) and the Regulation of Agricultural Environment Protection of Shandong Province (2004) have definitely included soil protection under the catalogue of agricultural environmental protection.
27 For example, the Regulation of the Agricultural Environmental Protection of Anhui Province prescribes that water quality of the nearest irrigation sources around industry areas should meet the irrigation water quality standard.
28 People's Republic of China, MEP, Decree No. [2009] 1020, September 29, 2009.
29 People's Republic of China, MEP, Decree No. [2009] 1312, December 10, 2009.
30 People's Republic of China, MEP, Decree No. [2010] 99, February 1, 2010.
31 People's Republic of China, General Office of MEP, Decree No. [2009] 918, September 18, 2009.
32 According to statics, Canada, Australia, Kingdom, Germany, Denmark, Belgium, Switzerland, and Taiwan District have all established specific land contamination law(s) to address land contamination issues. While other countries have no specific contaminated land law, there are several specific provisions related to contaminated land issues. This is very common in southern Europe, eastern Europe, and Russia.
33 As reported, the making of a national-wide contaminated land law has been incorporated into the legislation plan of the 12th Standing Committee of the National People's Congress. According to the plan, 11 new laws (or amendments) will relate to environmental protection.
34 Part IIA of the Environmental Protection Act 1990 was brought into force in England on April 1, 2000, by insertion of section 57 of Environment Act 1995 into the 1990 Act. For more details on the Environmental Protection Act 1990, see Chapter 5, section 5.1.
35 Pub L No. 96-510, 94 Stat 2767 (1980) (codified as amended at 42 USC§§9601-75 (2006).

36 Under CERCLA, PRPs may include: (1) current or former owners of a facility or vessel; (2) current or former operators of a facility or vessel; (3) generators who sent hazardous substances to the site, and (4) transporters who brought hazardous substances to the site. See CERCLA, §107(a).

37 While discussing the drawbacks of the polluter pays approach, Boyed (1999) points out that in countries where site contamination has mainly been caused by state-owned entities, such principle would be difficult to apply.

38 Detailed comparisons of the US and UK environmental insurance have been made by Fogleman (2005).

39 As at January 2011, in China, there were more than 10 insurance companies that had developed environmental insurance products. More insurance companies started an environmental pollution liability dialogue based on pilot programs with the support of local governments. However, due to low demand, resources allocated to this liability line are much poorer than those devoted to other lines of business such as property insurance, where the risk landscape is clearer and the premium contribution is larger.

40 Such problems have been noted by several Chinese researchers.

41 In order to ensure the achievement of the environmental targets of the 11th Five-Year Plan, the MEP has developed the 11th Five-Year Plan for the Building of National Capacity in Environmental Supervision, a first self-development plan in the history of environmental protection in China. The Plan, approved and supported by the NRDC and the Ministry of Finance, envisages total investment of almost 15 billion RMB, including 7.8 billion RMB from the central government.

42 However, administrative costs, such as indirect costs, of grant administration with the exception of financial and performance reporting, together with proposal preparation costs have been excluded from the funds usage.

References

Bartsch, C. and Wells, B. (2003). Financing Strategies for Brownfield Cleanup and Redevelopment. Northeast-Midwest Institute. Retrieved from http://brownfield.cberdata.org/files/Bartsch%20and%20Wells,%20(2003).pdf

Boyd, J. (1999). Environmental Remediation Law and Economies in Transition. Retrieved from www.rff.org/Documents/RFF-DP-99–21.pdf

Brandon, E. (2013). *Global Approaches to Site Contamination Law*. Netherlands: Springer.

Chen, H. (2002). *Behavior of Chemicals in Soils and Environmental Quality*. New York: Science Press.

China Council for International Cooperation on Environment and Development (2006). Environmental Issues and Countermeasures Facing New Rural Development in China. Special Policy Group on Environmental Issues Facing New Rural Development. Retrieved from www.cciced.net/encciced/policyresearch/report/201205/U020120529451221797895.pdf

Ching-Fu, L. (2013). *Taking China's Food Safety Problem Seriously (I)*, October 10, 2013. Retrievedfromhttps://blogs.law.harvard.edu/billofhealth/2013/10/10/taking-chinas-food-safety-problem-seriously-i

Conradie E. M. and Field, D. (2000). N*ugent and Western Cape Provincial Council of Churches – A Rainbow over the Land: A South African Guide on the Church and Environmental Justice*. South Africa: University of the South Cape.

Davis, T. S. and Sherman, S. A. (2010). *Brownfields: A Comprehensive Guide to Redeveloping Contaminated Property* (3rd edn). Chicago, IL: ABA.

De Roo, G. (2003). *Environmental Planning in the Netherlands: Too Good to Be True – From Command-and-Control Planning to Shared Governance*. Aldershot: Ashgate, 168–169.

Department of Research Center of the State Council (2006). Statute Quo of the Agricultural Pollution in China and Suggested Countermeasures. *Studies in International Technology and Economy*, 9(4), 17.

Enfeng, L., Ji, S. and Xingqi, L. (2005). Geochemical Features of Heavy Metals in Core Sediments of Northwestern Taihu Lake, China. *Chinese Journal of Geochemistry*, 24(1) 73.

EPA. (2010). Proposal Guidelines for Brownfields Revolving Loan Fund Grants. Retrieved from www.ct.gov/dep/lib/dep/site_clean_up/brownfields/bfrlfgrant fy11guideline s.pdf

FAO. (1996). *Report of the World Food Summit*. Rome: FAO.

FAOSTAT Database. (2014). China Country Profile. Retrieved from http://faostat.fao.org

Fletcher, T. H. (2003). *From Love Canal to Environmental Justice: The Politics of hazardous Waste on the Canada–US Border*. Colorado: Broadview Press.

Fogleman, V. (2005). *Environmental Liabilities and Insurance in England and the United States*. London: Witherby.

Food and Rural Affairs Department for Environment (2006). Environmental Protection Act 1990: part 2A contaminated land. Dept. for Environment Food and Rural Affairs. Retrieved from www.defra.gov.uk/environment/quality/land/contaminated/documents/circu lar01-2006.pdf

Gould, K. A. and Lewis, T. L. (eds.) (2009). *Twenty Lessons in Environmental Sociology*. New York: Oxford University Press.

Grazer, W. (ed.) (2009). *Catholics Going Green: A Small-Group Guide for Learning and Living Environmental Justice*. Notre Dame, IN: Ave Maria Press.

Jin, Z., Cheng, H., Chen, L., Li, X., Zhu, G., Zhuang, G. and Qian, N. (2010). Concentrations and Contamination Trends of Heavy Metals in the Sediment Cores of Taihu Lake, East China, and Their Relationship with Historical Eutrophication. *Chinese Journal of Geochemistry*, 29(1), 33–41.

Landcare Research (2012). Risk Assessment for Contaminated Sites in New Zealand Retrieved from http://contamsites.landcareresearch.co.nz/risk_assessment_fundamentals.htm

Li, Z. (2006). Soil Quality Deteriorating in China, Threatening Public Health and Ecosystems. Retrieved from www.worldwatch.org/node/4419

Lin, C. F. (2013, October 10). Taking China's Food Safety Problem Seriously (I). *Harvard Law*. Retrieved from http://blogs.law.harvard.edu/billofhealth/2013/10/10/taking-chinas-food-safety-problem-seriously-i

Luo, L., Ma, Y., Zhang, S., Wei, D. and Zhu, Y. G. (2009). An Inventory of Trace Element Inputs to Agricultural Soils in China. *Journal of Environmental Management*, 90(8), 2524–2530.

Luo, O., Catney, P. and Lerner, D. (2009). Risk-based Management of Contaminated Land in the UK: Lessons for China? *Journal of Environmental Management*, 90(2) 1123–1134.

McCaffrey, C., Challis, K., Cranstone, D., Trueman, M. and Nathanail, C. P. (2005). Guidance on Assessing the Risk Posed by Land Contamination and its Remediation on Archaeological Resource Management. Retrieved from www.helm.org.uk/upload/

pdf/Full_Guidance_on_Assessing_the_Risk_Posed_by_Land_Contamination_and_its_Remediation_on_Archaeological_Resource _Management.pdf

Ministry of Environmental Protection of PRC. (2104, April 17). *Gazette of the National Soil Pollution Survey*. Retrieved from www.zhb.gov.cn/gkml/hbb/qt/201404/W020140417558995804588.pdf

National Bureau of Statistics of China and Ministry of Environmental Protection of China. (2009). *China Environment Statistical Yearbook 2009*. Retrieved from www.stats.gov.cn/tjsj/ndsj/2009/indexeh.htm.

OECD. (2009). *Ensuring Environmental Compliance: Trends and Good Practices*. Retrieved from www.oecd.org/env/tools-evaluation/ensuringenvironmentalcompliancetrendsandgoodpractices.htm#Additional_info

People's Daily Online. (2010). Some Chinese Cigarettes High in Heavy Metal Content (9 October 2010). Retrieved from http://english.peopledaily.com.cn/90001/90782/90872/7160898.html

Project Group of National Program on the Development of Basic Research (973 Program). (2007). Newsletter for the 'Soil and Air Quality Changing Regularity and Rule of Control in Yangtze River and Pearl' (Project No 2002CB410800, Project Office of the 'Soil and Air Quality Changing Regularity and Rule of Control in Yangtze River and Pearl').

Quingxin, Cui and Sibei, Wang (2013). The 12th Standing Committee of the National People's Congress Published the Legislation Plan. Retrieved from Xinhua.news.cn www.npc.gov.cn/npc/zgrdzz/2013-12/12/content_1816288.htm

Ritter, W. F. and Shirmohammadi, A. (2001). *Agricultural Nonpoint Source Pollution: Watershed Management and Hydrology*. Boca Raton, FL: Lewis.

Swiss, R. (2011). Environmental Pollution Liability Insurance in China: A Bumpy Road Leading to a Bright Prospect. Retrieved from www.swissre.com/clients/insurers/property_casualty/Environmental_pollution_liability_insurance_in_China.html.

Switzer, C. S. and Bulan, L. A. (2002). CERCLA: comprehensive environmental response, compensation, and liability act (Superfund), American Bar Association, 3.

Tromans, Stephen and Turrall-Clarke, Robert (2008) *Contaminated Land* (2nd edn). London: Sweet & Maxwell, p. 495.

Wang, S. (2008). Some Considerations on Promulgating Soil Contamination Prevention and Control Law. *PRC*, 3.

Weili, Z., Shuxia, W. and Hong, J. (2004). Estimation of Agricultural Non-Point Source Pollution in China and the Alleviating Strategies I. Estimation of Agricultural Non-Point Source Pollution in China in Early 21 Century. *Scientia Agricultura Sinica*, 37(7), 1008.

Wendong, Z. (2007). The Impact of Sewage Irrigation on Farm Production. *Journal of Anhui Agricultural Science*, 35(12), 3623.

Wenyin, Z. (2011). Interim Measures for the Soil Environment Management of Contaminated Sites Got Approved by the EPM Committee Conference. Retrieved from www.zhb.gov.cn/zhxx/hjyw/201103/t20110325_207637.htm

Wong, E. (2013, December 30). Pollution Rising, Chinese Fear for Soil and Food. *New York Times*. Retrieved from www.nytimes.com/2013/12/31/world/asia/good-earth-no-more-soil-pollutio n-plagues-chinese-countryside.html?_r=0

Wong, E. (2014, April 17). One-Fifth of China's Farmland Is Polluted, State Study Finds. *New York Times*. Retrieved from www.nytimes.com/2014/04/18/world/asia/one-fifth-of-chinas-farmland-is-p olluted-state-report-finds.html?_r=0

Wong, J. L. (2010). The Food–Energy–Water Nexus. *Harvard Asia Quarterly*, 12, 15–19.

Xiaomiao, Q. (2009). 'Contaminated Land Remediation in China Is Still a Vacancy,' interview with Zhou Qixing, Dean of the College of Environmental Science and Engineering Nankai University. *Science News Bi-weekly*.

Ying, X., Tao, B. and Bin, W. (2007). Suppositions of China's Environment Pollution Liability Insurance. *Modern Law Science*, 29(1), 24.

Yingbin, Z. and Xiaohui, W. (2010). Study on the Environmental Liability Insurance Legal System in China. *Journal of Beijing University of Aeronautics and Astronautics (Social Science Edition)*, 23(4).

Zhao, X. (2013). *Developing an appropriate contaminated land regime in China: lessons learned from the US and UK*. Berlin: Springer.

Zijun, Li. (2006). *Soil Quality Deteriorating in China, Threatening Public Health and Ecosystems*. Retrieved from www.worldwatch.org/node/4419

10 Life-cycle regulation of food safety in China

A legal perspective

Qin Tianbao and Wei Lele

The life-cycle regulation

Life-cycle control of food security refers to the full supervision of the food safety management system, covering all food-related aspects, from farm to table. In this process, we need to focus on the foundations of food security, with emphasis on the safety of consuming agricultural products and concerns about producing food items from raw materials. This includes their transportation, storage, sale, and post-consumer aspects of food and consumer treatment of food, in an effort to supervise the whole food safety process.

Currently, China's agricultural product is not subject to food safety regulations. This is because China's agricultural soil is seriously polluted. The main sources of pollution are biological contamination (mainly refers to viral contamination, microbiological contamination, and transgenic contamination), chemical pollution (mainly includes pesticide pollution, heavy metal pollution, and non-metallic material), and radioactive pollution. These pollutants also become the sources of food safety hazards through the soil. Many of the causes of food safety problems in China are due to the pollution of the agricultural environment. Food security encompasses the production of primary agricultural products to storage, transportation, distribution, and consumption. Regulators need to pay special attention to the supervision of food safety supervision at the post-consumer stage. As environmental pollution is worsening, more attention needs to be paid to food safety regulations.

Current situation and problems

At present, China's food industry has been overextended. The focus on food safety has shifted from the raw materials of food to production, storage, transportation, distribution, consumption, and final disposal. Regulation of all these aspects, and food safety issues after consumption, needs to be taken into account.

The current situation

The current laws have been formulated to regulate the different stages of the food safety processes. However, the law has played a distinctive role in each different stage of the process without proper connection with one another and the provisions are too abstract or somehow outdated. The analysis undertaken in this chapter of current food regulation processes occurs at each different stage.

Regulation of raw food materials

Agricultural production requires land, water, and air as basic conditions. Currently soil, water, and air pollution are worsening, with each factor having an adverse effect on the other. Soil, water, and air pollution, pose a serious risk to the food safety of agricultural products. Special attention must be paid to the current laws on pollution, which are closely relevant to food safety.

In China, the existing laws concerning the regulation of raw food material include: 2009 Food Safety Law; 2002 Agriculture Law; 2006 Agricultural Product Quality Safety Law; Special Rules on Strengthening the Supervision and Management of the Safety of Food and Other Products. Articles with regard to raw food materials regulation are set out in Table 10.1.

The Articles mentioned in Table 10.1 have regulated the production of raw food materials and designated responsibilities for a variety of subjects. Great progress alongside rapid development in China has occurred; however, the environment has been seriously polluted and is harmful to the people living in it. The soil environment in China is not ideal, with several serious issues present, including heavy soil pollution in some areas, poor quality soil for cultivation and the waste from industrial and mining contaminating soils. Over the years, due to imperfect laws and regulations for agriculture and the lack of legal basis for effective supervision, people have taken advantage of the legal loopholes and undertaken agricultural management practices that jeopardize the safety of food in China (Pingjun, 2013). In agricultural production, the lack of technical knowledge and health and safety rules leads to higher costs of agricultural products and also increases security risks. There are various pesticides, veterinary drug residues, heavy metal pollution, and other food safety issues, which are becoming more and more serious (Ying and Erpeng, 2013). During primary production, improper use of agrochemicals, fertilizers, and pesticides in the field, and antibiotics and antiphrastic agents in animal production, are the most important causes leading to the presence of unsafe compounds in food products (Lam et al., 2013). There are also shortcomings in agricultural safety standards for food for human consumption, with current safety standards needing to fully meet the needs of social development. An effective agricultural products safety traceability system has not been established and this is urgently needed. Contamination of soil and water with heavy metal cadmium, can lead to its presence in agricultural products and when consumed

Table 10.1 Provisions on raw food materials

Law	*Content*
Food Safety Law of the People's Republic of China	Article 35 The producers of edible agricultural products shall apply agricultural inputs such as pesticides, fertilizers, growth regulators, veterinary drugs, feed, and feed additives in accordance with food safety standards and relevant State regulations.
	Article 36 Food producers shall check the license of the supplier and compliance certificate of the product when purchasing food raw materials, food additives, and food-related products. In the absence of a compliance certificate, the food raw material shall be tested in accordance with food safety standards. Food producers shall not purchase or use raw materials, food additives, and food-related products that do not comply with the food safety standards.
2002 Agriculture Law	Article 65 The competent administrative departments for agriculture at all levels shall provide guidance to farmers and agricultural production and operation organizations in their adoption of biological measures or use of highly effective, low-toxic and low-residual pesticides and veterinary medicines to prevent and control animal and plant diseases, insect pests, weeds and damage by rats. Straws and other residual materials after the reaping of agricultural products shall comprehensively be utilized and properly disposed of in order to prevent environmental pollution and ecological destruction. Units and individuals engaged in raising livestock and poultry in scale shall conduct decontamination or make comprehensive utilization of their excrements and urines, waste water and other waste materials; and units and individuals engaged in aquaculture shall rationally use feedings, fertilizers and medicines in order to prevent environmental pollution and ecological destruction.
	Article 58 Farmers and agricultural production and operation organizations shall keep their arable land well-maintained, make rational use of chemical fertilizers, pesticides and agricultural plastic films, increase the application of organic fertilizers and apply advanced techniques, in order to protect and improve soil fertility and prevent the land for agriculture from pollution, destruction and soil fertility declination.
Agricultural Product Quality Safety Law (2006)	Article 17 It is prohibited to produce fish or collect edible agricultural products or to build up bases for production of agricultural products in the areas where the toxic and harmful substances exceed the prescribed standards.

Law	*Content*
	Article 18 It is prohibited to violate any law or regulation to discharge or dump waste water, waste gas, solid wastes or other toxic and harmful substances to a place of origin of agricultural products. The water used for agricultural production and the solid wastes used as fertilizers shall meet the standards prescribed by the state.
	Article 19 A producer of agricultural products shall use chemical products such as chemical fertilizers, pesticides, veterinary drugs and agricultural films, etc. in a reasonable way, and prevent such chemical products from polluting the place of origin of agricultural products.
	Article 45 Whoever violates any law or regulation by discharging or dumping waste water, waste gas, solid wastes or other toxic and harmful substances to a place of origin of agricultural products shall be penalized in accordance with the relevant environmental protection laws and regulations; if it/he causes any damage, it/he shall bear liabilities for indemnity in accordance with the law.

will pose a range of health risks, from renal failure to osteoporosis to some cancers (Bernard, 2008). The most serious risk to food safety is the violation of the law on agricultural planting and breeding methods where hazardous substances, chemical fertilizers, pesticides, hormones, and antibiotics are used. This could lead to a direct use of large doses of hormones, epidemic antibiotics, and a variety of feed additives, which have the potential to endanger human health (Shujing, 2015).

Even though there are a lot of laws on food safety, and there have been improvements, issues still arise. What will happen if producers comply with the existing regulations but as their soil is polluted this has caused food materials to be contaminated? Liabilities for indemnity are limited to economic loss and there is no consideration for damage caused to ecosystems and human health. The current laws pay more attention to the limited requirement for environmental protection but have little consideration for food safety. Therefore, the laws on raw food material do not go far enough and have not played a sufficient role in food safety regulation.

Regulation of food production

There are many laws that regulate the processing of food in China, including the 2009 Food Safety Law, 2000 Product Quality Law, 2006 Agricultural Product Quality Safety Law, and 2009 Regulations on the Implementation of the Food Safety Law. The 2009 Food Safety Law is the most important law and the production of food is the most significant process covered. Article 28.1 of the 2009 Food Safety Law provides that

> food products made using non-food raw materials or recycled raw materials, food products with chemical substances added, other than food additives, or other food products which are potentially harmful to the human body … are prohibited.

Based on this provision, China has stated that in food production certain items, such as non-food raw materials, recycled raw materials, chemical substances and food additives, are prohibited, as they may be harmful to human health. Development in China has led to food being consumed in areas other than where it was produced. Food additives are used to maintain food safety in the transportation and storage process and therefore are necessary in China. However, some food producers are not following the guidelines relative to food additives and this could be harmful to food consumers. A few criminals use modern science and technology to make dirty money through fraud, ignoring relevant state regulations, e.g. the unlawful usage and addition of chemical substances and other prohibited materials (Shen-ping and Kun, 2009). In China, the Sanlu Company used non-food additives, including melamine, to produce milk powder for children, which caused serious illness (Office of the United Nations Resident Coordinator in China, 2008). Article 46 of the 2009 Food Safety Law states

> Food producers shall use food additives in compliance with provisions relating to the category, usage range and dosage of food additives set out in the food-safety standards. Under no circumstance shall food producers use chemical ingredients or other potential harmful substances other than food additives.

The article provides that the use of food additives should follow the food safety standards. However, the law was not well enforced. One of the issues is that the food safety standard is low and does not fully meet the needs of consumers; and investigations only occur once there is an incident, there is no ongoing monitoring. To resolve these problems the law must be amended.

Regulation of food storage

Food storage is very important in the food supply chain. With economic and technology development, food can be kept for a much longer time than before, but, at the same time, it may lead to higher risk of improper storage. The Food Safety Law 2009 states

> Containers, tools and equipment used for the storage, transportation, and loading/unloading of food products shall be safe and free of pollutant/

> toxic substances, meet special food-safety requirements (e.g. temperature criteria) and be kept clean to protect food products from infection.
>
> (Article 27.6)

> Food business operators shall store food products in accordance with relevant food-safety requirements, check food products in stock on a regular basis, and sort out spoiled or expired products in a timely manner.
>
> (Article 40)

The 2009 Rules on Food Safety Management in Circulation Field also play an important role in the regulation of food storage. However, violations still occur in the safe storage of food. In 2012, farmers in Shandong used formaldehyde to keep cabbage fresh, which caused risk to consumers' health. Empirical research has demonstrated that the liability of the operators is limited. In the Food Safety Law 2009, liability provisions for the food storage and the safety standard for the food storage are unclear.

Regulation of food transportation

Through fast and convenient food transportation, consumers can enjoy a greater variety of food produced in different places, even from foreign countries. Food transportation is an important stage of the food cycle as it provides the link between food production and consumption. Food transportation is under strict regulation. Article 27.6 of the Food Safety Law (2009) states that

> Containers, tools and equipment used for the storage, transportation, and loading/unloading of food products shall be safe and free of pollutant/toxic substances, meet special food-safety requirements (e.g. temperature criteria) and be kept clean to protect food products from infection. Food products shall not be transported alongside toxic or harmful objects.

The Rules on Food Safety Management in Circulation Field 2009 also provide regulation for food transportation. One practical example of issues in food transportation occurred when frozen dumplings produced in China, exported to Japan, were contaminated by chemicals during their transportation causing serious harm to consumers. Based on the regulations and what happens in practice, the implementation of laws is inadequate and has the potential to cause harm to the consumers.

Regulation of food distribution

Food distribution through sales occurs regularly in daily life. Regulation of food distribution is very important because it directly connects the food production with food consumption. In China, 2009 Food Safety Law and the

2009 Rules on Food Safety Management in Circulation Field provide us with the regulation on food distribution. Article 17 of the 2009 Food Safety Law states

> Containers, utilities and equipment, used by food operators for storing, transporting, loading and unloading food, shall be safe, harmless and clean, thus preventing food from contamination. Food operators shall guarantee that the relevant containers, utilities and equipment satisfy the special requirements such as the temperature required for food safety and shall not transport food along with toxic or harmful articles.

One practical issue in food distribution was the sale of sausages in many cities that caused harm to the consumers. Why are there problems in this stage of the food distribution? Limited regulation of food distribution, absence of control measures, and the limited means of supervision are the reasons for this.

Regulation of consumption

Consumption is another important stage of the food life cycle, which plays an important role in daily life. To better safeguard the consumers' healthy and safety, more attention needs to be paid to the regulation of food consumption. In China, there are many laws regulating food consumption, including the 2009 Food Safety Law, 2009 Rules on Food Safety Management in Circulation Field, 2010 Measures for the Supervision and Administration of Food Safety in Catering Services, 2010 Measures for the Administration of Permits for Operating Food and Beverage Services, and the 2005 Law on the Protection of Consumer Rights and Interests. The laws outline the punishment for the violation of these provisions among other things. However, there are still some food safety issues regarding food consumption. The punishment for violating the 2009 Food Safety Law is too light. The violator is only subject to light administrative liability for their violation and criminal punishment is also too light. Most regulation occurs after the violation has occurred which is not adequate.

Regulation of final disposal

To better regulate food safety, the overall regulatory system needs to be developed. Yet, the regulation of the final disposal of food has not been given enough attention, causing damage to consumers. Examples include

- in 2002 Guanshengyuan's moon cakes were filled with out-of-date recycled fillings (causing the bankruptcy of the company);
- the 2011 Shanghai stained bread incident where tainted steamed buns were made out of old steamed buns and colorant; and
- in 2011, the edible waste oil event.

There are many laws on food final disposal, including the 2009 Food Safety Law, 2009 Implementing Regulations for the Food Safety Law and 2009 Rules on Food Safety Management in Circulation Field. Although these contain some provisions on food final disposal, the effectiveness of the regulations is still limited. There are no more specific regulatory guidelines on the final disposal of food. The law has not provided adequate measures for regulating the regulator. Supervision of the food disposal process only deals with issues after they happen. The regulation of final food disposal is not enough. The Food Safety Law has been an obstacle to achieving food safety development.

Analysis of the current food safety regulation

Deficiency in the legal system

There are some deficiencies in the Chinese legal system regarding food safety law. The fragmented nature of the laws on the issue has been an obstacle. Based on the above analysis, the source of control has not been established. With the ongoing development and expansion of the Chinese food industry, more food is consumed in our daily life, and greater control to ensure basic food safety regulations is needed. However, the laws and the organizations responsible for control are not clearly established and do not provide sufficient mechanisms to ensure food safety. Based on the current laws, when consumers face the food safety problems at the stage where the food is sourced, they cannot fully get compensated for any harm caused. The 2009 Food Safety Law provides guidance on food safety regulation; however, the articles are too abstract, and lack specific legal provisions. The environmental situation in China is more serious than ever before. Soil contamination is also increasing in severity and will have a negative effect on food production. There is also a lack of specific legal provisions on the safety of raw food materials, especially when damaged through soil contamination and water pollution. There is an indirect and weak link between soil contamination, water pollution, and food safety in the legal provisions.

Historically there has been poor coordination of laws in the food safety legal system. In the 1989 Environmental Protection Law, there is no provision on farmland, which does not provide any guidance on environmental protection in rural areas. Article 20 of the 1989 Environmental Protection Law, stated that

> The people's governments at various levels shall provide better protection for the agricultural environment by preventing and controlling soil pollution, the desertification and alkalization of land, the impoverishment of soil, the deterioration of land into marshes, earth subsidence, the damage of vegetation, soil erosion, the drying up of sources of water, the extinction of species and the occurrence of other ecological imbalances, by extending the scale of a comprehensive prevention and control of plant diseases and insect pests, and by promoting a rational application of chemical fertilizers, pesticides and plant growth hormone.

Based on this provision, we need to take action to protect the rural environment. However, the provisions on rural environmental protection are so abstract that in practice they cannot fully meet the needs.

Deficiency in law enforcement

Law enforcement is an important part of the legal system, as it allows the goals of a specific law to be realized. The deficiency in enforcement of food safety law is a contributing factor to the weak food safety regulation.

Food production and circulation are interconnected and it is difficult to segregate and define the power of each authority and department. In the current segmented multi-sectoral regulation mode, each item of food is likely to be passed through multiple areas in China, being subject to different departmental regulations leading to an uncertainty in authority where regulatory gaps often appear (Guo, 2013). However, based on the current food safety provisions and practical examples of food safety breaches, all regulation and enforcement of the law only happens after an incident has occurred. The regulations concerned with post-incident investigations have made great progress for food regulation in China, however regulations overseeing the food transportation and distribution stages are too weak. Only after there is a food incident does food regulation play a role in attempting to find the violators and hand out the appropriate punishment. When food incidents happen, consumers have been put at risk of eating unsafe food, with the risk of becoming ill. Therefore, the existing legal system does not do enough to ensure food is safe for human consumption and fails to meet the goal of food safety regulation.

The weak implementation of food safety law is another deficiency in the system. In the 2009 Food Safety Law there are provisions on the subject of liability. Article 85 states:

> Under any of the following circumstances, any food producer or trader in violation of the Law, shall have any and all illegal benefits, including foods or food additives illegally produced or traded, and tools, equipment and food raw material, used for illegal production or trading confiscated by the relevant authorities according to their respective duties and responsibilities, and be subject to a fine of RMB 2,000–50,000 if the total value of the commodity is less than RMB 10,000; and subject to a fine between 5 and 10 times the total value of the commodity if the total value of the commodity exceeds RMB10,000; and for the serious cases, be revoked the business license:
>
> 1) Producing food with non-food raw material or adding non-edible chemicals or other substances possibly hazardous to human health to food, or producing food with recovered food as raw materials;
> 2) Producing or trading food which exceed food safety standard limits in content or concentration of pathogenic microorganisms, pesticide

residues, animal medicine residues, heavy metals, contaminants, and other substances that in food may be hazardous to human health;

3) Producing or trading staple and supplementary food exclusively for babies or other specific population, the nutritional ingredients of which fail to meet food safety standards;
4) Trading food which is rotten or spoilt, or has rancid fat, mildew or insects, or is contaminated or dirty, or contains foreign material or displays any other organoleptic irregularity;
5) Trading or producing meat or products of any bird, livestock, beast, or waterborne animal which has been killed by disease, poison or any unidentified cause;
6) Trading or producing meat or meat products which have not been quarantined or inspected by animal health supervision authorities or fail to pass such quarantine or inspection;
7) Trading food exceeding the shelf life;
8) Producing or trading food expressly prohibited by the State from production and trading for disease prevention and control purposes;
9) Using new food materials to produce food, or producing new types of food additives and food related products, but failing to pass the safety assessment;
10) Refusing to call back or stop operations when the relevant authorities order to call back or stop operations of foods not conforming to foods safety standard.

As we can see, the punishment for violations of food safety law is weak, thus the effectiveness of the law is poor and food safety outcomes are insufficient. The actions taken when a food safety violation occurs is inadequate, which includes fines, confiscation, or revocation of licenses, the issuing of a warning, suspension of the business, and criminal liability, etc. Under Article 85, the punishment is too light and does not act as enough of a deterrent to stop offenders undertaking activities which may violate food safety law. Poor law enforcement of food safety law is the basic reason for deficiency in food safety regulation in China.

Issues of inequality in the food safety system in China

The legal system of food safety in China consists of not only laws, rules, and regulations, but also food safety standards. China's food safety legal system is quite strict. The legal regulation of food safety focuses more on strengthening government regulation, and aims to increase administrative responsibility and prosecute criminals as a means to suppress food safety violations. It neglects the construction of the civil liability system, which is a big defect in the regulation system. There is inequality in the food safety system in China. Food safety standard can be divided into three categories: national standard, industrial standard, and local standard. Different departments promulgate a variety of standard policies, for example, forestry, agriculture, commodity inspection, commercial, supply and marketing, and light industry. Conflicts are prevalent across the standards, because there are duplicate sections and some questions cannot be answered. There are also a number of standards and requirements, and multi-management situations for one type of food product. Some of China's food exports and domestic standards also vary, e.g. for carbonated drinks, which make the already chaotic food safety standards worse (Ming and Jing, 2013, p. 91). There is inequality in the food safety system and standards in China, which makes it more difficult to fully enforce the legal framework. There are other laws in China that require attention to be paid to food safety issues including the Water Pollution Prevention and Control Law, and the Atmospheric Pollution Prevention and Control Law. However, the content of these laws is more a statement of principle and is not comprehensively implemented in practice. Similarly, there is poor convergence of the content of other comparable provisions contained in the Food Safety Law, Water Pollution Prevention and Control Law and Atmospheric Pollution Prevention and Control Law. In China, there are multiple departments which are responsible for the food safety regulation. In the process of regulation, they may enforce the regulation promulgated by them, which may be different from regulations issued by other departments on the same subject, potentially leading to inequality and unfairness. These inequalities in the food safety system are hindering food safety regulation in China.

Based on the above analysis, there are deficiencies in the different stages of the food life cycle leading to poor food safety regulation in China. The legislators need to take action to improve food safety law and law enforcement.

Some implications or lessons from cases outside China

China has established a legal system on food safety and put in place several governmental departments who are responsible for food safety regulation. The legal system on food safety has been enforced; however, some improvements are needed. To improve the legal system, China can look to the lessons learned on food safety from other countries.

Legal framework on food safety in other countries

Many countries have established legal frameworks on food safety. The USA developed the National Meat Supervision in 1890, the Federal Food and Drug Act in 1939, followed by the Federal Food, Drug, and Cosmetic Act, Food Quality Protection Act, Federal Milk Imports Law, Public Health Service Act and Dietary Supplements Health and Education Act. Over 100 years, the USA has established laws and regulations that encompass almost all types of food, covering various aspects of food manufacturing and sale, for food safety assessment and also providing a basis for certification and regulation. Japan also introduced its first food safety law in 1947, the Food Sanitation Law followed by the Pesticide Control Act, Fertilizer Management Law and Food Safety Basic Law. The legal system on food safety in Japan continues to improve. The European Union (EU) has played a big part in developing food safety laws and regulations. The EU has created over 20 food safety regulations as well as the Common Food Law and Food Sanitation Law, and continues to develop systems for drug residue control, food production, and health standards, as well as an official monitoring system for imported food and other food safety regulations, establishing a comprehensive system of food safety laws (Zhuolan and Jingbo, 2012, p. 104). In 2006, the EU implemented the new EU Food and Feed Safety Management Regulations, which focused on regulating the use of food additives, stopping food chain contamination and implementing a system of supervision at various points in the food life cycle (primarily raw material production, processing, sales, importation and exportation of food products) to create a comprehensive, seamless convergence of the food safety system. To better meet the need of regulation of the whole food life cycle, China needs to improve the legal framework on food safety.

Methods of food regulation

The regulating bodies need to pay attention to food safety systems in other countries to learn from their experiences to develop China's legal framework.

Germany conducts strict daily inspections to ensure food safety at the different stages of food production, circulation, and sales. For meat, at each stage of the food life cycle (slaughtering, processing, warehousing, transportation, and sales) strict rules apply. According to the regulations, meat that is not fresh cannot be sold (Yanping, 2005). In 2002, Germany set up a Federal Institute to oversee consumer protection and food safety. Denmark has formed a nationwide unified management agency for food safety by combining the agriculture, fisheries, and food ministries. France has set up a food safety evaluation center and the Dutch have established a national food authority (Ningsong, 2009). The characteristics of the European food safety regulations are embodied in three aspects: to establish a comprehensive farm-to-table food safety responsibility and enforcement system; to establish modern mechanisms to allow for constant supervision and the communication of information to ensure that any food safety incidents are quickly contained and the risk analysis undertaken is objective; and to ensure that human health is protected and the demands from higher level consumers for food products are met (Hoffmann and Harder, 2010). In South Korea, a committee is responsible for food safety management, dealing with policy, and the coordination between departments when food hygiene incidents occur. The Ministry of Agriculture and Food and Rural Affairs (MAF) security management is responsible for the production of crop, livestock and other agricultural products, and the quarantine of imports. The Fisheries Department is responsible for ensuring that aquatic production and management is safe, and it conducts security checks of imported seafood. The Health, Welfare and Family Affairs Department is responsible for inspecting imported food and farming products to ensure they are safe, and for also producing a guide listing the safety checks that aquatic produce must undergo.

The food safety regulation system in the United States operates under a meta-pattern management model (Zhongwei and Yuji, 2010). The federal, state, and local governments in the USA are independent, but function with mutual cooperation when it comes to the "food safety supervision and management of the network" (Zhaohua and Jiasu, 2004). The federal and local government departments responsible for food safety supervision constitute a comprehensive and effective food safety supervision system, with strict supervision of all aspects of the food life cycle, from production to sale. The majority of state laws identify the Federal Ministry of Health as responsible for overseeing food safety in the region, and for assisting with the training of food safety supervision staff and employees of the food industry. There are specific state departments that are responsible for various areas of food testing. The State Food Safety Supervision Department works cooperatively with the Federal Food and Drug Administration and the Ministry of Health and the Environmental Protection Department. The USA has established a regulatory model where an early warning mechanism to detect food safety concerns operates. This occurs through a series of processes, including the hazard analysis critical control point (HACCP) management system, and it is through the control of food products at each stage of the process that it is possible to achieve complete food safety. The USA also uses the Good Agriculture Practice (GAP) and International Organization for Standardization (ISO) standards to regulate food safety. The Food Safety Management System ISO22000 Guidelines were released by the ISO, on May 4, 2005 and they outlined the requirements for all types of organizations in the food chain. The Guidelines cover the whole process of the food chain, for food and beverages, for the planting, breeding, primary processing, manufacturing, distribution, stages, until the product reaches the consumer (Hui, 2011). In the USA, in order to overcome the serious consequences caused by market and government regulatory failure, the government has vigorously pursued a third-party monitoring system for food safety. This includes the establishment of a number of combined industry, consumer, and independent expert systems to whom regulatory agencies give information disclosure powers. Important actors in the system include various food industry associations and consumers. Health institutions at all levels hire food inspectors, microbiologists, epidemiologists, and other professions for continuous monitoring. Self-regulation of corporate behavior has become an important, day-to-day process for organizations and business involved in the food production and distribution stages. Competitors within the industry have become more conscious of each other as regulators.

In western countries, there are many government departments who are responsible for and undertake action on food safety regulation. In China, government departments also establish the regulations on food safety and undertake some operational tasks. However, the effectiveness of food life-cycle regulation in China is low. To improve food safety regulation, action is required to improve the life-cycle regulation and the implementation of food standards, such as the ISO22000 and GAP.

Suggestions for improvement

Improve the food safety laws

To improve regulation of the life cycle of food safety and better promote the development of food safety legal system, food safety laws should be improved. This will reduce the obstacles that exist in daily life with regard to food safety in China.

Coordination between different legal provisions

Food safety law is at the core of the food safety legal system and plays an important and daily role in food safety regulation. Some provisions are uncoordinated with other provisions in different laws and this is an obstacle in the enforcement of law. Therefore, the coordination between different legal provisions is very important.

Environmental protection of farmland and food safety are so interlinked in that, if the polluted area is used to produce food, this food may also be polluted, thus potentially causing harm to consumers. The food life cycle involves a multitude of processes from many sectors. Every process that alters the food product can lead to food safety issues, and if an aspect is even subtlety neglected this could lead to an outbreak of food safety issues (Wei and Liyuan, 2014). In China, environmental law, especially those provisions with regard to rural environment protection, guides pollution abatement. To better regulate the production of raw food materials, different legal provisions, especially those between environmental law and food safety law need to be coordinated. China should align its food safety law provisions with those of its environmental laws. Legislators also need to coordinate food safety and agricultural law as well as any other laws and regulations regarding food safety to develop a comprehensive, coordinated, and enforceable legal system.

Strengthen legal responsibility

Food safety incidents are increasingly occurring in daily life. Regulators cannot fully apply the full force of the provisions on legal liability to control the activities of violators. To strengthen legal liabilities, legislators need to pay more attention to administrative punishments and the civil liability of violators. In food safety law, a fine of between RMB 2,000 and RMB 50,000 can be imposed, in cases where the total value of the illegal food products and/or food additives is less than RMB 10,000. Otherwise, the fine shall be up to five times—but not less than two times—the total value of the illegal food products and/or food additives involved (Article 84 of 2009 Food Safety Law).

Compared with the profits that can be gained from the violation, the fine is insignificant and cannot prevent violators from breaking the law. To deter violations, the punishments should be tougher. Restricting food enterprises from undertaking illegal activity are examples of administrative punishment that can deter illegal business. The magnitude of the punishment will directly affect the behavior of food enterprises. By passing legislation to improve penalties for illegal business behavior, the law can effectively restrict illegal acts by food enterprises (Weihui, 2013).

Strengthen law enforcement

Improve food safety standards

Food safety standards are the basic conditions that are used by regulators to identify when there is a violation. Food safety standards are important, and China must place more emphasis on them. In China, as mentioned before, there are three kinds of food safety standards: national standard, industrial standard, and local standard. In recent years, as a result of a lack of clarity of and contradiction between standards, China's food safety standards have been simplified and refined. There are 303 national food safety standards, covering more than 6,000 food security indicators that encompass dairy safety standards, mycotoxins, agriculture veterinary drug residues, food additives and nutritional supplements, pre-packaged food labeling, and nutrition labeling (National Health and Family Planning Commission, 2014). The standards are not always consistent, which means food producers cannot follow all the requirements. Legislators should improve the food safety standard systems by conducting more research on food safety issues to develop a better food safety standard system. The government needs to play a larger role in food safety regulation, especially in the establishment, enforcement, and implementation of food safety standards, safety monitoring, information disclosure, and enforcing legal responsibilities. The food safety standard, ISO 22000, will play an important role in the development of food production processes. China should introduce the ISO 22000 system and allow it to fully play a role in the process of food safety regulation.

Strengthen regulatory means

In China, the government plays a leading role in the process of food regulation. However, food regulations are only enforced after a food safety incident occurs. Regulation occurring after the fact cannot meet the needs of China's society. Food safety law in China is weak and provides little regulatory guidance for daily regulation activities. Useful regulatory guidance is also needed for the regulation of China's food safety systems. Regulators should strengthen regulatory activities by

1 Encouraging consumers to participate in the process of regulation. Public participation mechanisms can protect people's right to know basic information about their food, rights, and obligations to participate in the decision-making and implementation process.
2 Regulators should encourage scientists to join in the process of formulating food safety standards. Scientists are very knowledgeable about food safety issues and can help regulators create effective food safety standards for China.
3 Regulators should expand the regime of the food safety regulation activities. Currently, regulation does not fully meet the need for social development and the content of regulations needs to be expanded. Regulators should pay more attention to the food market and other aspects of the system to promote food safety regulation. According to the regulatory link, institutions and staff are set up to achieve the functions of the food safety regime, and all levels of government are important. Looking forward, regulatory resources and regulators can increase production, monitoring, and law enforcement to build effective regulation of the food source.

(Ming, 2013)

The HACCP is being introduced into the regulatory system. Through the HACCP, China can regulate food safety from all perspective of the food life cycle, especially at the food material production and final disposal stages. The conditions for players entering the food market should be tight, as food safety is very important. Governmental departments who are responsible for food safety regulation should introduce the GAP into regulatory actions. Using the GAP, regulators could establish the conditions for entrance into the food market system and achieve the goal of food safety.

Food safety electronic information recording

The electronic recording of food safety information is one aspect of China's regulations that could be improved. This would allow information on food safety to be recorded at each stage, and could also be used to inform consumers of the status of the food. Regulators would easily be able to access food safety information via the electronic information recording. Based on this information, the government and consumers would have more access to information about the condition of the specific food item and could use this to determine whether the food is safe for use or consumption. The technical development of the electronic information recording system would allow regulators to decide which information should be recorded for food safety. Food safety supervision organizations and relevant government departments should create a consumer-friendly interactive platform for food safety information that provides both accurate scientific food safety information to the public and also allows the government to collect and use consumer feedback on the food safety information (Yonghong, 2014, p. 99).

Improve the implementation mechanism

Food safety risk assessment mechanisms

As society develops, there are heightened food safety issues. To reduce the occurrence of food safety incidents and the harm caused by food safety risks, regulators need to conduct scientific food safety impact assessment on various food production and utilization activities. As environmental pollution, which may affect the safety of raw food materials, is fairly serious in some parts of China, one important factor of the risk assessment to be considered is the environmental and health risk. Based on the risk assessment, regulators could determine the likelihood of a food safety issue occurring, and then take appropriate action to reduce the risk posed. Risk assessment procedures should include the following:

1. The members of the risk assessment panel should be determined and include experts in the field of risk assessment, legal systems, food production and distribution, sociology, psychology, and informatics. The experts should be identified and selected by specific administrative departments with knowledge and access to expert databases. The risk assessment should be carried out by experts randomly selected from a database.
2. The specific procedures that should be undertaken when conducting a risk assessment should be identified. Food safety supervision and management should be coordinated and the work carried out in accordance with the science and technology standards to demonstrate what is occurring in the local situation. By collecting information, feedback, re-evaluating the process, and the timely assessment of food safety risks, the public release of information would be effective and efficient, ensuring that food safety incidents are avoided.
3. Risk assessment regulators should organize relevant personnel and decision-makers to assess the instructions given by the expert group to make a reasonable decision based on a full understanding of the assessment. The expert panel should also indicate the corresponding legal responsibility in relation to the risk assessment. The China National Center for Food Safety Risk Assessment was established in 2011, and coordinates national efforts to monitor chemical hazards, food-borne pathogens, and disease according to the principles set forth in the Rules for Monitoring Food Safety Risk (Provisional) released in 2010.

   (Lam et al., 2013)

A sound risk assessment system can make the food safety legal system more complete and work better to achieve the goal of food safety. The legislators should further develop and improve the food safety risk assessment method by:

- determining how the implementation and management of rules and procedures occur;

- specifying the object and scope of the method;
- stating the basic principles and legal liability; and
- establishing the scientific nature, rationality, validity, and feasibility of the risk assessment contents and standards to ensure the controllability of major food safety problems or events.

(Guofeng, 2014, p. 132)

Coordination mechanism

The Food Safety Commission of the State Council (FSCSC) is a high-level consulting and coordinating body, whose remit is to implement the Food Safety Act. The FSCSC is tasked with strengthening the leadership of food safety and to supervise and manage the coordination of food safety in China. The FSCSC is not one of the main departments of the State Council. And, at a time when many groups and departments are working to ensure their existence, doubts are cast over its longevity, and the work it is tasked with is sometimes compromised. The main duty of the government as market regulator is to supervise the business activities of food-producing organizations, provide an environment for fair competition and the development of society as a whole. Improving the security and development of food safety is a government responsibility (Kezhen, 2013). Under the requirements of current food safety supervision and management departments, the FSCSC should play an active role to achieve improved coordination of functions. These functions include supervising food safety procedures, establishing a coordination mechanism for the positive interaction of various procedures, including information disclosure, risk assessment, comprehensive management, joint law enforcement, accident prevention, education and training. The FSCSC should also undertake a comprehensive analysis of the various departments to understand the food security situation and current issues to develop an overall food safety work plan that can be incorporated into policy (Dansong, 2012). For the FSCSC to fulfill the role of both supervisory and management departments, regular coordination meetings to address the oversight of management issues are needed to achieve coordination. The FSCSC works to coordinate and provide guidance in order to play an important role in the organization, coordination, supervision, and punishment within the food safety system. As a system, food safety administrative coordination mechanisms can reach the executive level to achieve integration and improve policy performance by executing considerable administrative functions (Tang, 2007). Simultaneously, regulators can organize regular joint meetings and call all agencies that deal with food safety together to take action toward developing the food safety system. The FSCSC can engage with a wide range of stakeholders, including government, business, social organizations, and encourage public participation in the governance of food security issues. This would allow food safety issues to change from only concerning a political, single regulatory body to involving enterprises, social organizations, and other public regulatory body in an effort to create co-governance mechanisms (Wei and

Liyuan, 2014, p. 79). The 12th Five-Year Plan (2011–15) was issued in 2011, and it included a national plan for food safety regulation systems with a detailed blueprint for a unified set of national food safety standards, an optimized, science-based food safety regulatory mechanism, and a plan for implementing food safety regulations (General Office of the State Council, 2012). The Food Industry Association is a national voluntary, non-profit, social organization formed by food industry businesses, relevant research institutes, professional organizations, and industry workers. As to the association, it sets up subsidiary bodies, information center offices, and training centers. The association should actively carry out research on food safety issues, develop and oversee the implementation of guild regulations and standard industry practices to strengthen self-discipline and fully perform their functions (Chen, 2014).

The current food safety regulation system does not fully meet the need for food safety in China. Regulators need to take action to develop the regulation of the whole food life cycle and the provisions of food safety law should be improved. Accountability, via a tracking system should be implemented to locate the origin of food safety issues. The surveillance systems should be strengthened and improvement in the enforcement of food safety laws will be key to a comprehensive and effective food safety regulation system in China (Lam et al., 2013).

References

Bernard, A. (2008). Cadmium and its adverse effects on human health. *International Journal of Medical Research*, 128, 557–64.

Chen, C. (2014). Food safety status quo and multi-angle supervision system. *Science and Technology Management Research*, 7, 36–39.

Dansong, L. (2012). Current research and analysis of legal practice food safety regulatory issue. *Contemporary Law*, 3, 156–160.

General Office of the State Council. (2012). *National Plan for the Food Safety Regulation System during the Period of the Twelfth Five-Year Plan*. Beijing: Chinese State Council.

Guo, Y. (2013). The problems and solutions of the food safety supervision in China. *Social Scientist*, Vol.8, 80.

Guofeng, D. (2014). Reflection and improvement for China's food safety risk assessment system. *Jianghuai Tribune*, 1, 132.

Hoffmann, S. and Harder, W. (2010). Food safety and risk governance in globalized markets. Retrieved from www.rff.org

Hui, J. (2011). On the crux and outlet of China's food safety supervision. *Legal Sciences*, 8, 154–162.

Kezhen, X. (2013). Safety, the government is duty-bound. *Qiushi magazine*, 14.

Lam, H. M., Remais, J., Fung, M. C., Xu, L. and Sun, S. S. M., (2013). Food Supply and food safety issues in China. *NIH Public Access, Lancet*, 381(9882), 6.

Liu, P. (2010). Tracing and periodizing China's food safety regulation: A study on China's food safety regime change. *Regulation and Governance*, 4, 244–260.

Ming, F. (2013, August 8). Short board and road skills to solve the food safety regulatory system. *Guangming Daily*.

Ming, F. and Jing, X. (2013). On the binding force of food safety standards in the food safety regulation. *Jiangsu Social Science*, 6, 90–95.

National Health and Family Planning Commission. (2014, October 12). Press Conference Record. Retrieved from www.moh.gov.cn/xcs/wzbd/201307/7ab6468ecd704ad89f68f07cd286c8fb.shtml

Ningsong, G. (2009). The food safety supervision model of United States, the European and its significance to China. *Contemporary Social Science Vision*, 1, 39–42.

Office of the United Nations Resident Coordinator in China (2008). *United Nations in China Occasional Report: Advancing food safety in China*. Beijing: United Nations.

Pingjun, Z. (2013). China's food safety problems and cause analysis. *Gansu Agriculture*, 23, 49–51.

Sheng-ping, W. and Kun, Z. (2009). Research on source management of foodstuff quality security. *Productivity Research*, 19, 81–84.

Shujing, Z. (2015). Explore food safety system based on the supply chain. *China Reform News*. Retrieved from www.crd.net.cn/2011-08/26/content_5148712.htm

Tang, Z. A. (2007). Legal analysis and legalization of administrative coordination bodies to build. *Wuhan University (Philosophy and Social Science)*, 7, 525–528.

Wei, W. and Liyuan, C. (2014). Issues on inter-ministerial coordination of food safety governance. *Journal of the Party School of the Central Committee of the CPC*, 18, 75–80.

Weihui, L. (2013). An in-depth analysis of food safety issues. *Journal of Shanghai Normal University (philosophy and Social Science Edition)*, 42, 55–65.

Yanping, L. (2005). Health inspection and management thinking in Germany and Britain. *Journal of Chinese Health Inspection*, 12, 205.

Ying, H. Z. and Erpeng, W. (2013). Chinese food safety regulators: A general framework. *Macroeconomic*, 4, 21.

Yonghong, H. (2014). New developments in food safety laws and governance in the United States and its Implications for China. *Law review*, 3, 92–101.

Zhaohua, W. and Jiasu, L. (2004). Research on food safety monitoring and management system in developed countries. *China Soft Science*, 7, 19–24.

Zhongwei, Han and Yuji, Li (2010). From multi-department swatch management to Administrative balance regulation. *Seeker*, 6,156.

Zhuolan, C. and Jingbo, Z. (2012). Reform and Improvement of the legal system of food safety regulation in China. *Jilin University Journal Social Science Edition*, 52, 102–108.

Index

For Product Safety Concerns and Information please contact our EU
representative GPSR@taylorandfrancis.com
Taylor & Francis Verlag GmbH, Kaufingerstraße 24, 80331 München, Germany

www.ingramcontent.com/pod-product-compliance
Ingram Content Group UK Ltd.
Pitfield, Milton Keynes, MK11 3LW, UK
UKHW022129190926
475702UK00013B/1711
* 9 7 8 1 1 3 8 6 1 8 2 9 9 *